Why We Must Work

Jon D. Wisman

Why We Must Work

Economic Freedom, Fulfilling Work, and Workplace Democracy

Jon D. Wisman
Department of Economics
American University
Washington, DC, USA

ISBN 978-3-031-98504-1   ISBN 978-3-031-98505-8 (eBook)
https://doi.org/10.1007/978-3-031-98505-8

© The Editor(s) (if applicable) and The Author(s), under exclusive license to Springer Nature Switzerland AG 2026

This work is subject to copyright. All rights are solely and exclusively licensed by the Publisher, whether the whole or part of the material is concerned, specifically the rights of translation, reprinting, reuse of illustrations, recitation, broadcasting, reproduction on microfilms or in any other physical way, and transmission or information storage and retrieval, electronic adaptation, computer software, or by similar or dissimilar methodology now known or hereafter developed.
The use of general descriptive names, registered names, trademarks, service marks, etc. in this publication does not imply, even in the absence of a specific statement, that such names are exempt from the relevant protective laws and regulations and therefore free for general use.
The publisher, the authors and the editors are safe to assume that the advice and information in this book are believed to be true and accurate at the date of publication. Neither the publisher nor the authors or the editors give a warranty, expressed or implied, with respect to the material contained herein or for any errors or omissions that may have been made. The publisher remains neutral with regard to jurisdictional claims in published maps and institutional affiliations.

Cover credit: eStudio Calamar

This Palgrave Macmillan imprint is published by the registered company Springer Nature Switzerland AG
The registered company address is: Gewerbestrasse 11, 6330 Cham, Switzerland

If disposing of this product, please recycle the paper.

For Josette

Preface

This book is a sequel to *The Origins and Dynamics of Inequality: Sex, Politics, and Ideology* (2022). That book claimed that the struggle over inequality has been the driving force of all human history. Near the conclusion, that investigation identified the explosion of inequality over the past half century as the source of most contemporary social dysfunction and malaise. If this extreme inequality is not reversed, there lies ahead not only increasing misery and social discord but also the continuing erosion of democracy and the increasing likelihood of ecological Armageddon. What blocks this reversal is laissez-faire ideology that legitimates inequality by justifying the social institutions that sustain it. That book concluded that the only hope for delegitimating this ideology is an attractive blueprint for a superior social arrangement. It also indicated the bare bones of some critically necessary elements of reform centering on the domain of work.

This book puts flesh on the bones of the potential to free a majority of the voting population from the persuasive power of the elite's ideology. It does so by offering an attractive alternative vision of our future grounded in explaining why work is essential to human flourishing and what must be secured and restructured to further freedom and happiness.

My interest in the potential of work to serve as a source for meaning, a vent for creativity, a site for community, and a realm where individuals can gain social recognition and self-respect dates back decades. This interest was continually stimulated by the inescapable contrast between my own privileged work and what I observed in the work of so many others. My own work as an academic has provided me with tenured job security, virtually full control over my work activities of teaching, researching, writing, and participating in some committee deliberations. It has provided me with the positive benefits that properly structured work can provide to all workers. Indeed, the very word "work" seems inappropriate; had I been independently wealthy, I would have done what I've been doing. By contrast, many less fortunate workers face the threat of unemployment in jobs where they have little control over their work process, occasionally in toxic environments under superiors who boss them about. Their work conditions compel them to suffer insecurity, stress, and at times humiliation.

The question that came to occupy me is why, in rich societies whose abundance surpasses basic needs and far surpasses the expectations of past visionaries, so many workers lack jobs where they can flourish. Why must they suffer the threat of unemployment, the paucity of control over their work, and the indignity of being bossed about? This book began as my attempt to answer this question.

This question could usefully be restated as follows: with the primordial problem of scarcity solved in today's rich countries, to what domain of life might attention turn to increase human flourishing and happiness? The answer is simple. That domain is work, where most working-age people spend about a third of their time when preparing and commuting are included. Yet in today's rich countries, there is little public discussion of why work for so many is not fulfilling, why it is not a major life activity in which they can find meaning, be creative, find community, and enjoy social and self-respect. Instead, work is widely understood as not of value itself, but instead as primarily a means to income to enable consumption. Even the science of economics—my specialty—views work negatively as disutility, as that which people must endure to earn income with which to consume.

What makes this limited view of work striking is that our species evolved to experience work as pleasurable, and it remained pleasurable for the first 98 percent of our existence as hunter-gatherers when we lived with primitive technology and produced so little beyond the necessities for survival. However, with the rise of the state 5500 years ago—the last two percent of human history—exploitation and extreme inequality degraded work as workers lost ready access to productive wealth (principally land, and much later capital) that came to be owned and controlled by elites. To survive, most workers had to work for and take orders from these owners, which they have done as slaves, serfs, indebted peasants, and wage laborers.

But today, two reforms can be implemented to recapture critical aspects of the pleasurable, fulfilling work that prevailed during the first 98 percent of our history. These two reforms are guaranteed employment at living wages with benefits and retraining where necessary, and measures to establish worker ownership and management of workplaces. Guaranteed employment would recreate security of access to productive resources and eliminate poverty. Worker ownership and self-management would recreate freedom and democratic control of work. That is, the political ideals of freedom and democracy would be extended to the realm of work.

Although these reforms would dramatically enhance worker security and bring freedom and democracy to the realm of work, laissez-faire ideology has kept them out of public discourse. No political party in the United States or Europe, even those proclaiming to represent workers' interests, include either of these reforms in their political platforms. Labor unions seldom mention them. Consequently, the public generally remains unaware of their nature or desirability.

Even the science of economics ignores the issues of guaranteed employment and workplace democracy. Some years ago, in preparing to teach a course on labor economics, much to my surprise, I was unable to locate among the highly respected textbooks any mention whatsoever of either guaranteed employment or workplace democracy.

These two proposed reforms can serve as the new foundation for an attractive vision to replace that of laissez-faire. It should be emphasized that these reforms would leave in place capitalism's two principal institutions of private property and markets. The economy would remain capitalist, but with far greater freedom and democracy and without extreme inequality and exploitation.

Workers, constituting the overwhelming majority of the electorate, possess the political power to rewrite the social script and convert such a vision into social reality. The only prerequisite is workers' awareness of its desirability and feasibility. It is hoped that this book will contribute to this awareness.

The title of this book: *Why We Must Work* stems from the fact that once basic material needs have been met, it is in work rather than in consumption that the greatest potential for human flourishing is to be found. Flourishing in work entails enacting reforms that create greater economic security and extend freedom and democracy to the realm of work—hence the book's subtitle: *Economic Freedom, Fulfilling Work, and Workplace Democracy.*

There is urgency that a new vision of our future replace laissez-faire ideology. The public policies laissez-faire ideology legitimates are not only increasing inequality but also threatening the future existence of democracy and humanity's ability to avoid ecological Armageddon.

Washington, USA   Jon D. Wisman

Acknowledgements I am indebted to Bronwyn Geyer, my editor at Palgrave Macmillan, for seeing promise in my book, shepherding it through the review and acceptance process, and offering invaluable editorial assistance for improving its style. My dear friend, the polymath Philip Newman Lawton, also brought his great editorial skills to improving my prose, while offering helpful suggestions on content. Economics professors Aaron Pacitti and John Willoughby offered valuable comments on an earlier draft of Chapter I. Evolutionary psychologist Satoshi Kanazawa generously guided me through some critical issues in the dynamics of natural selection.

I am also indebted to generations of gifted undergraduate and graduate students at American University. Their quest for understanding and participation in intellectual discourse has continually suggested novel perspectives on the human condition.

I am grateful for Palgrave Macmillan's permission to draw upon portions of my chapter "The Urgent Need to Delegitimate Laissez-Faire Ideology," in *Neoliberal Economic Policy and the Rise of Right-Wing Populism: Western Civilization at the Crossroads,* John Komlos, editor, Palgrave-Macmillan, 2024: 223–248 for Chapter 6 of this book.

Competing Interests The author has no competing interests to declare that are relevant to the content of this manuscript.

Contents

1	We All Must Work	1
2	Work in a State of Nature	23
3	Eden Lost: The Rise of the State and Work Degraded	45
4	Victory Over Material Scarcity	77
5	What Abundance Promised Got Crushed	95
6	The Urgent Need to Humanize Work and Recover Community	119
7	Creative Destruction and Security with Guaranteed Employment	143
8	Creating Democracy, Freedom, and Community in the Workplace	171
9	Final Reflections	201
References		213
Index		245

1

We All Must Work

In our quest for a better environment, we must always remember that the most important part of the quality of life is the quality of work, and the new need for job satisfaction is the key to the quality of work.
—President Richard Nixon, Labor Day message, September 6, 1971

Without work all life goes rotten. But when work is soulless, life stifles and dies.
—Albert Camus, cited in O'Toole 1974, 186

Work is central to human flourishing and happiness. This was a result of our evolution as *Homo sapiens*. During this long formative period, we evolved to experience activities necessary for our provisioning to be pleasurable to motivate their performance and our survival. Among these activities was democratically coordinating work with others.

These highly positive work conditions endured for the first 98% of our history. But since the rise of the state 5500 years ago, extreme inequality and exploitation has resulted in much work becoming debased. Workers lost control over their work and came to be bossed about. Work came to be viewed as a curse, as mythically captured in *Genesis*.

Nevertheless, some workers today continue to experience work as fulfilling, as an activity in which they can be creative, find community with others, and find social and self-respect. They are privileged. Many, if not most, other workers are not so fortunate. For them, work itself is not fulfilling or pleasurable. Instead, it is something they must do to avoid the humiliation of being unemployed and to gain income to enable consumption. Indeed, this is the dominant understanding of work. It is a necessary means, often unpleasant, to the end of consumption. Even the science of economics depicts work negatively as disutility and that which would be avoided in favor of leisure if not necessary for consumption.

Work can and must be rehumanized. Why this is critically important and how this can come about will become clear in the following pages. As will be seen, this challenge is made far easier by the fact that in today's rich societies, the material problem of scarcity has been solved. With appropriate reforms, we can enjoy both our abundance and the principal aspects of work to which we evolved to experience as fulfilling and pleasurable.

And just how rich are we in today's wealthy nations? In the United States, for example, although highly unequally distributed, per capita income in 2024 was $72,579, the amount each individual would receive if all income were equally divided. That's $290,316 for a family of four (St. Louis Fed 2025). Per capita wealth in the United States in 2020 was $505,420, or over 2 million dollars for a family of four (Buchholz 2021). We are rich far beyond what was imagined by past visionaries who reasoned that once material needs were met, humans would be able to focus on other aspects of their lives. And what domain of our lives might best be improved? The answer is easy. It is work which takes up a third of our lives when including work time, commuting, and preparations.

The urgency of the challenge to rehumanize work is that people in today's rich nations live in an absurdist reality. Although the primordial problem of scarcity has been solved for over half a century in rich nations, the quality of the prime life domain of work is, for so many, debased and most workers are not free in their workplaces. As opposed to being a realm in which they can vent their creativity, find purpose, develop their potential, democratically participate with co-workers, and find community, workers frequently have little ownership or control over the work process and suffer the humiliation of being bossed about.

It is noteworthy that in the quarter century following World War II, victory over the problem of material scarcity was sensed and the liberation it promised began to be realized, especially among youth who embraced postmaterialist values. They held that happiness or fulfillment was to be found in greater freedom, meaningful work, and richer community life as opposed to ever more consumption. However, since the late 1970s, a hard political turn toward laissez-faire and austerity has generated degrees of insecurity and stress exceeding what existed prior to this triumph over material scarcity. As economist and happiness researcher Richard Layard puts it, "what madness [that] as we become richer, we also become less secure and more stressed.... Both security and a quiet mind are goods that should increase, not decrease, as people become richer" (2006, 164).

The source of today's conundrum of abundance accompanied by rising insecurity and stress is laissez-faire ideology that over the past 50 years has legitimated public policies that have resulted in extreme and growing inequality, more debased work conditions, and eroded community.

Laissez-faire doctrine sets forth the following claims: Government is incompetent and must be minimized; the economy should be deregulated to permit businesses and household to seek their own self-interests in free markets; taxes, especially on the rich and corporations should be cut to stimulate investment and economic growth; welfare, including unemployment benefits and social security must be eliminated to force the unemployed to seek jobs and poor workers to work harder and save for their retirements; in a free market economy, everyone gets their just rewards—the rich have earned their wealth and the poor their poverty. This doctrine also reinforces the view that ever greater consumption is the key to greater happiness, while work is viewed negatively as a mere, often unpleasant, means to the income necessary for consumption.

Laissez-faire ideology's dominance in contemporary politics must be eliminated if the insecurity, stress, and social decline accompanying unparalleled abundance are to be overcome. This requires an attractive alternative vision that recognizes the central importance of work and community for human flourishing and privileges measures to enhance their quality. Such a superior vision would promise work security and reform the workplace to better satisfy deep fundamental needs generated during human evolution. In support of this argument, this book makes and defends six claims:

1. To ensure provisioning, humans evolved over the first 98% of the human story to experience work, generally democratically coordinated with others, as pleasurable and thus essential for human flourishing or happiness.
2. Since the rise of the state and civilization 5500 years ago, workers have been exploited, and their work experience has been debased.
3. Perpetuated by laissez-faire ideology and inequality, a vision of material progress has accompanied the eventual achievement of widespread abundance, locking us into mistakenly believing that ever greater material abundance and consumption are today's keys to improving human welfare. Work is widely understood as a mere means to greater material abundance.
4. To escape the absurd contemporary condition of rising insecurity and stress accompanying ever greater abundance, contemporary capitalism can be reformed to create the security and quality of work and community necessary for human flourishing while retaining capitalism's two principal institutions of private property and markets. These reforms are guaranteed employment at living wages with reskilling where necessary and measures to democratize the workplace.
5. These reforms, by better enabling social and self-respect through work, would reduce the pressure to consume, thereby reducing the risk of ecological Armageddon.
6. These proposed reforms are politically viable because they offer an attractive alternative to the elite's laissez-faire ideology by building upon and expanding widely embraced contemporary values such as freedom and democracy while preserving the dynamism of capitalism's "creative destruction" and its institutions of private property and markets.

This book opens with the extraordinary story of much of the world's ascent from bare subsistence to stupendous economic abundance. It reveals the enormous costs of this success following the rise of the state and civilization which came in the form of exploitation, extreme inequality, and the debasement of work and community. This historical exploration lays the groundwork for an understanding of what is necessary to avoid further degradation of social and psychological well-being and to reverse environmental devastation that threatens the end of the human story. Attention then turns to focusing on what more specifically is required for harvesting the full benefits of humanity's economic achievement. Although the needed institutional changes are auspicious, they accord with, deepen, and expand the contemporary values of freedom and democracy and do not dramatically alter the foundations of today's societies. For these reasons, guaranteeing employment and democratizing the workplace offer a renewed vision of our future, one that replaces the ideology of laissez-faire that legitimates unfair and irrational social institutions that impede human flourishing.

Our Biologically Evolved Guidance System

One of the greatest Reasons why so few People understand themselves is, that most Writers are always teaching Men what they should be, and hardly ever trouble their heads with telling them what they really are.
— Bernard de Mandeville 1970, 77

Happiness has generally been recognized as the ultimate human goal in cultures throughout history. It has been viewed as the self-evidently good that should be pursued. To be happy is not, of course, the goal of evolution. Instead, through the course of human evolution, happiness or life-satisfaction came to serve as the principal overall motivational force, guiding behavior toward fulfilling those conditions that contribute to happiness.
— Luis Rayo and Gary S. Becker 2007

Definitions of what constitutes happiness have varied. Nevertheless, there has been widespread agreement on what constitute the major prerequisites. They generally include basic material security, good health, fulfilling work, community, close personal relationships, freedom, and a sense of social standing and self-worth. These elements are interdependent, and work plays an especially large role in each of them.

Happiness is not achieved by direct pursuit. In fact, directly pursuing it may thwart its attainment. Happiness is more what comes with a life well lived. Happiness is a composite sense of well-being resulting from the satisfaction of life activities that we were selected to experience as pleasurable because they further the odds of surviving and reproducing. For instance, we evolved to find pleasurable activities such as eating, sex, and maintaining friendships because they enhanced the individual's potential for survival and reproduction. We evolved to find activities that would reduce that potential to be disagreeable or painful to prompt retraction and avoidance of such behaviors. Success in experiencing pleasure and avoiding pain contributes to a sense of well-being, a sense of happiness.

Thus, the dynamics of biological evolution provide animals, humans included, with pain-pleasure guidance systems to steer behavior in ways that favor survival and reproduction. Those who fail to possess this innate guidance, or do so imperfectly, are less likely to survive and mate to send their unique genes into the future. Their inadequate guidance systems are likely to be eliminated from the future gene pool of the species.

Although the state of happiness is an individual privilege, seeking it does not necessarily mean self-centeredness or selfishness. Indeed, our individual happiness might be fullest when we are successful in helping others attain the same state. Individual happiness is more readily achieved in societies where others are happy.

But rather than such "happy" conditions, malaise appears to be widely prevalent in today's wealthy societies. It is the project of this book to uncover what is needed for expanding happiness in today's world. Because of its central importance for human flourishing, this entails examining the role of work in human evolution. Work is foremost for human happiness not merely because it provides the material provisioning necessary for survival and reproduction, but also because we evolved to find it pleasurable, a vent for creativity, a means for community, and a means for attaining social and self-respect.

Work as Pleasurable

> The genius of hunter–gatherer society... lies in its ability to accomplish the tasks that must be accomplished while maximizing each person's experience of free choice, which is essential to the spirit of play.
> — Peter Gray 2009a, 505

To survive and reproduce, all animals must provision themselves with food, shelter, and defense. When performed by humans, we call this provisioning "work." However, when we think of animals provisioning themselves, we neither use the term work nor imagine it to be unpleasant. It is just what they must do. Birds flit about locating food, taking shelter, and hiding from predators. Some animals hunt other animals, some graze, bees seek flowers, and fish swim about in pursuit of nourishment. Not only do we not call it work, but we are also not likely on reflection to believe it disagreeable. And correctly so.

The dynamics of biological evolution have selected animals, including humans, to find provisioning activities pleasurable to guide behavior to their accomplishment.[1] Why then have so many humans found their own provisioning activities, what they call work, unpleasant necessities to be minimized or avoided? Does this suggest that our social institutions have put us out of phase with our evolutionary heritage to the detriment

---

[1] The following studies in evolutionary biology, evolutionary psychology, and neuroscience lend support to the claim that animals evolved to find their provisioning pleasurable. Animals prefer working for food even when free food is available (Inglis et al. 1997; Osborne 1977; Balcombe 2009). Primates exhibit increased dopamine levels during tool use for provisioning (e.g., termite fishing), indicating reward in the process, not just the outcome, and birds such as corvids and parrots show play like manipulation of food items and tools, suggesting intrinsic enjoyment in the provisioning activity (Panksepp 1998; Balcombe 2009; Wayner 2011). Domestic animals such as dogs, cows, and pigs, exhibit behavioral and physiological signs of pleasure when allowed to choose how to obtain food or interact with mechanisms that enable access to food (Rault et al. 2020).

of our well-being and happiness? This book explores why "yes" is the correct answer and what we should do about it.

It is critically important to note that until recently in the human story, humans, like other animals, did not find their provisioning unpleasant. Our species, *Homo sapiens*, has existed for about 300,000 years, and for almost the entire period, the first 98%, practically all lived as hunter–gatherers with a high degree of political and economic equality, without social classes or hierarchy.[2] Beyond gender and age specialization, there was no division of labor. Humans are by nature social beings, and they typically carried out their provisioning collectively without bosses. Their work was chosen and performed democratically. Anthropologists have found that they made no distinction between work and leisure. Indeed, they lacked a word for work. As with other animals, in youth their play fostered the development of the skills needed for provisioning, as kittens make us delightfully aware. Developmental psychologist Peter Gray reports that for adults in hunter–gatherer societies, work is simply an extension of children's play. Children play at hunting, gathering, hut construction, toolmaking, meal preparations, defense against predators, birthing, infant care, healing, negotiation, and so on; and gradually, as their play becomes increasingly skilled, the activities become productive. The play becomes work, but it does not cease being play. It may even become more fun than before, because its productive quality helps the whole band and is valued by all (2009b). Indeed, research suggests that the lives of hunter–gatherers were as a whole generally playful. Anthropologists have noted their good humor, their joking, teasing, and laughter. Such playful behavior served to strengthen their social bonds (Gray 2009a, 490).

But there is a second reason why primordial work was not experienced negatively. It was not compelled by social coercion. There were no bosses with authority to tell others what to do.[3] Living as hunter–gatherers with

---

[2] About 2% of hunter–gatherers were sedentary and had formal class structures characterized by wealth and political distinctions. Their sedentary condition was due to fishing on food rich waterways (Flannery and Marcus 2012, 72–80; Garfield, von Rueden, and Hagen 2019, 6).

[3] Economist Robert Heilbroner chose to reserve the word work for what is performed by unfree labor: "The essence of work is that...tasks are carried out in a condition of subordination imposed by the right of some members of society to refuse access to vital resources to others"

a high degree of economic and political equality, decisions were made without leaders, with the exceptions of those they needed to collectively choose during war. As social beings, we were selected to find participating in activities in coordination with others, whether in work or play, to be pleasurable. Teamwork, where all participate in determining how the work is to be carried out, remains pleasurable in many contemporary workplaces and it is especially evident in team sports, which evolved in all societies to develop the skills and coordination necessary for success in provisioning the community, especially with defense.

Work aims to produce something. It may be anything that we or others find of value. But because we evolved to seek approval and status, almost all work is undertaken because we believe others will find it worthy.[4] From this perspective, prophecies of the end of work are misguided; they fail to recognize and understand what motivates us. People will always strive to produce things that others appreciate, even if it is a cake or a party. This is the nature of work we were selected to do.

Work Debased

> There is no point in work
> —unless it absorbs you
> —like an absorbing game.
> If it doesn't absorb you, if it's never any fun,
> don't do it.
> — "Work," a poem by D. H. Lawrence

However, as will be seen in Chapter 3, the quality of work was radically degraded upon the rise of the state and civilization about 5500 years ago, the last 2% of the human story. Although civilized life is widely assumed

---

(1985, 12). The word "labor" in its Latin and French etymology means "toil, exertion, hardship, fatigue, distress, pain, work" (Klein 1971, 855).

[4] Charles Darwin wrote, "We may...conclude that primeval man, at a very remote period, would have been influenced by the praise and blame of his fellows. It is obvious, that the members of the same tribe would approve of conduct which appeared to them to be for the general good" (1871, 1:165).

superior to pre-civilized or primitive life, civilization brought a dramatic debasement of work and a severe decline in the quality of life for most of its members. Much work came to be socially coerced, most extremely as slavery. For the masses, work was grueling and often cruelly imposed, to be endured to survive.

This debasement of work and quality of life came forth in Eurasia as warrior elites' command of superior metal weaponry, military organization, and persuasive ideology permitted them to take control of productive resources and subjugate all others, forcing them to work on the elites' land or with their capital as slaves, serfs, and indebted peasants. Elites expropriated their surplus output, that above which the workers needed for their bare survival. Although producers often retained considerable control over their work processes, their exploitation meant working long hours in tasks that were far less varied than was the case for hunter–gatherers. Poorer nutrition and urban living left them shorter and more diseased. They could be raped, tortured, and killed by those with higher status and greater power.

But, seconded only by slavery, the most degraded work process accompanied the rise of capitalism.[5] Workers were separated from any ownership, control, or ready access to productive wealth. They were proletarianized, forced to find work with the capitalist owners of land and capital. Workers no longer had control over when and how they worked. Through the division of labor, their work was broken down into small repetitive tasks which, Adam Smith claimed, made them "as stupid and ignorant as it is possible for a human creature to become" (1776, 734). Karl Marx and Friedrich Engels added that under capitalism, the worker was reduced to a mere "appendage of the machine" (1848, 479). Although in recent decades many workers have gained greater control over their workday, for most their work is not highly varied, and most still remain unfree as they can be ordered around.

---

[5] However, as will be discussed later, this debased condition of work was not due to capitalism as an economic system, but instead to the extreme inequality in the ownership and control of productive wealth that accompanied its evolution.

The Growth Trap

> Consumerism is only the other side of the degradation of work—the elimination of playfulness and craftsmanship from the process of production.
> —Christopher Lasch 1985, 27

Although capitalism further debased work, it has made an increasingly large number of societies rich beyond the imagination of past visionaries. It has unleashed a dynamic that economist Joseph Schumpeter called *Creative Destruction*, which he characterized as capitalism's very essence—a "process of industrial mutation… that incessantly revolutionizes the economic structure from *within*, incessantly destroying the old one, incessantly creating a new one" (1962, 83).[6] The long-term fruit of this creative destruction is that, as noted above, in today's rich countries, the primordial material problem has been solved, although extreme inequality means some of their members continue to suffer material privation. Today's wealthy economies produce far more output than necessary for secure and abundant provisioning.

Unfortunately, however, their members are locked in a growth trap, driven by a vision that views ever greater material abundance as the key to well-being and happiness. Workers succumb to this material progress vision for two reasons: First, their lack of ownership or control of productive wealth leads them to support economic growth to generate employment and raise wages; Second, the debased character of work nudges them to place greater importance on seeking social validation through consumption.

Despite the rich country's post-World War II victory over the problem of scarcity, and the extension of this victory to all the world's populations being within reach, we remain saddled with the institutions and mindsets of a world of scarcity. This is especially true as concerns work, to which we give about half of our waking lives but which we continue to

---

[6] Marx and Engels had earlier recognized what Schumpeter called capitalism's creative and destructive dynamism, not only in the economic domain, but in all of human culture, such that "All that is solid melts into air, all that is holy is profaned" (1848, 476).

understand as predominantly a means to the end of consumption and material accumulation, as opposed to the development and enjoyment of self-expression, creativity, teamwork, and community.

All social attitudes and institutions impact the distribution of wealth, income, and privilege and, not unexpectedly, perpetuating this vision of material progress benefits elites. Productive wealth is overwhelmingly owned and controlled by a very small portion of society, and returns to their productive wealth depend upon robust growth.[7] Because most workers lack ownership or control over productive assets, their employment and wages depend upon economic growth that generates profits to encourage wealthy owners to create and maintain jobs. Where growth and profits are lacking, workers face unemployment. The institutional conditions by which a wealthy elite owns productive assets and all others must seek contracts with them for their livelihoods lead workers also to embrace the material progress vision.

The second dynamic underlying why workers embrace the material progress vision is that the demeaned character of much work leads them to seek social status less through work and more through the conspicuous consumption that so irked economist and social critic Thorstein Veblen (1899). Because a high level of consumption confers high status, people sacrifice job satisfaction for higher pay and abandon communities for the same end. Inequality intensifies the consumption arms race that results from this pursuit of status through consumption. As the wealthy increase their consumption, those below do so as well in an attempt to maintain their relative social standing. Largely sacrificed to this economic growth compulsion are such essential components of human welfare and happiness as more creative and fulfilling work; greater equality in the distribution of opportunity, income, and wealth; richer and more supportive communities; a sustainable environment; and more time for family, friends, and reflection. All of these desirable things can

---

[7] Since the rise of the state, this ownership has always been extremely concentrated. In the U.S., for instance, in 2020, according to Federal Reserve data, the wealthiest 1% of Americans owned 51.8% of stocks and mutual funds, and the richest 10% of the population owned 87.2%, leaving the bottom 90% in possession of only 12.8% (Pisani 2020). The world's richest 1% owns an estimated 45% of global assets; the richest 10% an estimated 85% (Suzman 2021, 395).

be treated as subsidiary issues because strong material growth is held to be the key to a better future. For the sake of maximizing economic growth and augmenting everyone's potential consumption, capitalism's creative destruction must be fully unleashed—even if this results in ever more intense competition, insecurity, stress, and environmental destruction.

Mainstream economics reinforces this privileging of consumption over work as a source of satisfaction. It depicts work as a necessary disutility serving as a means to income, which in turn is viewed as a means to consumption. It does this, economist Tibor Scitovsky contends, because "the satisfaction the worker himself gets out of his work is not an economic good because it does not go through the market and its value is not measurable" (1976, 17). Further, families benefit from the incomes work provides, but not so clearly from the quality of work life. Consequently, to the detriment of the worker's happiness, work becomes a means to higher consumption, as opposed to an outlet for creative self-expression and workplace community.

Philosophers and heterodox economists have been less prone than mainstream economists to ignore the intrinsic value of work. For instance, two centuries ago, Friedrich Hegel pointed to the central importance of rewarding work for a full life, contending that "recognition from his professional peers…would save the individual from the temptation to seek recognition through the display of wealth, and from the 'bad infinity' of unlimited wants" (1821, para 250–255). Socio-economic thinkers such as Jean Charles Léonard de Sismondi, Louis-Marie Prudhomme, François Marie Charles Fourier, Karl Marx, and Thorstein Veblen envisioned a non-exploitative future society in which work would become an end in and of itself rather than a mere means to income.

This book embraces economist Robert Heilbroner's claim that "Work is the inescapable starting point for all social inquiry" (1985, 9). It explores the central importance of work not just for meeting material needs, but also for psychological and social well-being. Although during evolution we were selected to find work or provisioning pleasurable and it also served as a cement holding communities together, its quality was debased following the rise of states and civilization. Nevertheless, technological progress and superior modes of social organization accompanying the rise of capitalism have enabled victory over the problem of scarcity in increasing numbers of societies. However, laissez-faire ideology legitimates extreme inequality in ownership and control of productive wealth, which perpetuates the debased character of work, while devastating the environment and threatening humanity's future.

It is ironic that although much work is degraded, in today's societies all must work, including the extremely rich.[8] We must do so for social standing and self-respect. By working, we are seen as worthy, as contributing to society's well-being. Yet, that all must work does not mean it must be the 35- to 40-hour weeks typical in today's rich nations. Anthropologists reveal that in hunter–gatherer society—the socio-economic condition during the first 98% of our history when we evolved to be who we are and technology was extremely rude—work weeks averaged 12–20 hours.

Post-Scarcity's Promise of Liberation

> If our ancestors knew what tools and resources stand at our command, they would have surmised that we must be enjoying celestial tranquility, free of all cares and worries.
> — Yuval Harari 2017, 218

The extraordinary prosperity in the wake of World War II in the rich nations made it possible to note that producing ever greater material output need no longer trump all other social values. This was most vividly recognized by the first generation born following World War II that, for the first time in human history, came of age without fear of dire material privation. Many of this generation sensed the liberation this abundance made possible. The combination of robust economic

---

[8] It is true that historically elites were comfortable not working. But their status was ascribed by birth. They believed themselves superior by birth and that others should work for them. In today's meritocratic world, this is no longer possible. Hence today's super-rich work. Retirees are comfortable not working because society views them as having earned through decades of work a right to old-age leisure. Notable also is that many winners of large sum lotteries continue to work, albeit generally at reduced hours (Picchio et al. 2018).

growth, low unemployment, rising wages, labor empowerment, lessened inequality, and liberation from the fear of extreme privation set the conditions for a cultural revolution, most visibly expressed in the so-called counter-cultural and hippie movements of the 1960s and 1970s. But that was merely the flashy tip of the iceberg. Massive cultural and socio-economic effects were to be found much deeper.

Sociologist Ronald Inglehart has found that this extraordinary victory over the harshness of scarcity generated a shift from materialist to postmaterialist values, from "an overwhelming emphasis on material well-being and physical security toward greater emphasis on the quality of life." These "Postmaterialists … are Postmaterialists precisely because they take economic security for granted" (1989, 5, 238). They sought to satisfy such nonmaterial needs as more meaningful and fulfilling work, community, belongingness, and self-expression. They also demanded greater freedom and justice in all domains of personal and social life. They decried war and imperialism, and they agitated for free speech, economic equality, and racial and gender justice.

With the problem of scarcity solved, humanity was poised to fulfill the dreams of past visionaries in which all could achieve their full potential. Appropriate social institutions and continuing technological progress would make life ever richer and more rewarding.

Liberation Choked in Infancy

The cultural revolution in the Western Hemisphere was unleashed by post-World War II abundance of economic output and increased equality. Both were historically unique. Greater equality followed upon substantial delegitimization of the laissez-faire ideology that accompanied the hardships of the Great Depression of the 1930s. Between the 1930s and 1970s, the relative share of income and wealth declined for the rich as it increased for all others. Conditions of life significantly improved for most Americans.

But economic and social conditions in the 1970s set in motion a political reversal built upon a revived laissez-faire ideology in the form of supply-side economics.[9] The consequence over the subsequent 50 years has been exploding inequality, a heightened sense of insecurity, and widespread malaise. Two severe recessions, the most punishing to workers since the Great Depression, sharply reminded workers of the insecurity of their jobs. Unemployment in the recession of 1973–1975 reached 9%; in that of 1981–1982, 10.8%. Simultaneous high unemployment and inflation—"stagflation"—delegitimized Keynesian economics, creating an opening for the resurgence of laissez-faire ideology that put the blame on government policies that had greatly benefited non-elites. Interests serving elites captured both political parties, enabling legislation such as massive tax cuts that benefited the wealthy. Deregulation of the financial sector added to elites' wealth, as did lax anti-trust enforcement and more extensive intellectual property rights. Lacking substantial political support and facing hostile courts, organized labor saw its political clout collapse, leaving workers without a powerful political advocate. Inequality soared to levels not seen since the 1920s, providing elites with additional resources to finance politicians who in turn rewrote laws in the elite's favor. Productivity growth weakened, leading to sluggish growth. Public services such as education declined in quality, falling below the levels in other wealthy nations. American opportunity and social mobility, which had earlier been the world's greatest, fell below that of all other industrialized countries.

And then, during the early decades of the twenty-first century, and especially after the financial crisis of 2008 and the consequent Great Recession, conditions for the least privileged workers unimaginably worsened. So hopeless did many become that an epidemic of low self-esteem and self-abuse generated what economists Ann Case and Angus Deaton (2020) call deaths of despair. Insecurity and stress fueled an epidemic of obesity, depression, drug abuse, and suicide.[10] For the first time

---

[9] Laissez-faire doctrine began in the late eighteenth century as an argument against mercantilist state interference in the economy, claiming that minimal government and free markets would make the economy more dynamic and less unequal. However, over time, it became an ideology justifying inequality.

[10] Cultural historian Yuval Harari reports that "For the first time in history, more people die today from eating too much than from eating too little; more people die from old age than from infectious diseases; and more people commit suicide than are killed by soldiers, terrorists and criminals combined.... In 2010 famine and malnutrition combined killed about 1 million

since the Spanish Flu of 1918–1920, life expectancy declined for three consecutive years after 2014. Realizing that the Democratic Party had betrayed them, many workers threw their support in two presidential elections to an authoritarian personality lacking in political experience. Inequality has surged yet higher. A sense of betrayal by political parties in Europe that had earlier advocated for labor has also cultivated the rise of undemocratic leaders.

The extreme inequality and debasement of labor in contemporary capitalist economies threaten the future of the democracy and freedom capitalism had done much to create. The quasi-utopian future that visionaries had imagined and that seemed to be aborning over the three decades following World War II was smothered in early infancy, before it could deliver the liberation that post-scarcity conditions had promised.

What Is to Be Done

> Work is the spine which structures the way people live, how they make contact with material and social reality, and how they achieve status and self-esteem.
> — Herbert Applebaum 1992, ix

Capitalism has been undeniably the most dynamic wealth-creating socio-economic system in human history. It is now enabling a rapidly increasing portion of humanity to live free of material privation. It has also created the conditions that have generated the greatest political freedom.

It is ironic, however, that transcending the most fundamental of all insecurities, that of material scarcity, has been accompanied by rising social and psychological insecurity. A major source of this malaise is due to the stagnation of wages and increased insecurity of employment resulting from a speed up of capitalism's creative destruction expressed

---

people, whereas obesity killed 3 million" (2017, 2, 6). For an analysis of the obesity epidemic in terms of rising insecurity and stress, see Wisman and Capehart 2010.

in technological change and economic globalization that have disproportionately benefited the wealthy elite. Legislation and court decisions favoring these elites have complemented creative destruction in worsening labor's fate. Extreme inequality in ownership and control of productive wealth not only impedes advances in freedom and the quality of life but also threatens democracy and portends ecological disaster.

The vast number of people who suffer the consequences of high and rising inequality hold the overwhelming majority of votes and could in principle peacefully and democratically rewrite the social script to diminish inequality in wealth, income, and privilege. Why do they not do so? The reason is that the persuasive power of the elite's laissez-faire ideology convinces an adequate percentage of voters that more egalitarian measures would not be in their best interest. A critical message of this ideology is that there is no viable and attractive alternative to classical highly inegalitarian capitalism. This message has been especially persuasive since the fall of Eastern European state socialism. To a substantial extent, the dominance of the elite's laissez-faire ideology persists because, as political economist Thomas Piketty puts it, "The fall of communism led to a certain disillusionment concerning the very possibility of a just society…. it extinguished all hope of truly fundamental socio-economic change" (2020, 648; 831). Capitalism in its current form is, as political scientist Francis Fukuyama claimed, the "end of history" (1992).

Only an attractive alternative to classical capitalism can delegitimize the elite's laissez-faire ideology. As Hariri writes, "While it is a favorite pastime of Western academics and activists to find fault with the liberal package, they have so far failed to come up with anything better" (2017, 269). This book fills this lacuna by presenting an alternative built upon two reforms that preserve the fundamental structure of capitalism—its private property and markets—while conforming to social values generated by the spread of these capitalist institutions. These reforms are guaranteed employment and measures to advance workplace democracy.

Guaranteed employment at a living wage for all able to work, and, where appropriate, the training necessary to enter the regular job market is a relatively low-cost solution to job insecurity and poverty that would increase workers' skills (human capital) and reduce inequality. Not only would it eliminate poverty, but also welfare for those who can work while appealing to the widely embraced value that all should work and thus contribute to society's economic well-being. It would enable society to adjust to and embrace capitalism's ever-quickening pace of creative destruction, currently expressed in artificial intelligence, robotization and globalization. It would set the material and social foundation for human flourishing, especially by providing everyone with the social status and self-respect of being a productive member of society. Guaranteed employment would eliminate one of the principal sources of insecurity and unhappiness.[11] It would recreate the security of employment that accompanied our species' evolution prior to the rise of the state.

Although guaranteeing employment may sound radical, it is not a novel idea. In the United States, from Franklin Delano Roosevelt in the 1930s and early 1940s to 1978, proposals were advanced in the American political arena to guarantee jobs for all willing and able to work. These proposals fell out of political discourse as laissez-faire ideology resurged to dominance in the late 1970s.

Whereas guaranteed employment at a living wage and reskilling where appropriate would end economic insecurity for everyone, workplace democracy would empower workers with control over the tools and resources with which they work. It would promise to recreate work conditions similar to those which humans evolved to fit during the first 98% of their history—democratic workplaces without bosses.[12] As in political democracy, members of a firm would elect those who direct and coordinate operations. These directors would serve for specified terms after which, to continue, they would have to stand for reelection. There could also be procedures for their impeachment. No one would take directions from anyone they had not participated in democratically choosing. Democratically elected directors would be in service to their electors. The firm would be private property, and firms would compete

---

[11] Frey points out that "One of the most consistent results identified by happiness research is the devastating effect of unemployment on happiness" (2008, 157).

[12] The point is not to romanticize primordial human existence, but to highlight the fact that life practices evolved to be pleasurable in order to steer behavior toward conduct that would enhance chances of survival and reproduction, and that recreating some of these practices can enhance human flourishing.

within markets. Thus, capitalism's two principal social institutions would continue to exist, but they would no longer impair workers' democratic freedom of self-determination.

Today's advanced capitalist societies depict themselves as grounded in human freedom. This conception of freedom evolved with the struggle of a rising bourgeoisie against the landholding aristocracy's monopoly on political power. It celebrated the individual's freedom to own and sell property, move in search of better opportunities, and participate in markets. But this conception of freedom does not extend freedom to the workplace. It does not recognize the unfreedom of workers being separated from ownership, control, or ready access to the productive wealth they need to work and flourish. It emphasizes the workers' freedom to choose among employers, but not freedom from being bossed around. That is, it does not include workplaces as sites in which freedom should prevail, even though preparing for work, commuting, and working take up about one-half of workers' time awake, not to mention time thinking about and discussing work with others. Nor does it include freedom from the scourge of unemployment.

With work, as with all other situations where exploitation takes place, the prevailing ideology depicts unfree labor as free, captured fictionally by George Orwell's "doublespeak" and historically by German fascism's *Arbeit Macht Frei* (work makes you free) over the entrance gates of concentration camps.

The dominance of the elite's self-serving ideology of laissez-faire has been successful in keeping these freedoms absent from public discourse to such an extent that they are rarely even mentioned. They are seldom addressed in education or in the media. No contemporary political party or labor movement expresses substantial support for either guaranteed employment or workplace democracy.

Yet, if widely embraced and advocated by progressives, a political platform based on workplace democracy and guaranteed employment at living wages, with reskilling as needed, holds promise of being highly attractive to electorates. Democracy and freedom would be extended from the political domain to work life. The curse of unemployment, poverty, and inadequate professional education would be eliminated. Moreover, such a vision would not appear all that different from classical capitalism, retaining its two principal institutions—private property and markets—without concentrating power in the state or in a small rich class owning and controlling productive wealth. It would constitute the next major progressive step in freedom's historical unfolding.

Workers, constituting the overwhelming majority of the electorate, possess the political power to rewrite the social script and bring such a vision into reality. They need only awareness of its desirability and feasibility.

Humanity faces the threat of environmental catastrophe, making it urgent that laissez-faire ideology be delegitimized. Those who benefit from and perpetuate this ideology have possessed the political power to block environmental measures. Further, guided by this ideology, public policies have been enacted over the past decades that have been debasing conditions of life and generating a loss of faith in democracy. Without democracy, there is little hope that catastrophic environmental consequences can be avoided.

How This Book Unfolds

The next chapter explores work within the dynamic of evolutionary biology and humanity's primordial condition. It then turns in Chapter 3 to the degrading of work that began with the rise of the state and civilization and became more extreme for even "free workers" during the industrial revolution. Whereas the first three chapters address work in the broadest terms, beginning with Chapter 4, attention is narrowed to focus principally upon work and social conditions in the United States. The reason is to develop the more in-depth analysis that focusing on one country permits. However, as will be noted, most of the analysis applies equally to Western Europe. Chapters 4 and 5 address in turn the promise held forth by the post-World War II victory over the problem of scarcity in the rich countries and the dynamics by which this promise was betrayed. Chapter 6 addresses contemporary economic, social, political, and environmental conditions that make it urgent that work be humanized. Chapter 7 details the need for guaranteed employment and how it would function. Chapter 8 speaks to how workplace democracy would function and how it can be implemented to restore the nobility of work and render it pleasurable and supportive of community as it had been during the first 98% of human history. A concluding chapter summarizes the book's arguments and assesses whether employment security, fulfilling work, and post-scarcity liberation are humanity's likely future.

2

Work in a State of Nature

> Work is a necessity, part of the meaning of life on this earth, a path to growth, human development and personal fulfilment.
> — Pope Francis, n.d.

> A consistent aversion to whatever activity goes to maintain the life of the species is assuredly found in no other species of animal.
> — Thorstein Veblen 1898, 187

Writing was invented following the rise of the state 5500 years ago, and the written evidence we possess for early civilized history reveals work to have been viewed negatively. These writers were elites who thought work to be beneath them, done by subservient and inferior people. Aristotle, for instance, claimed that for fully flourishing lives and "growth in goodness," citizens must not be engaged in work (2000, 1328b–29). But even in modern times, when workers have been freed from the debased conditions of slavery and serfdom, work continues to be depicted negatively. For instance, mainstream economics—which its practitioners view as the queen of the social sciences—depicts work negatively as something people will do only if bribed with income with which to meet their consumption needs and desires. Work yields disutility, and workers long for leisure time "after hours" and on weekends, holidays, and vacations.

The traditionally disparaging depiction of work in social thought and popular culture has blinded us to its importance for human flourishing beyond material provisioning. Ignored have been work's potential to serve as a vent for creativity, for community belongingness, and for social esteem and self-respect. This chapter removes those blinders by demonstrating that, prior to the rise of the state, work was experienced and viewed positively. This pre-state world constituted the first 98% of the human story when our species, *Homo sapiens*, lived as hunter–gatherers and then early agriculturalists. Humans had free access to productive wealth (hunting and gathering territories and stone tools and then cultivable land), and they organized and carried out their group work democratically and without bosses. Social oppression and exploitation did not exist.[1]

An exploration of the primordial conditions of work is important for two reasons: first, this is the period when humans physically and psychologically evolved to became virtually who we are today; second, examining early social and economic arrangements might suggest how the workplace could be restructured to advance human flourishing.

This chapter begins by reviewing anthropological evidence supporting the claim that until the rise of civilization work was experienced and viewed positively. It then examines how during evolution, humans were selected to experience work as pleasurable. A third section draws support from the new field of happiness research to show why work, without oppression or exploitation, can be fulfilling.

---

[1] Among hunter–gatherers there was the exception of sedentary peoples on food rich waterways who developed social hierarchy and even slavery.

Anthropological Reports on Work

> The world's most 'primitive' people have few possessions, but they are not poor. Poverty is not a certain small amount of goods, nor is it just a relation between means and ends; above all it is a relation between people. Poverty is a social status. As such it is the invention of civilization. It has grown with civilization, at once as an invidious distinction between classes and more importantly as a tributary relation.
> — Marshall Sahlins 2004, 129

It seems ironic that when technology was most primitive, when humans possessed the least control over nature, work was neither perceived nor experienced negatively. Historians and anthropologists inform us that, prior to the rise of civilization, people did not clearly distinguish between work time and leisure time. Their vocabularies did not typically include a specific word for "work" or "toil" (Curle 1949, 41; Gray 2009a, 477).

It was long believed that the lack of a work-leisure distinction among pre-state people was because the scarcity problem was so extreme as to preclude the very possibility of leisure time (Graeber and Wengrow 2021, 137). However, since the late 1960s, anthropologists have rejected the view of hunting and gathering people as never resting from an unrelenting struggle just to survive. In fact, the opposite appears to have been true. Such people enjoyed a great deal of time that was not devoted explicitly to meeting their material needs. Indeed, they typically spent only between 12 and 20 hours per week in activities related directly to subsistence. This was true even of those dwelling in the earth's least hospitable environments such as the hunter–gatherer !Kung of the Kalahari desert (Leakey and Levin 1978, 95). Hunter gatherers would often work intermittently, stopping when they had enough for their needs (Sahlins 1974, 17). Because foragers worked to meet their needs as opposed to accumulating wealth, they took any productivity gains in increased non-work time (Sahlins 1974, 86). Interestingly, research has found that even today people are most productive when they work only four to five hours a day (Pang 2018).

It is this short workweek imposed by necessity that prompted Marshall Sahlins to refer to foraging people as "the original affluent society," and observe that to accept that hunters and gatherers are affluent is therefore to recognize that the present human condition of man slaving to bridge the gap between his unlimited wants and his insufficient means is a tragedy of modern times. (1974, 3).[2]

Whereas foragers viewed their world as one of abundance, modern economics views the principal human problem as one of scarcity. Anthropologist Rodney Needham points out that the behavior of hunter–gathering people exhibited "a confidence in the capacity of the environment to support them, and in their own ability to extract their livelihood from it" (quoted in Leakey and Levin 1978, 106). Foragers predominantly lived in the present with a "studied unconcern" for their future food needs (Sahlins 1974, 30). They did not see themselves as involved in a struggle with nature, but as living harmoniously in it.

Not only did hunter–gatherers not distinguish between work and leisure, but more strikingly, they did not distinguish between "work" and "play" (Sahlins 1974, 64; Gray 2009). Developmental psychologist Peter Gray claims that "play and humor lay at the core of hunter–gatherer social structures and mores....[and] They do not confound productiveness with unpleasantness.... Work for them is play" (2009a, 477; 501). He characterizes play as an "activity that is (1) self-chosen and self-directed; (2) intrinsically motivated; (3) structured by mental rules; (4) imaginative; and (5) produced in an active, alert, but nonstressed frame of mind" (2009a, 480).

Conquering "civilized" peoples found these natives "congenitally lazy," unwilling to do the arduous work of their new masters (Sahlins 1974, 55). But these natives were socialized to work without supervisors, or as Gray puts it, "They deliberately avoid telling each other how to behave, in work as in any other context. Each person is his or her own boss"

---

[2] Anthropologists David Graeber and David Wengrow note "all the other things [than food] paleolithic foragers got for free, but which we ourselves would expect to pay for: free security, free dispute resolution, free primary education, free care for the elderly, free medicine, not to mention entertainment cost, music, storytelling and religious services. Even when it comes to food, we must consider quality: after all, we're talking about 100% organic free range produce here, washed down with purest natural spring water" (2021, 527).

(2009a, 504). In accomplishing their necessary group tasks cooperatively without bosses, they were "maximizing each person's experience of free choice, which is essential to the spirit of play" (Gray 2009b).[3] Work was necessitated directly by nature rather than coerced by unequal social power. Further, except for sexual and age divisions of labor that were natural and viewed as such, all shared more or less equally in scarcity-compelled tasks. No parasitic class lived off the labors of others. As anthropologist Marvin Harris puts it: "People did what they had to do, but the where and when of it was not laid out by someone else. No executives, foremen, or bosses stood apart, measuring and counting" (1991, 101). They shared everything in such a way that the highest producers get no larger shares of food than any other member of their band (Gray 2009b).

Short work weeks, cooperative work carried out without bosses, and work experienced as play suggest a high quality of life. This is the conclusion reached by many anthropologists. Graeber and Wengrow, for instance, report that the

> colonial history of North and South America is full of accounts of settlers, captured or adopted by indigenous societies, being given the choice of where they wished to stay and almost invariably choosing to stay with the latter. This even applied to abducted children. Confronted again with their biological parents, most would run back to their adoptive kin for protection. By contrast, Amerindians incorporated into European Society by adoption or marriage, including those who…enjoyed considerable wealth and schooling, almost invariably did just the opposite: either escaping at the earliest opportunity, or—having tried their best to adjust, and ultimately failed—returning to indigenous society to live out their last days. (2021, 19)

---

[3] "Hunter–gatherers maintained their egalitarian ethos by cultivating the playful side of their human nature. Social play—that is, play involving more than one player—is necessarily egalitarian. It always requires a suspension of aggression and dominance along with a heightened sensitivity to the needs and desires of the other players. Players may recognize that one playmate is better at the played activity than are others, but that recognition must not lead the one who is better to lord it over the others…. The drive to play, therefore, requires suppression of the drive to dominate" (Gray 2021).

Benjamin Franklin observed that the Indians of the Iroquois Confederacy viewed the "laborious manner of life" of the colonists as "slavish and base," revealing them to be hostage to "infinite Artificial wants, no less craving than those of Nature," whereas the Indians possessed only "few…wants," which could be satisfied by "the spontaneous productions of nature with the addition of very little labor, if hunting and fishing may indeed be called labor when Game is so plenty." Thus, compared to the colonists, the Indians enjoyed an "abundance of leisure" (cited in Suzman 2021, 244).

Graeber and Wengrow report that "some of the first European travelers to the Americas compared savage males to nobleman back home because like these nobleman, they dedicated almost all their time to politics, hunting, raiding and waging war on neighboring groups" (2021, 190).

Hunters were capable of extreme work effort, pursuing game for days on end with little rest (Leo Marx 2000). But once the hunt had succeeded, they would be idle until their food supplies were used up. A proclivity for idleness in all animals has survival value, since it reduces energy expenditure (Barash 1986, 308). This preference for hard labor followed by idleness appears to have remained with humanity.[4]

Darwin's Evolutionary Biology

In the first place, as the reasoning powers and foresight of the members became improved, each man would soon learn that if he aided his fellow-men, he would commonly receive aid in return. From this low motive, he might acquire the habit of aiding his fellows. And the habit of performing benevolent actions certainly strengthens the feelings of sympathy which gives first impulse to benevolent actions… But another and much more

---

[4] Writing about free workers such as craftsmen in the seventeenth century, historian E. P. Thompson notes, "The work pattern was one of alternate bouts of intense labour and idleness, wherever men were in control of their own working lives." He speculates that because this "pattern persists among some self-employed—artists, writers, small farmers, and perhaps also with students—today, [it] provokes the question whether it is not a 'natural' human work-rhythm" (1963, 73).

powerful stimulus to the development of the social virtues is afforded by the praise and blame of our fellow-men... and this instinct no doubt was originally acquired, like all other social instincts, through natural selection.
— Charles Darwin 1871a, 1:146–47

[The] reasons why people have particular preferences and priorities cannot be satisfactorily addressed without consideration of the ways in which our long history of natural and sexual selection pressures shaped the emotional, motivational and information-processing mechanisms underlying the expression of values and preferences.
— Evolutionary psychologists Margo Wilson, Martin Daly, Stephen Gordon, and Adelle Prat 1996, 144

Because humans are first and foremost biological beings, our understanding of their motivation must be consonant with what has been revealed by the biological sciences, especially evolutionary psychology with roots in the work of Charles Darwin. The necessity of this grounding, as behavioral economist Robert H. Frank puts it, is that the "Darwinian framework is the only scientific framework available for trying to understand why humans and other animals are motivated to behave as they do" (2011, 24). Evolutionary biology takes research in human behavior to the level of ultimate causation, and as evolutionary biologist David Sloan Wilson and economist John M. Gowdy note, "Thinking in terms of ultimate causation is one of the most important tools in the evolutionary toolkit" (2013, S5). Accordingly, our understanding of work must be grounded in how our species evolved biologically.

Biological evolution occurs when a genetic change survives in the population of an organism over successive generations. Cultural evolution occurs when cultural traits like ideas and behaviors change over time. But biological and cultural evolution are interdependent. In a process called gene-culture co-evolution, they mutually affect each other. Genes set the conditions for cultural expression, or as biologist Edward O. Wilson quipped, "G*enes hold culture* on a *leash*" (1978, 167). However, over time, where a cultural practice provides survival advantage to the group and its members, the genes that privilege this cultural expression are carried into future generations. In this manner, over time, cultural changes have changed humans biologically. In an important sense, to some degree humans have made themselves.[5]

According to evolutionary psychology, work would be expected to be experienced positively. During evolution, humans have been selected to experience activities that enhance survival chances, including work, to be pleasurable, and not the biblical curse "of painful labor all the days of your life" (*Genesis* 3: 17). That is, because the provisioning activities we call work improve the likelihood of continued existence, they would be expected to be pleasurable (Inglis et al 1997; Osborne 1977; Balcombe 2009). This accords with Darwin's view that "nothing is more common than for animals to take pleasure in practising whatever instinct they follow at other times for some real good" (1871b, 2:54). It is, in fact, hard to imagine how a species could have survived if it had been selected to experience work, an activity necessary for survival, to be a curse or a disagreeable activity to be shunned.

Through the second Darwinian dynamic of sexual selection, those who performed work well would be appreciated by their communities, and would therefore enjoy a degree of status, especially insofar as early humans shared food. Potential mates are attracted to those well appreciated by the community, and hard and effective work would signal promise that offspring would be adequately nourished.

Mainstream economists claim that self-interested individuals will not voluntarily contribute their fair share of a public good, a lesson poignantly made in Garrett Hardin's *The Tragedy of the Commons* (1968). In their understanding, in small groups, contributing to a group's welfare might be an expression of reciprocal altruism or useful as insurance or risk-reduction. But this narrowly utilitarian view abstracts from the wider

---

[5] Without explicit biological grounding, some notable social scientists have recognized this self-creation. Karl Marx claimed that man, by "acting on the external world and changing it, he at the same time changes his own nature" (1859, 177). Political philosopher Hannah Arendt noted "the seemingly blasphemous notion of Marx that labor (and not God) created man or that labor (and not reason) distinguished man from other animals" (1958, 86). Anthropologist V. Gordon Childe titled his now classic work *Man Makes Himself* (1936).

outlook that people's preferences are interdependent, and that community approval and reproductive advantage can result from what appears to be, is felt to be, and is believed to be, generosity.

How, in fuller detail, each of Darwin's two principal dynamics of natural selection and sexual selection clarify the nature of work are addressed below in turn.

Natural Selection and Work

The evolution of our humanoid ancestors dates back about 6 million years when they diverged from other primates to exploit the environmental niche of savannahs created by climate change that cooled Africa, reducing forest habitats and expanding grasslands. Savannahs hold more protein per square kilometer than any other landscape (Dutton 2010, 19–20). As they began exploiting this rich environment to provision themselves, genetic adaptations were selected that enabled them to do so more effectively—the drawn-out process of a species adjusting to fit its environment. Examples include maintaining an erect position to better see prey and predators over tall grasses while freeing hands to carry tools and weapons. Standing upright also permitted the larynx to drop, expanding capacity for making vowel and consonant sounds. Elongated feet permitted greater running speed to chase down game and escape predators. Body hairlessness and sweat glands enabled more efficient heat dissipation than that of furred prey and predators. Excess brain neurons may have been selected as backup for dysfunction due to extended exposure to the sun's intense heat (humans have three times as many neurons in the cortex as chimpanzees, our nearest relatives, who remained shielded from sun in the forests).[6] More meat in the diet allowed a smaller gut, smaller teeth, and muscles to develop that could make finer movement of the tongue within the oral cavity, facilitating a diverse and high-quality range of sounds.

---

[6] Retention of hair on the top of the head moderated heat absorption and enable humanoids to outlast other scavengers feeding on killed prey under the sun. Pubic and underarm hair served to transmit signals by odor.

Because the pace of biological evolution is glacially slow, contemporary humans' mental and emotional processes, as well as behavior, are to a considerable extent those which humans were selected to possess during our evolution to fit a savannah environment. Evolutionary psychologist Satoshi Kanazawa identifies a "savannah principle," according to which "the human brain has difficulty comprehending and dealing with entities and situations that did not exist in [this] ancestral environment" (2009, 26).[7] Polymath Nassim Nicholas Taleb agrees, arguing that "black swan" events (unpredictable events with massive consequences) have been increasing in frequency since the adoption of agriculture, such that "The world has changed too fast for our genetic makeup. We are alienated from our environment" (2010, 85). It is for this reason that, in our striving to craft social institutions conducive to human flourishing and happiness, we must take into account our evolution in our ancestral environment.

Homo sapiens, evolved about 300,000 years ago (Lawton 2020). Although there was substantial evolutionary change over the 290,000 years when these humans lived as hunter–gatherers, evolutionary biologists believe that contemporary humans remain virtually the same, biologically, as when agriculture was adopted about 10,000 years ago.[8]

The dynamics of natural selection provide animals, humans included, with guidance systems that steer them to behave in ways that favor their survival. To motivate appropriate behavior, humans evolved to experience these activities to be pleasurable or painful. Thus, just as evolution would select humans to experience as tasty those foods that are nutritious, and to experience the pursuit and act of sex as highly pleasurable, so too the activities needed to procure nutrition and general wellbeing. That is, as is true for all living animals, behavioral mechanisms evolved

---

[7] Philosopher of art Denis Dutton implicitly endorses the savannah principle, reporting that "people in very different cultures around the world [esthetically] gravitate toward the same general type of pictorial representation: a landscape with trees and open areas, water, human figures, and animals...landscapes of a fairly uniform type" (2010, 14). They also prefer one with a climbable tree, presumably to see at greater distance as well as to escape predators.

[8] Often cited exceptions are the development of lactose tolerance within pastoral populations and adaption to high altitudes by mountain peoples.

to steer humans to acquire the necessary resources for survival and reproduction.[9]

Because humans are social beings and social coordination in work is generally more productive, humans evolved to carry out their provisioning in cooperation with others. This provisioning, or what we have come to call work, in community with others was pleasurable, motivating and steering behavior to best assure its success. Humans enjoy carrying out tasks in concert with others, especially when they freely participate in determining how it is to be done. Because humans have changed little biologically since the adoption of agriculture, work and community remain central to their sense of wellbeing, to their happiness.

Cultural historian Johan Huizinga, in *Homo Ludens* (1938), claimed that it was through play that human culture arose and advanced. Gray concurs: "one evolutionary function of play is to generate... novel behaviours and creations, some of which turn out later on to be useful in survival-promoting ways. According to this theory, play, not necessity, is the mother of invention" (2018, 94). Hunter–gatherer societies that have been studied in remote regions of all continents have been found "to be extraordinarily playful," both among children and adults. This playfulness is evident in activities as diverse as work, religious practices and dispute resolution. Work and games are conducted cooperatively as opposed to competitively. Because their work benefits and is valued by the community, it is especially rewarding (Gray 2009b).

Play also exists among mammals other than humans and serves the same basic functions. It is not something the young need to be taught to do. They are instinctually driven to it. They practice in play "the skills they must develop for survival into and through adulthood" (Gray 2009a, 516). Play, then, is "a means by which individuals (1) practice skills that are essential to their survival and reproduction; (2) learn to cope physically and emotionally with unexpected, potentially harmful events; (3) generate new, sometimes useful creations; and (4) reduce hostility and enable cooperation" (Gray 2018, 84).

---

[9] In terms expressed by psychologist Mihaly Csikszentmihalyi, humans "experience a positive state of consciousness when they use their skills to the utmost in meeting an environmental challenge [to] improve their chances of survival" (1993, 190).

Hunting was a principal male activity during the first 98% of human history, generally carried out in small bands. It is telling of its pleasurable nature that long after it ceased to be an important provisioning activity, it continued to be a sought-out leisure pursuits for individuals, often in participation with others.[10] Indeed, in later highly inegalitarian times when wild animals were in short supply, elites restricted hunting grounds for their own amusement, denying game to the poor for whom it would have been a needed source of protein. Today, many partake of "catch and release" fishing, clearly revealing that its end is pleasure and not nourishment. Gathering was generally an even more important source of nourishment and was generally carried out in groups. It too continues to be a highly pleasurable group activity today, notably in search of mushrooms. After the Neolithic revolution—the adoption of agriculture—growing and tending plants became the prime provisioning activity. Today, gardening remains a favorite pastime, not only highly pleasurable to its practitioners, but also providing physical and psychological health benefits.[11]

Animals were selected to respond to signals such as discomfort and pain to steer them to retreat from and avoid harmful behavior and conditions. Humans, as social animals, suffer the pain of loneliness that motivates them to seek company with other members of their group among whom they are safer and thus better able to survive and reproduce (Csikszentmihalyi 1993, 45). Those who lack adequate innate guidance signals, or possess them in weakened form, are less likely to survive to mate and send their unique genes into the future.

Sexual Selection and Work

Among the behavior that would draw favorable attention of the opposite sex would be diligent and high quality work. A reputation for being a

---

[10] Many productive activities of early humans other than the hunting and gathering, such as cooking, woodworking, pottery, knitting, sewing, weaving, and leather work have become hobbies in contemporary wealthy societies.

[11] In the United Kingdom, for instance, in a population of 64 million, 27 million partake in "leisure" gardening (Evergreen Garden Care 2020).

good worker would signal to potential mates good promise for parenting their offspring. Accordingly, individuals would be motivated to perform high quality work and find pleasure in doing so. If this resulted in being selected for mating, their unique set of genes would make it into posterity, carrying forward this behavioral trait.

Early anthropologists such as Richard Thurnwald recognized that people seek good reputations through work, although they did not link it to Darwin's dynamic of sexual selection. Thurnwald noted that in primitive societies, "It is for social distinction that work is done, not for the acquisition of money or material goods" (1932, 178). Similarly, Bronislaw Malinowski observed that what motivates the Trobriand Islands' male to work is that "He wants…to achieve social distinction as a good gardener and a good worker in general" (1922, 62).

What led Darwin to formulate his theory of sexual selection was the difficulty his theory of natural selection faced in explaining the existence of unfit traits such as the ornate and heavy male peacocks' feathers, or the huge racks of antlers found on stags. Such traits are handicaps that reduce their carriers' survival potential. This enigma led Darwin to formulate his theory of sexual selection. Species may evolve physical or behavioral traits that reduce their survival fitness but enhance their attractiveness for mating and thus the probability that their unique genes will survive into the future.[12]

Among humans, sexual attraction may be physical. Social behavior, however, is often equally if not more important. Those who behave in a manner sufficiently attractive to the opposite sex will successfully mate and the genes that carry these behavioral traits will be found in their offspring. Individuals, no matter how fit they might be, who are unsuccessful in mating, will have a unique complex of genes that

---

[12] It is noteworthy that most of these unfit survival traits evolved in males because they were preferred by females, and where this was the case females effectively directed aspects of the males' evolution. This empowerment of the female drew the attention of feminists and progressives at the end of the nineteenth century to Darwin's theory of sexual selection. Cultural historian Kimberly Hamlin writes that "The woman who did the most to popularize the feminist potential of Darwinian sexual selection was a Bellamy disciple who went on to become the most influential American feminist thinker of the early twentieth century: Charlotte Perkins Gilman" (2014, 164).

will become extinct.[13] The expressions of behavior that are attractive to potential mates become instinct driven, the dynamic of gene-culture co-evolution, a dynamic, as discussed above, that comes into play when cultural changes make certain genetic adaptions fitness or reproduction-enhancing.

Aristotle held that, by their nature, human beings are curious and seek knowledge. Because knowledge enhances the potential for survival, those who possess or pursue it are sexually attractive to mates. Accordingly, seeking knowledge and making cognitive connections could be predicted to be pleasurable.

The roots of human behavior in sexual selection have generally been ignored by social scientists and historians.[14] This is due, at least in part, to that fact that people generally lack awareness of the extent to which their behavior is motivated by sexual competition. As Kanazawa puts it, "evolved psychological mechanisms mostly operate behind and beneath conscious thinking..." (2009, 26).[15]

It is because of the centrality of sexual competition in human behavior and the fact that human society requires cooperation and internal peace that considerable cultural practices have evolved to mask or temper its expression. How striking upon reflection that humans are the only animals that have not only come to hide their genitalia, but taboos on nudity are enforced by punitive laws.

---

[13] Kanazawa points out that "we are all descended from those who chose to reproduce. None of us inherited our psychological mechanism from our ancestors who remained childless. Everything else in life, even survival, is a means to reproductive success.... [reproduction] is the ultimate goal of our existence" (2009, 26). It should be noted, however, that modern reproductive technology enables reproduction outside of mating.

[14] Thorstein Veblen was rare among social thinkers in recognizing the need to ground understanding of human behavior in Darwinian dynamics. However, he failed to draw on Darwin's theory of sexual selection. Had he done so, he would have perceived that the conspicuous consumption that so vexed him, signaled that spendthrifts were so well-off economically that such waste was affordable, making them appear wealthy enough to be promising mates. This behavior, although not irrational for individuals, is so for society. Adam Smith's invisible hand fails (Wisman 2019).

[15] Cognitive scientist Steven Pinker elaborates: "ultimately people crave sex in order to reproduce (because the ultimate cause of sex is reproduction), but proximately [many contemporary humans] may do everything they can not to reproduce (because the proximate cause of sex is pleasure)" (2002, 54).

Historically, for a society to be successful in surviving and reproducing, it was necessary that its members succeed in acquiring food, shelter, and providing defense. This is the provisioning we call work. As noted above, those most valued as workers would command higher status and be more attractive to potential mates for parenting their children.

One form of work, warfare, is extremely dangerous, and highly successful warriors were, until quite recent times, highly attractive sexually. Warring requires being willing to put one's life at risk for the welfare of the community. Although this might seem altruistic, the fact that successful warriors parented more children reveals its self-interestedness from an evolutionary point of view.

Frequently, capturing women was a principal aim of war. Evolutionary psychologist David Buss provides a vivid report:

> Among the Yanomamö [a contemporary foraging-horticultural people in the Amazon rainforest], there are two key motives that spur men to declare war on another tribe—a desire to capture the wives of other men or a desire to recapture wives that were lost in previous raids... It seemed silly to them to risk one's life for anything other than capturing women (1994, 219–20).[16]

It would appear that hunters and gatherers did not conform in their relations with surrounding peoples to Jean-Jacques Rousseau's image of the noble peaceful savage, living as "a free being, whose heart is at peace, and body in health," during an era he claimed to be "the best for man" (1755, 150; 167). Hunter–gatherers were anything but peaceable beyond their own group. Darwin observed from his travels that "tribes inhabiting adjacent districts are almost always at war with each other; for the social instincts never extend to all the individuals of the same species"

---

[16] Anthropologist Napoleon Chagnon calculated that among the Yanomamö, those who had killed enemies had an average of over two and a half more wives and more than three times as many children (Diamond 2012, 163). Victorious hunters were also more successful in reproduction. The skills required of warriors are common to hunters and the latter were also attractive to potential mates. Anthropologist Eric Alden Smith points out that "better hunters tend to have younger wives and...these men also have harder-working (more economically productive) wives....[Further] women cite 'good hunter' as the single most valued trait in a potential husband.... better hunters receive preferential treatment when incapacitated" (2004, 346; 351).

(1871a, 1:85). Anthropologist Lawrence Keeley reports that 87% of pre-agricultural societies fought more than once a year and 65% were continuously at war. A single battle might result in the death of a tenth of a band's population. They took women as captives and generally killed their enemy men to preclude revenge. About 30% of males were killed in warfare, a rate found among chimpanzees, our nearest primate relatives (1997, 174).

Because warring contributed to group survival, warriors performing this extreme expression of work could be expected to gain social status and find it pleasurable. This is supported by the reported positive psychological experiences of soldiers. Philosopher Friedrich Nietzsche, and others since, have noted that men are more closely bonded in combat and its threat than at any other time. This bonding appears to be intensely exhilarating (Gat 2008, 662). War historian John W. Dower adds that "Psychological drives that may run deeper than group identity or thirst for collective revenge enter the picture, such as constructs of masculinity or the compelling attractiveness of 'limit experiences'" (2010, 223).

Self-Creation Through Work

> Labour is… a process between man and nature, a process by which man, through his own actions, mediates, regulates and controls the metabolism between himself and nature…. He sets in motion the forces belonging to his own body, his arms, legs, head and hands, in order to appropriate the materials of nature in a form adapted to his own needs. Through this movement he acts upon external nature and changes it, and in this way changes his own nature.
> — Karl Marx 1867, I:197–98

Numerous scholars in addition to Marx have noted the manner in which humans have participated in their own creation, and arguably, as Marx claimed, the principal way has been through work, and especially through the development of tools. As humanoids crafted the tools that increased the efficiency of their provisioning, they also changed themselves through the dynamic of gene-culture co-evolution. Using tools is not unique to humans. Anthropologist James Suzman reports that it has been found among "fifteen species of invertebrates, twenty-four species of birds, and four species of non-primate mammals, among them elephants and orcas" (2021, 63). Nevertheless, its prevalence and consequences have been overwhelmingly greatest among humans.

Of all tools, none has had a greater importance in altering our species during evolution than fire (Suzman 2021, 98). The ability to control fire dates back a million to two million years. It made the diet more diverse. Some plants are toxic or too fibrous while raw but become edible when cooked. Meat became safer and easier to digest. Cooking, in effect, accomplishes part of the digestive process prior to eating, permitting a smaller digestive system and making more energy available for brain functions.

Fire served other functions. It permitted humans to survive in cold climates, even extremely cold ones. With fire, the day extended later into the darkness of night. Foragers could set fires to clear terrain to make it attractive to plant-eating prey, as well as using it to drive animals into traps or ambushes. A campfire deterred predators.

Human brains are energy hogs, constituting only 2% of body weight but consuming 20% of the body's energy. By contrast, chimpanzees, our closest relatives, have brains only one-third the size of humans' that consume about 12% of their energy. Suzman hypothesizes that it was the extraordinary energy windfall permitted by the adaption of the tool fire that enabled the brain to grow among humanoids (2021, 104), another striking example of gene-culture co-evolution.

As a labor-saving technology, fire expanded the amount of free time, and in doing so, increased the time available for boredom, a mental setting for creativity. Csikszentmihalyi points out that "Boredom directs us to seek new challenges, while anxiety urges us to develop new skills; the net result is that, in order to avoid such negative feelings, a person is forced to grow in complexity" (1993, 190–91). Suzman notes that "Some of Newton's, Einstein's, Descartes's and Archimedes' greatest insights have all been attributed to boredom.... [and] Psychologists ... remind us that boredom is a more fertile mother of invention than necessity" (2021,

109; 110). Further, "As our ancestors gained more free time, making or keeping peace by humoring, entertaining, persuading, and engaging others—rather than beating them into submission—will have become an ever more important skill" (Suzman 2021, 112).

Through work, other tools developed that transformed humans physically, mentally, and socially. Early human species and other primates are unable to throw objects with force and accuracy. But about two million years ago, as a consequence of throwing objects to kill game, fight enemies, and deal with bullies, human shoulders underwent changes that enabled them to throw stones or other projectiles with greater accuracy and force, yet another example of a cultural practice leading to genetic change. This ability to throw lethal projectiles from a distance also allowed humans to hunt big game more safely. Along with the ability to form coalitions, the ability to throw projectiles such as stones, spears, and later bow-powered arrows enabled the weaker to cut down and eliminate bullies from a safe distance. By eliminating bullies and others behaving in ways that are detrimental to the community, humans domesticated themselves into a less violent species (Wrangham 2019). Stone Age weaponry, inexpensive and relatively available to all, was critical in bringing forth and maintaining a high degree of economic and political equality among foragers.[17] This weaponry also reduced the advantage of large body size for males, thereby reducing gender size differences (dimorphism).

Suzman captures humanity's self-creation through work in the following terms:

> The story of *Homo sapiens*' ability to master skills from microsurgery to masonry is written into our hands, arms, eyes, mouths, bodies, and

---

[17] Gray writes that

> The hunter–gatherer version of equality meant that each person was equally entitled to food, regardless of his or her ability to find or capture it; so food was shared. It meant that nobody had more wealth than anyone else; so all material goods were shared. It meant that nobody had the right to tell others what to do; so each person made his or her own decisions. It meant that even parents didn't have the right to order their children around; hence the non-directive childrearing methods.... It meant that group decisions had to be made by consensus; hence no boss, 'big man,' or chief (2021).

brains. It tells us not only that we are physically and neurologically the product of the work our evolutionary ancestors did, but also that, as individuals, we have evolved to be progressively remolded over the course of our lives by the kinds of work we do. (2021, 64)

The evolutionary history of humanity has substantially been a process of self-creation through advancing work practices.

Happiness Research and Work

The truth seems to be that as human nature is constituted, man rapidly degenerates unless he has some hard work to do, some difficulties to overcome, and that some strenuous exertion is necessary for physical and moral health. The fullness of life lies in the development and activity of as many and as high faculties as possible.
— Alfred Marshall 1890, 136

As discussed above, the pleasurable character of work in societies without oppression and exploitation is confirmed by the dynamics of evolution and by extensive anthropological evidence. This evidence receives further support from the findings of a new interdisciplinary body of study called happiness research, where the term happiness stands for well-being and life satisfaction.[18] Economist and happiness researcher Bruno Frey notes that the new field "explicitly takes into account the genetic, socio-demographic, cultural, and political determinants of happiness" (2008, xi; 3). This research gives more attention to the intrinsic importance of work as an end in and of itself, as opposed to a means to income with which to purchase consumption items.

Some of the findings of happiness research concerning work were earlier recognized by social scientists who found that, above a certain

---

[18] The scientific study of happiness is relatively new. It developed as behavioral scientists grounded their findings in testable hypotheses, longitudinal and controlled experimental studies, using varied measurement techniques (Biswas-Diener, Diener, and Tamir 2004, 19). The stature of this new science of happiness research was recognized in 2002 when psychologist Daniel Kahneman, one of its founders, received a Nobel Prize in economics.

material threshold, it is in the realm of work that well-being is most readily achieved. For instance, following his own research, Gunnar Myrdal, 1974 Nobel Laureate in Economics, reported that "Most people who are reasonably well off derive more satisfaction in their capacity as producers than as consumers. Indeed, many would define the social ideal as a state in which as many people as possible can live in this way" (1968, 136). More recently, political scientist Robert E. Lane reported that "It is in work, not in consumption and, as research reports show, not even in leisure, where most people engage in the activities that they find most satisfying, where they learn to cope with their human and natural environments, and where they learn about themselves" (1991, 235). Indeed, the psychological benefits of increased consumption appear to be short-lived. Individuals experience rising utility or pleasure for only about a year following an increase in income (Frey 2008, 131).[19]

Substantial evidence reveals that humans experience a strong sense of well-being when they are involved in working on a project, whether alone or with others, that they find interesting and worthwhile. Indeed, they often become totally focused on and immersed in the activity, much as athletes do in sports. When in this state they are highly energized, they feel in control, there is a loss of self-consciousness, negative or pessimistic thoughts disappear, the activity seems worth doing for its own sake, and they report being in their element or being happy. Csikszentmihalyi has chosen the term *flow* for this phenomenon because some experiencing it have characterized it as a flow-like experience (1993). He likens the term flow to psychologist Abraham Maslow's "peak experiences" (1954) and the feeling philosopher Bertrand Russell described in *The Conquest of Happiness* (1930, 229), and notes that "it is surprising how many people have come independently to the same conclusions regarding the real sources of human happiness" (1993, 299).[20] These conclusions lend

---

[19] Economists Milena Nikolova and Carol Graham report that "work meaningfulness is a eudaimonic dimension of well-being at work... [finding] that autonomy, competence, and relatedness explain about 60% of the variation in work meaningfulness perceptions. Meanwhile, extrinsic factors, such as income, benefits, and performance pay, are relatively unimportant for work meaningfulness" (2020, 23).

[20] Csikszentmihalyi poses the question of "Why should full immersion in a challenging activity be so rewarding?" He answers that

support to the argument that humans evolved to experience work as pleasurable.

On the central importance of work for happiness, polymaths John Ruskin and William Morris equated work with "fellowship, with love, with the liberating vitality of the artist" (Gillespie 1965, 77). Sociologist Ronald Mason writes, "The more work becomes expressive and a means of developing individual potentials, the more work comes to resemble art" (1982, 134). Much earlier, Marx argued that in a future society without exploitation, the distinction between work and art would disappear (Gulli 2005).

Extensive further studies confirm the importance of work to individuals beyond providing an income. For instance, a World Values Survey found that "only 22% of respondents agreed that a job is just a way of earning money, and 63% said that they would enjoy having a paying job even if they did not need the money" (Alesina, Glaeser, and Sacerdote 2001, 239). Psychologists Edward Diener and Martin Seligman, in reviewing the literature on the economic psychology of well-being, find two of the six major factors underlying well-being to be living in a democratic and stable society that provides material well-being, and having rewarding and engaging work and an adequate income (2004, 25).[21]

Within good workplaces, work provides a ready medium in which self-esteem can especially flourish. In work we contribute to society's wealth, as opposed to drawing upon it via consumption, and thus we have grounds for a sense that we are participating in achieving society's well-being. Possessing a degree of control over the work process provides a sense of accomplishment and pride as tasks advance and are completed.

Apparently, humans who experience a positive state of consciousness when they use their skills to the utmost in meeting an environmental challenge improve their chances of survival. The connection between flow and enjoyment may have been at first a fortunate genetic accident, but once it occurred, it made those who experienced it much more likely to be curious, to explore, to take on new tasks and develop new skills (1993, 190).

[21] The other four are: to have supportive friends and family, to be reasonably healthy and have treatment available in case of health problems, to have important goals related to ones values, and to have a philosophy or religion that provides guidance, purpose, and meaning to one's life (2004, 25).

Lane reports evidence that reveals control over the work process to provide more self-esteem than does possessing political rights (1991, 198). A later national survey of British workers found them to be substantially happier when possessing greater responsibility and control over their work. More striking, those with little such control suffered a 23% higher risk of heart attacks (Priestland 2012, 271). Moreover, in work we can aid our fellow workers and bask in their appreciation of our assistance and our skills.

******

As has been revealed in this chapter, extensive evidence from the dynamics of natural selection, sexual selection, anthropology, and interdisciplinary happiness research suggests that during evolution, humans were selected to experience work—provisioning to meet basic human needs—to be pleasurable. But if this is true, how did work come to be seen as a curse, undesirable and looked down upon, something that can only be brought forth by the threat of starvation, the whip, or by bribes with which to buy consumer goods, but otherwise avoided?

3

Eden Lost: The Rise of the State and Work Degraded

Why anyone not impelled by hunger, danger, or coercion would willingly give up hunting and foraging or pastoralism for full-time agriculture is hard to fathom.
— James C. Scott 2017, 18

A person who can acquire no property, can have no other interest but to eat as much, and to labour as little as possible. Whatever work he does beyond what is sufficient to purchase his own maintenance can be squeezed out of him by violence only, and not by any interest of his own.
— Adam Smith 1776, 365

The adoption of agriculture—the Neolithic revolution—about 10,000 years ago was not only the most transforming of all revolutions in human history, it was, according to anthropologist Jared Diamond, "the worst mistake in the history of the human race" (1987). Whatever the merits, or seriousness of Diamond's verdict, it is clear that the quality of the work experience was severely degraded. As hunter–gatherers, humans provisioned themselves—"worked"—by nomadically searching for food, as do other migratory animals. With agriculture, they became sedentary and produced food in a controlled manner. Although this has been generally viewed as an advance in human well-being, for most humans it was the opposite.

Not only did agriculturalists work far longer hours than hunter–gatherers (Gillingham 1979), they also became victims to a host of diseases transmitted from their domesticated animals and lived shorter lives. Human skeletons became weaker as bones became less dense (Feltman 2014, A3). Skeletons from Greece and Turkey reveal that after the adoption of agriculture, the average height for men declined from 5'9" to 5'3", for women from 5'5" to 5'. Life expectancy at birth fell from about 26 years to 19. Among hunter–gatherers, about five percent lived past age 50; among early agriculturalists, about one percent (Diamond 1987).

Cultivators were also relatively trapped geographically since survival would be difficult should they move before harvests. They would also have lost much of the complex knowledge and skills necessary to survive as foragers. Consequently, living in agricultural settlements made producers more vulnerable to domination by those who could amass superior physical force. Further, the greater their stock of animals or harvests, the more they would be targets for outside pillagers, and therefore face a need to fight rather than flee.

Planting and herding increased humans' orientation to the future. Whereas the economic existence of forager peoples was mostly short-run or practically day-to-day, centered on consuming the food from a few days of hunting and gathering, agriculturalists had to focus on the agricultural cycle. Over an agricultural cycle, they had to plan and save for planting and animal breeding. They had to be strictly disciplined in the sense that, no matter how hungry they might become, they could not eat their seed corn or breeding animals, lest they starve during the next agricultural cycle. Religious beliefs and practices often facilitated this harsh discipline. A notable, albeit much later example is the Christian Lenten period of belt-tightening that traditionally preceded the birthing of domesticated animals and planting of crops.

Cultivators' work was far less varied than that of foragers and thus so too was their knowledge and personal independence. Anthropologist Claude Lévi-Strauss reports that hunter–gatherer societies had meticulous scientific classifications of the natural world that in many ways resembled the later Linnaean model. The Subanun in the Philippines, for instance, had a botanical lexicon of more than a thousand terms (2021, 4). Anthropologist Peter Gardner writes that "while non-foragers tend to push children towards obedience and responsibility, foragers tend to press for self-reliance, independence and individual achievement" (1991, 543). Agriculturists' work was also more onerous. Nevertheless, early pre-state agrarian societies remained highly egalitarian, and its members retained control over the work process. They were not exploited or bossed about.

Agriculture set in motion the demographic, material, and cultural foundations that would enable greater social complexity and technological dynamism. It also was a precondition for the rise of the state and civilization, private property, extreme inequality, and the debasement of work. Yet, paradoxically, although it dramatically decreased the wellbeing for workers, the rise of the state eventually set the preconditions for the material wealth and freedom of our contemporary world.

The shift to agriculture permitted the accumulation of food surpluses, enabling some to eat without farming and so freeing them to engage in the development and production of other goods, services, and cultural artifacts. Increasingly sophisticated division of labor nourished technological advances. Progress for nomadic foragers had been constrained by limits to their division of labor, their inability to accumulate wealth, and their very small-scale social units. With sedentism, non-portable wealth, such as improved land, buildings, and workshops could be accumulated. Villages expanded into towns.

Population growth among foragers was slow, often nonexistent, and sometimes negative. Whereas population density averaged 0.05 persons per square mile among foragers, it increased in the Levant to about 35 per square mile following the adoption of agriculture. It rose as high as 155 per square mile with intensive irrigated agriculture.[1] Sedentary life enabled mothers to care for more children than was possible among nomadic foragers. Forager mothers had to nurse and carry children until about age four, braking population growth. Further, the grain diets of

---

[1] An alternative way to grasp this population explosion is to note that after about 290,000 years of existence, only between five and eight million humans foraged the earth at the outset of the transition to agriculture about 10,000 years ago. About 8000 years later, about 250 million did so as agriculturalists, leaving one to two million still foraging, principally in Australia, America, and Africa (Harari 2015, 98).

agriculturalists, softened by cooking, enabled children to be weaned earlier, permitting pregnancy at shorter intervals. High-carbohydrate diets also boost ovulation and thus frequency of pregnancy (Scott 2017, 114). The resulting population growth required more food production, resulting in long workdays, often from sunrise to sunset. It will be recalled that the workweek of hunter–gatherers was only between 12 and 20 hours. Because agriculture supported a larger and more dense population, there was no turning back. Their higher population-to-land ratio made it impossible for all humans to survive by foraging. As mythically captured in *Genesis*, humans lost Eden and were condemned to a harsh and degraded agricultural existence in which they would eat by the sweat of their brow.

The Rise of the State and Debased Labor

The spread of agriculture created the preconditions for the rise of the state and civilization about 5500 years ago (beginning the last two percent of human history). This was humanity's second greatest revolution. In Eurasia, technological advances in metallurgy, superior military organization, and ideology empowered warrior elites to gain ownership and control of the means of production. All others were forced into subservient roles to access the productive resources necessary for survival. The cost for this access was the elite owners' appropriation of their surplus, the output workers produced in excess of what they needed for survival. Over the course of civilization, to work and thus survive, workers have been exploited—their surplus expropriated—as slaves, serfs, indentured servants, indebted peasants, and wage earners. That is, workers have been unfree.[2]

Jean-Jacques Rousseau was thus correct when he claimed that, with civilization, the powerful "irretrievably destroyed natural liberty, established for all time the law of property and inequality…and for the benefit

---

[2] In 1772, 4 years prior to publication of Adam Smith's *Wealth of Nations*, political economist Arthur Young estimated that only 4% of the world's population was free, the remaining 96% living as slaves, serfs, servants, or vassals with obligations to landlords (1772).

of a few ambitious men subjected the human race thenceforth to labour, servitude and misery" (1984, 122). It is only in modern times that the existence of the state began becoming positive for most of humanity.[3] Although the rise of civilization has always been viewed as positive, political scientist and anthropologist James C. Scott reminds us that "It would be almost impossible to exaggerate the centrality of bondage, in one form or another, in the development of the state until very recently" (2017, 155). The most positive consequence of the rise of the state was the decline in deaths from violence and the acceleration of technological progress that would eventually promise today's abundance.

Foragers shared food and much else, and thus generally no one starved unless all did. And because they lived somewhat hand to mouth, they lived to a substantial extent in the present. This sharing of resources was also common among highly egalitarian pre-state agriculturalists (Bogaard, Fochesato, and Bowles 2019, 2). However, with the rise of the state, restricted or private rights to property, in the sense that some hold possession and exclusive control of resources such as land, radically transformed social conditions, enabling those who possessed property to eat while others starved. A radical form of insecurity was born where what is most fundamental—food and a right to life—might be available only to some, and those most likely to possess it would be the ones owning or controlling property. To survive, those without property would have to work with the owners' resources on the owners' terms.

Scott reports that "there is massive evidence of determined resistance by mobile peoples everywhere to permanent settlement, even under relatively favorable circumstances. Pastoralists and hunting-and-gathering populations have fought against permanent settlement, associating it, often correctly, with disease and state control" (2017, 8). However, escaping from the state and its exploitation was difficult and typically

---

[3] If the adoption of agriculture was the "worst mistake in the history of the human race," the rise of the state and civilization, for all but a thin elite, might be thought the second worst mistake. Freud seemed to have thought so, although he did not allude directly to exploitation. In *Civilization and Its Discontents,* he alluded to the widespread view that "our so-called civilization itself is to blame for a great part of our misery, and we would be much happier if we were to give it up and go back to primitive conditions.... The gratification of instincts is happiness.... [and] it is impossible to ignore the extent to which civilization is built up on renunciation of instinctual gratifications" (1930, 19; 13; 28).

impossible. Frequently states were surrounded by harsh terrain such as deserts and mountains inhabited by hostile peoples. But the greatest barrier was that their exploiters did all possible to preclude their escape. As historian Michael Mann puts it, they were *caged*: They could not escape their subjugated and exploited condition (2012, I:75). According to sinologist Owen Lattimore, the great walls of China were constructed not only to keep out barbarian invaders, but also to keep Chinese workers and thus taxpayers from escaping (Scott 2017, 30; 155).

In about 3100 B.C., a few centuries after the rise of the state, writing was developed as a technology of social control. It evolved in its earliest forms as accounting to keep track of who paid their proper amount of grain taxes. Early writing also permitted a means to maintain accounts of war captives, slaves, and to provide directives on how to discipline and recapture runaway workers. A Sumerian agricultural manual discusses how managers should make use of "whips, goads, and other disciplinary instruments to keep both laborers and beast working strenuously and continuously" (Mann 2012, I:154).[4]

Variety or complexity are among the aspects of work that contribute to its pleasantness. By contrast, repetitive tasks such as required by assembly line work have been found to be mentally debilitating, in part because the narrow and stressful goal is never to miss the exact same action, and, at the risk of penalty, the mind endures a form of terror. Although repetitive agricultural work such as planting, weeding, and harvesting is not as mechanical and time regimented as the assembly line work that would come with industrialization, it is far from the highly varied work of hunter–gatherers.

Nevertheless, there is reason to believe that work in early agricultural societies, where cultivators retained control over their activities, continued to be experienced and viewed positively. Work was a means not merely of gaining subsistence but also of achieving social standing

---

[4] A further possible costs to workers, if not to all of humanity is that work life appears to have been dumbed down following the adoption of agriculture and rise of the state. Anthropologists have often noted with awe the high level of skill and intelligence of hunter–gatherers. (Gray 2009b) Cultural historian Yuval Harari claims that they "were the most knowledgeable and skillful people in history." In fact, evidence suggest that brain size decreased after the adoption of agriculture (2015, 49). Foragers were better able to analyze parts and wholes than agriculturalists. They were also more independent and less conformist (Berry 1976).

and self-respect. In its social dimension, it also typically served as a religious way of maintaining harmony with the world.

Echoing Kanazawa's claim that our mentality and psychological needs were formed on the savannah, it has been found that modern humans suffer from the repression of the deep sentiments that evolved during our early tribal existence, such as cooperating rather than competing and sharing resources rather than individually retaining them. Benjamin Franklin noted the curious phenomenon that American Indians did not voluntarily join civilized society, whereas whites freed from Indian captivity soon expressed disgust at "our manner of life" and tried to return to their former captors They chose the egalitarian, sharing, and communal nature of primitive life over that of colonial civilization (Junger 2016).

Once the state came into existence, it commanded a comparative advantage in violence. That is, it could mete out greater violence than any other social agency. Accordingly, its physical force could be used to maintain the exploitative and degraded conditions of work and living conditions that followed upon its creation. However, using force is expensive and generates resentment. A far superior means of control would be doctrines that convince everyone that prevailing conditions are necessary, good, and fair. This is just what religions evolved to do, serving as ideology legitimating the extremely unequal distribution of societies' wealth and privilege. It did so by depicting the social world as created and sructured by gods, making everything, including extremely unequal social conditions as sacred. To contest these conditions was therefore blasphemy, an offense that could merit torture and death.

Access to the spiritual realm became the monopoly of a priesthood that used rituals and language incomprehensible to the lay populations to maintain their control over truth and meaning. Note the use of Latin in Catholic services until 1965, a language which few if any parishioner understood. The complexity and impenetrability of religious mysteries served to awe believers, revealing the limits of their possible understanding, and masking religion's social function of providing justification for the extremely unequal distribution of wealth, privilege and work's degraded condition.

Because everyone's status and social role was given and unchangeably fixed by birth, these *civilized* religions' prescription for preparing for a proper spiritual existence, and in many cultures, a blissful afterlife or higher status reincarnation, was to work hard, keep quiet, and respect superiors. If material conditions in this life are rude and filled with suffering, then little matter, since what is important is the eternal spiritual life that follows physical death.

There were limits to the ability of religion to justify highly unequal social conditions, such as when workers faced starvation and at times revolted. But a repressive response by the state was always swift and lethal.

Historical Forms of Unfree and Debased Labor

> Whenever the legislature attempts to regulate the difference between masters and their workmen, its counsellors are always the masters.
> — (Adam Smith 1776, 142)

Since the rise of the state, elites' monopoly ownership and control of productive wealth has meant that all others have gained access to means of production to work and survive only on the condition that they turn over to elites virtually all output in excess of the minimum required for subsistence. They have done so with portions of crops, as labor services, and in money form. These same owners of productive wealth could, and at times did demand sexual services, better ensuring that their genes survive into the future. Elites often had multiple wives and concubines, while rulers could have harems of over 1000 women (Betzig 1986).[5]

In predominantly agricultural economies, landlords constituted the ruling class—the class with the greatest political power—and laws, customs, and ideology tied agricultural workers to the land as slaves, serfs, indebted peasants, and indentured servants. In all instances,

---

[5] *The Old Testament* (King James version) reports that Solomon, third king of Israel (reigned c. 968–928 B.C.), "had seven hundred wives, princesses, and three hundred concubines" (1 Kings 11:3).

3 Eden Lost: The Rise of the State and Work Degraded

workers' control over the work process was compromised. Further, they were usually kept from fleeing their exploited condition by force, legal codes, lack of resources, and lack of safe havens.

The workers' living standards might rise when labor was in short supply, but the power of their exploiters would always manage to eventually extract that surplus and return workers' share to the bare subsistence that survival required. And, of course, the longer and harder they could be forced to work, the greater would be the surplus that owners of productive wealth could extract.

It is important to recognize that this history is not about good actors versus bad actors. People generally pursue what they perceive to be their self-interest within the social conditions they find themselves. Within these exploitative societies, elites faced four forces that compelled them to appropriate as much of the workers' surplus as possible. First, elites were in a continuous struggle among themselves for the very pinnacle of status. As has been seen, the human preoccupation with status or relative social position is understandable from an evolutionary perspective. Those with higher status, whatever its socially valued source, possess disproportionate access to resources and members of the opposite sex, thus permitting more and better cared-for progeny, and thus greater chances of winning the biological race to send their genes into the future. Humans were selected with a proclivity to seek status, and as behavioral economist Robert Frank puts it, "falling behind ones local rivals can be lethal" (2005, 183), especially for the future of one's genes.

Since the rise of civilization, much of the competition for status among elites has been manifested in conspicuous consumption, the point of Adam Smith's "trinkets and baubles" thesis for the decline of aristocratic power in late Medieval Europe and of Thorstein Veblen's focus on wasteful spending in late nineteenth century "gilded age" America.[6] Otherwise wasteful expenditure, not unlike the male peacock's tail or the stag's heavy rack, communicated to others, and especially to potential mates, how very worthy one must be to carry such handicaps. Interestingly, productive slaves and, even better, unproductive slaves and servants

---

[6] Smith contended that late medieval aristocrats competed through conspicuous consumption for status, impoverishing themselves and enriching a rising commercial class that would slowly take away their wealth, power, and privilege (1776, 389–92).

could serve the goal of conspicuous consumption, as was pointed out by Veblen (1899, 63).

The second reason for maximum exploitation is that to survive politically, ruling elites needed to command as many resources as possible to defend themselves against domestic and foreign contenders for their privileged status, as well as those below who might rebel against their exploitation. The threat of warfare with neighbors and the need to police subordinates were ever-present, requiring resources for soldiers, weapons, and the maintenance of fortifications.

Third, maintaining an ideological infrastructure that legitimates the status quo and helps maintain domestic social peace has always been costly and absorbed a substantial portion of the surplus. To be robust and convincing, ideologies needed to be delivered in ways that inspired awe. This entailed expensive physical structures such as temples, pyramids, cathedrals, churches, and priests robed in expensive garments. These expenses could be huge. For instance, on the eve of the French Revolution of 1789, the Catholic Church's share of national output was about 25 percent (Piketty 2020, 89).

Fourth, to reinforce their ideology, the elite also needed to spend resources to signal their superiority, and thus their right to rule. They were far better nourished, clothed, and sheltered, and received the best health care. They were also more sophisticated, cleaner, and with superior nutrition, on average taller and more robust. They also displayed fewer signs of ill-health such as deformed bodies, skin blemishes, and open or poorly healing wounds. Their inherent superiority was there for all to see.[7]

The principal forms that labor's exploitation have historically taken are briefly addressed below.

---

[7] Social psychologists John Jost and Brenda Major note that "members of low status groups are more likely to accept the legitimacy of their own inferiority… when there is a clear, well-established, non-overlapping status-related difference between their own group and a higher status outgroup" (2001, 21).

Slave Labor

Slavery has existed since the rise of the state 5500 years ago. It is the most unfree and debased condition possible for workers. Slaves are living commodities, not unlike beasts of burden, experiencing the extreme unfreedom of being bought and sold. Families can be broken up and members sold off individually. Female slaves can be raped, depriving them of choice as to the male parentage of their children.[8] As whips and goads were used to discipline horses and oxen, so too were they used to discipline slaves. Indeed, slaves were at times treated far worse than horses and oxen since they could be tortured and killed to set disciplinary examples for other slaves.

The extent of exploitation was at times extreme. For example, in Saint-Domingue (today Haiti), slaves, who constituted 90 percent of the population, absorbed about 20 percent of the value of their output for subsistence, mostly in the forms of food, shelter, and clothing. That means a rate of surplus extraction, or rate of exploitation, of 80 percent (Piketty 2022, 83).

Work conditions for slaves varied greatly. Where slaves were easily captured and therefore inexpensive, they might be worked literally to death (Ingraham 2020). One of the reasons why slave economies experienced little technological progress is that where slaves were so cheap there was little incentive to use or develop labor-saving machinery (Lilley 1966). Gang slavery in mines, plantations, and in ships' galleys was extremely harsh. Some slaves, however, had a degree of control over their work process, especially in households, crafts, and small-scale agriculture.

Most slaves were war captives, although some impoverished and indebted families were forced to sell their own children or themselves into slavery (Flannery and Marcus 2012, 480). Slave breeding, although relatively uncommon, was practiced where their high cost made it profitable.

---

[8] Graeber reports that "In ancient Ireland, female slaves were so plentiful and important that they came to function as currency…. slave girls also served as the highest denomination of currency in Medieval Iceland, and in the Rig Veda, great gifts and payments are regularly designated in 'gold, cattle, and slave girls'" (2012, 128; 408).

The widespread practice of slavery is economically understandable. Capturing and exploiting slaves yielded high profits. Little of value beyond precious metals and jewelry could be carted off from poor countries by conquering armies. What had considerable value was land and humans capable of labor and procreation. The land could not, of course, be carried off, but slaves could be cheaply walked over land. Water transportation, where available, was also relatively low cost.

Captured slaves represented an economic windfall. Raising children is extremely expensive. They must be fed and cared for at great cost in terms of resources and especially labor time. Only after many years might their labor pay for their daily keep. For society, raising children is an investment in labor for its collective future. For parents, children represent investments for care in old age—children are the principal part of kinship social security systems. To capture slaves is to steal an investment that others have borne the high costs of producing. Taking female slaves also represented a reproductive windfall for the male conquerors who, by mating with them, increased the probability that their genes would survive into the future.

The economic and reproductive utility of slavery for elites is evidenced by the tardiness of its legal abolition: Abolition only began to come about in the nineteenth century, mostly the second half. The last country to make it illegal was Mauritania in 1981. Although slavery is currently outlawed in all countries, the International Labour Organization estimates that in 2021, 50 million humans lived as slaves, 28 million in forced labor and 22 million in forced marriages (International Labour Organization 2022).

Since the rise of states and until its abolition, slaves comprised at least 30 percent of their populations, and in European colonies up to 90 percent (Piketty 2020, 217–20). Slaving was central to the growth and maintenance of the state (Scott 2013, 14–15). Crowd diseases, especially in cities, decimated populations and required capture or purchase of slaves to maintain labor supply for agriculture, construction, soldiers, and raising children. War was at times undertaken as much for acquiring slaves as for other ends (Scott 2017).

Due to its high profitability, capturing and selling slaves was undertaken by raiders throughout history. It was far more profitable than putting slaves to work and expropriating the surplus. When elites desired imported goods, but lack a means of purchasing them, selling slaves flourished. For instance, in the eighth century, Venice maintained a prosperous slave trade, selling Europeans to the Moors in Northern Africa. (Appleby 2011, 126). Another notable example is that of African rulers and elites who, lacking a valuable export commodity other than slaves, maintained a long history of slave trading across the Sahara between East Africa and the Arabian Peninsula. Later, West Africa supplied slaves to the Americas. Their leaders and elites sought not just foreign luxury goods, but also modern weapons, which solidified their rule and lowered the cost of capturing yet more slaves (Boix 2015, 170).

A principal "spoil of victory" during most of history was the capture of young women and girls taken as slaves. Defeated males usually suffered death unless taken as slaves. Their fate was legitimated in social thought, even by generally progressive thinkers.[9]

Upon conquering the Americas, European powers acquired abundant fertile land, but lacked labor to exploit it. Enslaving the indigenous populations was difficult due to their high susceptible to European diseases and their ability to escape into territories not controlled by Europeans. The solution was to import indentured servants from Europe and slaves from Africa who had not been captured as hunter–gatherers, who strongly resist working as slaves and can survive in the wild as runaways. They instead sought slaves who had worked in agriculture, mining, or manufacturing (Blackburn 1996, 166–67).

Wherever it existed, slavery readily found legitimation in ideology. Aristotle claimed that "the lower sort are by nature slaves, and it is better for them as for all inferiors that they should be under the rule of a master" (2000, 1254a). Although Christianity proclaimed all humans equal in the eyes of God, "Church Fathers from Paul to Jerome unanimously accepted slavery, merely advising slaves to be obedient to their masters and masters to be just to their slaves—true liberty, after all, was not to be found in this world anyway" (Anderson 2013, 133–34). In

---

[9] For stance, philosopher John Locke maintained that "captives taken in a just war [had] forfeited their lives and, with it, their liberties [and were therefore] subjected to the absolute dominion and arbitrary power of their masters" (quoted in Losurdo 2014, 24).

North America, the Catholic Church counted among the largest institutional slaveholders, and practically all southern churches possessed slaves. Eleven of the first 15 US Presidents were slave owners in a republic founded on the principals of freedom and that all humans are created equal.

Serf Labor

Serfdom and slavery share much in common, both existing in predominantly agrarian economies. Both slaves and serfs are unfree, the former property of slave owners, the latter bound to the land and ruled over by landlords. Both conditions were generally hereditary.

Nevertheless, there were distinct differences. Slaves were chattel, not unlike domesticated animals and could be bought and sold, even breaking up households. Serfs, by contrast, were considered members of society, with inherited rights to be on the land and they could not generally be sold. Slaves were often imported aliens, racially or ethnically different, reducing the cost of identifying and recapturing runaways. Whereas slaves possessed no civil rights, serfs were generally racially and ethnically like the landlords. Serfs might also find some protection from landlord abuses where there existed considerable political authority above the landlords.

Serfdom tended to exist where political power was highly decentralized into feudal manors whose lords could control and defend the immediate surrounding territory. Slavery tended to not exist where centralized state power did not exist or was weak, reducing the potential for acquiring slaves through conquest or recapturing runaways. And, lacking a strong state to protect trade routes, markets within which slaves and their output could be exchanged could not readily exist.

Where state power either did not exist or did so in weakened form, landlords acted as proto-states, providing serfs with law and order within the manor and protection within castle walls from external enemies. They also provided a degree of material security by maintaining granaries to survive disastrous harvests and enemy assaults. "No-man's-land" between and beyond manors provided serfs with potential escape from their bondage, but at the cost of giving up the protection and security the manor provided and the risk of harsh punishment if recaptured to set examples for others. To secure their ability to maximally exploit their serfs, neighboring landlords often formulated accords to preclude bidding for the serfs of each other's domains or providing sanctuary to runaways.

In medieval Europe, low population density and lack of centralized state protection of property rights meant prohibitively high costs ("transactions costs") of forming markets. Extensive markets require that property rights be defined and enforced by state power. As a result, to appropriate serfs' surplus, landlords forced them to work on their lands for typically two or more days per week. This permitted landlords greater control over what was produced for them than requiring a portion of the serfs' output on their own lands. Often serfs also had to work on community projects designated by landlords. Serfs spent their remaining time working on their own plots for their household subsistence with considerable control over their workday.

The dearth of markets also clarifies why workers were tied to the land as opposed to being hired as wage laborers. Without substantial labor markets, landlords could not hire replacements should their workers strike during critical times such as planting and harvesting. Without tying the serfs to the land, labor strikes could lead to ruin.

The quality of serfs' lives varied according to local conditions. Where labor was in short supply, serfs enjoyed better conditions to discourage them from running away into "no-mans-lands" or to more attractive prospects available at other manors or in towns. By contrast, where labor was relatively abundant and towns too politically weak to resist landlords' demands that runaways be returned, the serfs' status could approximate that of slaves, as was the case in much of Eastern Europe's serfdom.

Economic historian Richard Tawney wrote that "The very essence of feudal property was exploitation in its most naked and shameless form" (1926, 56). Yet despite the "shameless" exploitation of feudalism, the Catholic Church participated as a landowner. In fact, peasant revolts in Germany were more frequent and bitter on ecclesiastical estates (Tawney 1926, 119).

Debt-Bound Labor

As elites captured disproportionate shares of productive resources, especially land with the rise of the state, those with few such resources often could not endure bad harvests. Facing starvation, these less fortunates often had to borrow from elites or usurers. Debt bondage resulted when these loans, often at usurious interest rates, could not be repaid, forcing the indebted to become bonded to labor for the creditor. Extortionate interest rates could lead to the debt becoming ever more burdensome to payoff, trapping workers in perpetual indebtedness. The result could be slavery. For instance, to repay or reduce the debt, the indebtors' children could be sold into slavery or prostitution. Historian of ancient societies Moses Finley claimed that provoking insurrections in the ancient world was the call, "Cancel the debts and redistribute the land" (quoted in Graeber 2012, 8).

Debtors, even among elites, were usually blamed for their condition, accused of irresponsibly living beyond their means. This judgment is captured by the fact that the word debt in some Indo-European languages is related to the words for sin or fault (W. Thompson 2015, 86).

Indentured Labor

Indentured servitude existed from the rise of the state and extreme inequality until modern times. It is a form of unfree labor created by a contract whereby the worker must work for an employer for a specified number of years to pay off a debt or other obligation. It is not unlike debt bondage. After the specified years of contract were completed, the worker was free. This form of unfree labor played a major role in populating the American colonies with poor European immigrants. It was a response to the labor shortage where abundant and cheap land was available. To pay for their passage to colonial America, impoverished Europeans could obtain transportation in return for agreeing to work a specified number of years, typically four to seven, as indentured servants. Upon arrival, these contracts would be sold by the ship's captain to employers. From one-half to two-thirds of white immigrants are estimated to have been indentured servants between the 1630s and the American Revolution (Galenson 1984).

It could be a form of term-limit slavery where the contract, and hence the worker could be sold to another employer, earning it the name in North America of "white slavery." As in slavery, punishment for attempts to escape or failure to work diligently could be severe. Colonial leaders were contemptuous of the ragtag workers that had been brought over from Europe, many drawn from impoverished homes, prisons, and orphanages. Employers complained that they were generally lazy and often surly, and it was not uncommon for them to be tortured, mutilated and even killed. It is noteworthy that with abundant and inexpensive land, free workers could more readily refuse mere subsistence wages or poor and abusive work conditions. A response was to turn to importing African slaves (Bailyn 2013). Because of their skin color and different ethnicities, runaway black slaves could be more readily hunted down and returned to their owners.

Wage Labor

Accompanying capitalism's evolution, ownership and control of productive resources became concentrated in a capitalist class, separating workers from any ownership, control, or free access to the material wherewithal necessary for survival. Marx termed this process the proletarianization of labor. Under feudalism, workers had been tied to the land and although exploited, at times harshly, they had the security of a right to be on productive land that provided them with material subsistence and the security of living in a community. They possessed some control over the work process, especially when working their own plots. The security of community usually meant no one starved unless all did.

This proletarianization of labor occurred over centuries as workers were pushed off the land by enclosures of common lands on the manors or pulled into urban areas in expectation of better lives. In either instance, they lost guaranteed access to productive wealth and supportive communities. Because women and children were the primary exploiters of the common rights on the manor such as grazing pastures and woodlands, their loss reduced women's economic position within the family as it increased dependence of households on the male's wages (Humphries 1990, 21). In industrial urban centers, households were typically distant from the security of extended families, living in crowded, dirty, disease-ridden, and crime-filled slums. To survive and care for their children, women often had to turn to prostitution.

Although the enclosures were repeatedly opposed, often by the Crown eager to avoid insurrection, they came to be legitimated as essential for economic efficiency and moral behavior. The enclosures were ideologically depicted as "designed to eliminate idleness, intemperance and riotous behaviour, and to render the poor sober and respectable" (McNally 1993, 20).

Within this evolving system of capitalism, propertyless workers had to contract with the owners of productive wealth for access and survival. As Marx put it, the worker became "the slave of other men who have made themselves the owners of the material conditions of labour. He can only labour by their permission and hence only live by their permission" (1875, 526). Marx, however, was not the first to view wage labor as a form of slavery. First century B.C. Roman philosopher, lawyer, and statesman Cicero had written: "Unbecoming a gentleman…and vulgar are the means of livelihood of all hired workmen whom we pay for mere manual labour, not for artistic skill; for in their case the very wage they receive is a pledge of their slavery" (1913, Book 1: 42).

As capitalism expanded, relying on wages was widely viewed as disgraceful, although legal alternatives for workers became nonexistent (W. Thompson 2015, 190). And for centuries thereafter, working for wages was viewed as unfit and humiliating for free people. Historian Keith Thomas writes that "In the seventeenth century … wage labourers were thought to have 'lost their birthright': even Levellers excluded them from the franchise" (1964, 63). Wage workers lost control of the labor

3 Eden Lost: The Rise of the State and Work Degraded

process and were bossed about by overseers. Clocks rather than nature controlled their work time.[10]

Yet, as capitalism continued to evolve, markets eventually came to be understood as sites of freedom. Participants in market exchanges appear free since an exchange cannot be concluded unless all agree to the terms. Market exchange also fosters a sense that participants are equal insofar as each possesses the power to refuse the terms. Unlike feudalism where workers are tied to the land and under the rule of landlords, in a society of markets, human relationships appear to be consensually free. Understandably, wage labor would be seen as "free labor." Unrecognized was Marx's later understanding that workers "became sellers of themselves only after they had been robbed of all their own means of production, and of all the guarantees of existence afforded by the old feudal arrangements" (1894, 3:715).

The illusion of workers' freedom results from the fact that the worker "is compelled to sell himself of his own free will." But this compulsion is hidden because "Direct force, outside economic conditions, is of course still used, but only exceptionally" (Marx 1894, 3:766; 737). It is because markets appear as sites of freedom, and because forceful subjugation is not routinely used against wage workers as it was against slaves and serfs, that wage workers have been mistakenly perceived as free.

But did not workers freely choose among employers after comparing pay and work conditions? Yes, but not in a truly free sense insofar as competition between employers reduced pay and work conditions to the same low levels. The continual existence of unemployment insured that wages would be minimal, near or at subsistence, and work conditions poor. Further, early industrialization deskilled workers to the level of skill

---

[10] Social philosopher Lewis Mumford characterized the rise of capitalist labor and living conditions as follows:

> In the city new ways, rigorous, efficient, often harsh, even sadistic, took the place of the ancient customs and comfortable easy-paced routine. Work itself was detached from other activities and canalized into the "working day" of unceasing toil under a taskmaster; the first step in the "managerial revolution" which has reached its climax in our day. Struggle, dominion, mastery, conquest were the new themes; not the protectiveness and prudence, the holding fast, or the passive endurance of the village (1961, 27).

possessed by children.[11] Thus, in fact, the workers' freedom was only to work for these minimal wages and in these poor conditions or starve. But was the worker not free in choosing what to buy with their wages? No, because their low subsistence wages meant that they could only purchase the cheapest and poorest quality goods necessary for survival. Because their food, often a diet of oatmeal gruel or the equivalent, lacked adequate nutrients for good health, worker growth was typically stunted and their lives shorted (Allen 2001).[12] Worker freedom, then, was an illusion and the concept of the free worker served as legitimation for extreme inequality and the exploitation of workers.

In agrarian economies, workers' lives were guided by the rhythms of nature, where they could work irregularly and with a substantial degree of autonomy (E. P. Thompson 1967). Capitalist work, by contrast, reduced the work experience to the rhythm of machines and clocks. By 1500, due to entrepreneurs' pressure on local governments, most European towns where labor markets were significant had constructed clock towers to facilitate control of workers' time. Workers were required to report for work at assigned hours or suffer fines or firing. Rebellious workers often attempted to sabotage the tower clock bells (Van Bavel 2015, 75). Economic historian David Landes wrote that "Factory discipline… required and eventually created a new breed of worker, broken to the inexorable demands of the clock" (1969, 2). As schools became available for workers' children, they were trained by the clock for capitalist workplace discipline.

Working class lives in Western Europe dramatically deteriorated between 1500 and 1800. Real wages largely declined as the number of workdays a year increased (Appleby 2011, 106). The length of workdays also increased. In England, for instance, the workday increased from 12 hours in 1700 to 14–18 hours in 1800 (Willensky 1961, 34). Further,

---

[11] Suzman points out that "Children were such compliant and versatile laborers that by the turn of the nineteenth century, close to half of all Britain's factory workers were under the age of fourteen" (2021, 316–17). Children, as well as both parents often had to work for households to meet bare subsistence needs.

[12] Economist Angus Deaton reports that working class children in England were very short and skinny, with life expectancy of only about 40 years. By 1850 the gap in life expectancy between the aristocracy and the general population had widened to 20 years (2013, 83, 91).

more members of the family, at times even including children as young as 6 years of age, had to work to enable households to subsist.

Slave-owners and feudal landlords had an interest in the health and skill development of their exploited chattel or serf workers. And should they fall ill or die, slave owners and landlords would suffer income losses. But this was not true for early capitalists who had little investment in their unskilled workers. Should these workers die or become ill, there was no loss beyond inconvenience, since they could be replaced from what Marx termed the "reserve army of the unemployed." There has always been a percentage of the workforce in capitalist economies that has served to hold down wages and discipline workers. The ranks of the unemployed were incessantly replenished, in early capitalism by population growth and the enclosures that pushed peasants off the land, and in the maturing capitalism of the early nineteenth century and beyond, by labor-displacing technological change.

Scientific Management

> In handicrafts and manufacture, the workman makes use of a tool, in the factory, the machine makes use of him. There the movement of the industry of labor proceed from him, here it is the movements of the machine that he must follow…In the factory we have a lifeless mechanism independent of the workman, who becomes its mere living appendage.
> — Marx 1867, I:461

Already at the birth of industrialization, Adam Smith claimed that work was "toil and trouble," and launched the discourse on industrial worker alienation with his observation that, whereas the "understandings of the greater part of men are necessarily formed by their ordinary employments," the division of labor in factories renders workers "as stupid and ignorant as it is possible for a human creature to become…. [and by working for others the worker] must always lay down the same portion of his ease, his liberty, and his happiness" (1776, 30; 734; 33). Scottish politician David Urquhart went further, claiming that the "subdivision of labour is the assassination of the people" (cited in Schumacher 1979, 42). Marx also took note of this deskilling as the capitalist production process "progressively replaces skilled labourers by less skilled, mature labour power by immature, male by female, that of adults by that of young persons or children" (1867, I:697).

Smith, Urquhart, Marx, and many others were observing the debased character of work accompanying industrialization. Workers were assigned limited repetitive tasks. Bosses decided how work was to be done. That is, mental and manual labor were divorced. Whatever was done by workers could be better done by machines if engineers could design them. Machines do not need to be disciplined, and, although they break down, they do not tire and thus can be worked around the clock.

At the outset of the twentieth century, the separation of mental from manual labor was given scientific legitimacy by Frederick Winslow Taylor, the founder of the "scientific management" movement. He claimed that the greatest problem facing management "lay in the ignorance of the management as to what really constitutes a proper day's work for a workman.... Hardly a competent workman can be found...who does not devote a considerable amount of time to studying just how slowly he can work and still convince his employer he's going at a good pace" (1911, 53). A large part of scientific management consisted of strategies for getting the worker to reveal his or her full productive potential to enable managers to work them full throttle.

Given how dehumanizing the workplace had become by the early twentieth century, he was arguably right concerning worker shirking. But rather than improve the quality of work to draw workers' interest and diligence, Taylor would debase the work process yet more. His scientific management represents the legitimation of an extreme separation of mental and manual labor. All workplace decisions were to be removed from workers and placed in a new planning and scheduling department composed of engineers.[13] Productivity gains could be had by following three rules: break complex jobs down into simple components; measure

---

[13] "Under our system the workman is told minutely just what he is to do and how he is to do it; and any improvement which he makes upon the orders given him is fatal to success" (Taylor 1906, para 118).

all that workers do; and give bonuses to high-achievers and send sluggards packing ("rank and yank"). Henry Ford applied Taylor's ideas to his giant River Rouge car plant. Vladimir Lenin viewed scientific management as one of the building blocks of socialism. Today, Taylorism is thriving, now in the form of digital Taylorism where the three rules are applied to service workers, managers, and knowledge workers (The Economist 2015).

It was not that Taylor lacked sympathy for workers. Instead, like mainstream economists, he believed that work yields disutility and thus the sole reason people worked was to earn an income with which to purchase consumption goods. He failed to recognize that, beyond provisioning, meaningful work is essential for human flourishing.

Privileged Workers

Since the rise of the state and civilization, not all workers have been deprived of the ownership, control, or ready access to the productive wealth they need to work and survive. Some have been privileged to own and control the land or the capital with which they worked. Although they were often taxed heavily, forcing them to work long days to meet their basic needs, their ownership of the means of production provided them with control over their work process and the independent status such control entailed. These workers included peasant proprietors, pastoralists, fishermen, craftsmen, and freelance providers of skilled services. All were, in a sense, small-scale entrepreneurs—those who own and control a small concern and serve as their own bosses.

Among these privileged workers, the most rewarding work—and the work which is highly appreciated by others—requires skill, endurance, and especially inspiration. Thus, the work of artists, musicians, dramatists, and novelists has often provided them with status and social approval, explaining why these professions draw large numbers, most of whom earn low incomes due to the competition. Similarly, crafts have existed in virtually all societies and provide similar rewards to their practitioners.[14]

Craftsmen included masons, carpenters, stoneworkers, metal workers, tailors, dyers, weavers, tanners, bakers, and butchers, many of whom, prior to industrialization, were organized into guilds that dominated non-agricultural production. These guilds maintained elaborate regulations concerning the craftsmen's activities to strictly limit competition and so to keep the playing field level. Although these regulations restricted workers' control over their workplaces, the workers nevertheless were, as Thorstein Veblen put it, "skilled masterless workmen" (1914, 276)—their own bosses. In mid-sixteenth century London, for example, 75 percent of workers were found in guilds (Gadd and Wallis 2002). Because guilds restricted competition, their members' incomes were typically greater than those of non-skilled laborers. Many service workers also belonged to guilds or similar institutional associations that restricted competition, notably doctors and attorneys. Other professions of independent workers included tutors and teachers, architects, peddlers, wholesalers, and retailers,

Degraded Industrial Work and the Shift to Consumption for Status

> …emulation in expenditure stands ever ready to absorb any margin of income that remains after ordinary physical wants and comforts have been provided for, and, further, that it presently becomes as hard to give

---

[14] The social character of crafts is described by philosopher of work Edmund Byrne as follows:

> Three things in particular about crafts deserve our attention: 1) they gave practitioners not only a personal sense of accomplishment ("craft pride") but also social status; 2) practitioners of each craft typically sought through organizations known as guilds to exercise control over access to the craft and over the terms and conditions of its practice: and 3) authoritarians long opposed and by the time of the industrial revolution did in fact destroy the guilds (2010, 71).

3 Eden Lost: The Rise of the State and Work Degraded 69

up that part of one's habitual 'standard of living' which is due to the struggle for respectability, as it is to give up many physical comforts.
—(Thorstein Veblen 1919, 394–95)

As noted previously, workers were both pushed and pulled into industrial work. They were pushed first by land enclosures and then by declining relative incomes in agriculture due to falling produce prices brought on by productivity gains. Craft work declined as handicraft prices were progressively undercut by cheaper factory output, leading craftsmen to also be pulled into factory work as wage workers. The same dynamic increasingly confronted most independent workers. Accompanying industrialization and urbanization were rapid declines in transportation costs, facilitating the creation of regional, national, and even international markets for output. Over a protracted period that continues today, small local businesses began to be outcompeted by far larger firms that could capture economies of scale.

Industrialization dramatically increased productivity and economic output, but at the cost of degrading the quality of work and weakening community life. Traditional communities were weakened as workers were pushed and pulled into industrial urban areas. Further, whereas earlier workers' goods and services had been consumed primarily by other members of their community, purchases increasingly came from unknown consumers in faraway places. Community members were less economically and socially linked.

Within all industrializing economies, as more and more work took place in urban factories—some quite large—the final product came from the serial efforts of many individuals performing small tasks that required little skill other than attention to mechanical regularity. Workers progressively lost direct control not only over the quality of the product, but also over how quickly they worked as the pace came to be determined by machinery. The eventual rise of the assembly line set the same pace for all. As noted earlier, Taylorism provided scientific justification for this rather complete separation of intellectual and manual labor.

Within factories, the worker's skill and diligence were not clearly visible to those outside, or even frequently to co-workers. Where machines set the pace of work, there was no skill or work quality to be appreciated. A critical source for social and self-respect was thereby weakened. Only subjugation to bosses and endurance of mechanical routine could be observed. This degradation of work would nudge workers, when income arose above subsistence, to seek social certification of their worthiness through consumption. Their status would depend less on their qualities as workers and more on the conspicuous display of goods and services consumed.

Conspicuous consumption was not new to humanity. It had been a means for elites to signal their wealth and status since the rise of the state. It was a principal way in which elites competed among themselves for the pinnacle of status.[15] It was a form of competition reserved to them by the fact that only they received surplus with which to consume beyond their basic needs. All others, living near or at subsistence, only had the wherewithal to spend on necessities.

Consumption for status started to become more widespread in the latter part of the nineteenth century as worker militancy resulted in higher wages that enabled many workers to hold onto a portion of their surplus. The debased quality of work and the accompanying decline in its potential to provide social status, along with the example of the upper classes, turned workers toward consumption as a means to achieve recognition, social status, and self-respect. Workers entered a consumption arms race for status that had previously been the exclusive preserve of the wealthy. A self-reinforcing dynamic was set in motion: where a choice was possible, workers would trade off quality of work life for higher pay to finance more consumption. This put pressure on all workers to do likewise, reducing resistance to further loss of control over the work process. Workers' demands became increasingly biased toward higher wages to enable consumption as opposed to improved work conditions. A notable example is the 1950 "Treaty of Detroit" with General Motors in which the United Auto Workers (UAW) gave up attempts to gain

---

[15] With an acuity that would also mark the much later work of Thorstein Veblen, Adam Smith observed that the rich are always competing among themselves for the very pinnacle of status by flashing their wealth: "With the greater part of rich people, the chief enjoyment of riches consists in the parade of riches, which in their eye is never so complete as when they appear to possess those decisive marks of opulence which nobody can possess but themselves" (1776, 172).

control over the production process in favor of a 5-year contract with good wages, benefits, and pensions.

Thus, the further debasement of work brought on by industrialization and the rise of wages above subsistence for many workers, steered them to increasingly seek social certification through consumption. This trend could serve as an observable consequence, or gauge, of hard work, since harder work generally enables greater consumption. It should also be noted that, compared to work, consumption is a more efficient way of showing success to large numbers of people. Whereas hard work is evident only to those who can see or know of one's workplace performance, high consumption is visible to a great number of people, including neighbors and passersby. In the twentieth century, automobiles joined clothing, houses, and furniture as dominant examples of showy consumption.

As will be discussed in Chapter 6, the turn toward consumption to achieve social recognition has disastrous consequences for environmental stability.

Attitudes Toward Labor

> Aversion—not desire—is the emotion—the only emotion which labour taken by itself is qualified to produce…. In so far as labour is taken in its proper sense, love of labour, is a contradiction in terms.
> — Jeremy Bentham 1983, 104

As discussed in Chapter 2, the dynamics of evolution predict that provisioning, or what we call work, would be pleasurable where it is not socially coerced and workers are individually in control of their work or democratically participate in group work decision-making. Anthropologists reporting on forager and non-state agricultural societies lend support to this prediction, as does happiness research. Further, because work in these societies benefited the community, it was viewed positively. Indeed, those who worked with skill and diligence would be socially valued and therefore more sexually attractive as mates, and genes carrying their behavioral traits would more readily appear in future generations.

With the extreme inequality accompanying the rise of the state and civilization, workers were subjugated to those who owned or controlled land and other productive resources. Work became socially coerced, often brutally, and, with greater division of labor, robbed of variety. Evidence of how these workers felt about their work is unavailable. But given that elites had cause to work them to their physical limits in order to extract as much surplus as possible, it is plausible that many had unpleasant work lives, if not miserable ones, and that they viewed work negatively. Yet many workers who were economically exploited nonetheless retained some control over their work process and could gain pride and social respect from their efforts.

There is extensive written evidence of how elites viewed work. Where the state was weak or nonexistent, work appears to have been viewed positively. This is apparent in antique (pre-classical) Greek and Hebrew societies, the two main cultural sources of Christian thought. In both instances—as in other societies at similar levels of development—there was social stratification but little division of labor. The principal reasons were that population pressures had yet to lead to the emergence of substantial markets, the debasing of peasants into serfdom, and the establishment of significant state power. The primary social unit remained the kinship group and the primary production unit was the household.

In Homer's world, nobles also worked. In *The Odyssey*, the king Odysseus' work skills are mentioned as are those of his wife, Penelope, who worked as a weaver (Homer 1944, 233). Some deities even worked. This appears surprising insofar as slavery existed in Homeric society. However, the work performed by slaves apparently did not differ substantially from that of free workers. Moreover, slaves generally were part of households, often captured women who served as concubines, and are generally reported to have been well-treated (Gottschall 2008).

Early Hebrew thought appeared to share these general attitude toward work. Even leaders and rabbis worked. Moreover, according to the creation story in *Genesis*, it was through God's work that all came to be. Creation took God 6 days, and the fact that it was work is evident by his need to take the seventh day in rest. Human work reflected that they

3 Eden Lost: The Rise of the State and Work Degraded

had been created in God's image to continue his creation project. Work is good.

Nevertheless, *Genesis* is ambivalent about work. Work is depicted as God's curse cast on humans for their disobedience—their daring to taste from the forbidden tree of knowledge:

> And unto Adam he said, Because thou hast hearkened unto the voice of thy wife, and hast eaten of the tree, of which I commanded thee, saying, Thou shalt not eat of it: cursed *is* the ground for thy sake; in sorrow shalt thou eat *of* it all the days of thy life… In the sweat of thy face shalt thou eat bread, till thou return unto the ground (*Genesis* 3: 17, 19).

This textual passage often offered support for the negative views of work that would frequently be expressed by both Jews and Christians. It is also possible to view this story of Eden lost as representing the leaving behind of the pleasurable work life of hunter–gathers to take up the onerous demands of agricultural work.

With the extreme inequality accompanying the rise of the state, freedom from work conferred nobility. The appropriate domains for "noble" action were warfare and politics. Warring was viewed not only as a more fruitful means of enrichment than production but also as beneficial to human character.[16] Consequently, the prevailing objective was not with improving production so much as strengthening the military means of procuring tribute and booty.

Work became socially compelled and thus denigrated as it was performed increasingly by subservient inferiors and slaves. Because work was unfree, it was beneath the dignity of full humans.[17]

---

[16] Even as late as the mid-nineteenth century, aristocratic Tocqueville wrote: "I do not wish to speak ill of war; war almost always enlarges the mind of a people and elevates their character" (Tocqueville 1840, 2:268).

[17] In the following passage, Aristotle makes this strikingly clear:

> a state with an ideal constitution—a state which has for its members men who are absolutely just and not men who are merely just in relation to some particular standard—cannot have its citizens living the life of mechanics or shopkeepers, which is ignoble and inimical to goodness. Nor can it have them engaged in farming: leisure is a necessity, both for growth in goodness and for the pursuit of political activities (2000, 1328b–29).

Within Greek mythology, labor was included among the plagues unleashed by the opening of Pandora's infamous box (Byrne 2010, 72).[18] Even trade and commerce in classical Greece were predominantly performed by resident aliens (metics). Many of those who worked but were not enslaved were foreigners, peoples the Greeks considered barbaric and inferior.

Early Christianity evolved and was nourished by Rome's ethnically diverse working class, which it drew together by minimizing their differences, focusing on their common humanity, and depicting work as noble (Wisman 1998). In the eyes of the one universal God, all are equal. Christ's doctrine of brotherly love places emphasis on the inherent value and dignity of each individual, regardless of his or her station or origins. It established in spiritual terms what would later become so important in secular terms as a postulate of universal humanity during the Enlightenment: all humans are equal. Jesus was the son of a carpenter and is himself referred to as one (*Mark* 6:3). Paul, a leather worker or saddler (*Acts* 18:3), praises work for making independence and self-respect possible. It also enables charity: "by so laboring ye ought to support the weak and to remember the words of the Lord Jesus, how he said, it is more blessed to give than to receive" (*Acts* 20:35).

Yet Saint Paul wrote: "Slaves, in reverent fear of God submit yourselves to your masters, not only to those who are good and considerate, but also to those who are harsh" (1 Peter 2:18). Indeed, work was not always positively viewed within Christian societies, although a positive view was kept alive within monasteries.[19] In a manner reminiscent of classical Greek philosophy, later Catholic thought considered work to

---

[18] Plutarch praised Archimedes because, "regarding mechanical occupations and every art that ministers to needs as ignoble or vulgar, he directed his own ambition solely to those studies the beauty and subtlety of which are unadulterated by necessity" (quoted in Mokyr 1990, 196).

[19] A strong force within Christianity—the monastic orders founded during the Middle Ages—continued to extol the virtues of work. With the decline of urban centers that followed the disintegration of the Roman Empire, these orders became not only important carriers of learning but also the vanguard of much technological progress. Members worked, and their work was understood as the fulfillment of divine will. To work was to do God's will, or as Saint Benedict put it "*Laborare est orare*," to work is to pray. He claimed that all work, whether menial or mental, was a duty, and idleness an invitation to sin. The purpose of work was not merely to meet physical needs, but also to provide discipline and to enable charity. By ennobling work, the cultural barriers to technical invention and innovation were weakened.

be divided into higher and lower forms. The higher form was spiritual contemplation directed to the more important concerns of spirituality and the eternal hereafter. The lower form of work, was viewed as servile, to be performed by inferior beings, because it was involved with the transient present (Pieper and Schall 1963, 21). This attitude legitimated the practices of slavery and serfdom within Catholic orders. Christians even sold Christians into slavery. The papacy also participated in slavery.[20]

However, Protestantism's later expression of Christianity significantly renewed a positive view of work—blessed and sacred—that legitimized the rising power and status of the bourgeoisie (Wisman 2024). Paradoxically, as Protestantism became viable, although it viewed hard work as a virtue, it also justified institutions and attitudes, under which work conditions became more debased than in any other system except slavery.

Secular economic science, in its earliest form of mercantilism (1500–1750), arose alongside the rise of Protestantism. It viewed work negatively, as disutility, a mere means to the utility of consumption. This negative view is understandable, given the generally dehumanizing conditions of work under early capitalism. Only the bribe of an income, if not the threat of starvation, could bring work forth. Still today, mainstream economic science does not recognize that work may be of value in and of itself as a vent for creativity, social and self-respect, and community. It instead continues to view it as disutility, as what must be done for income with which to consume. Nevertheless, in the nineteenth century, a few heterodox and mostly ignored social thinkers began envisioning alternative social organizations that would not only fulfill provisioning needs but also enable workers to flourish psychologically and socially in their work.

Later still, however, giving renewed support to mainstream economics' negative view of labor, pioneer psychologist Sigmund Freud wrote that "as a path to happiness, work is not highly prized by men. They do not strive after it as they do after other possibilities of satisfaction. The great majority of people only work under the stress of necessity, and this

---

[20] For example, in 1452, Pope Nicholas V granted the Portuguese king the right to sell Muslims and heathens. Later, in 1488, Pope Innocent VIII happily received a Portuguese gift of 100 Moorish slaves, which he shared among his Cardinals (Lucassen 2021, 249).

natural human aversion to work raises most difficult social problems" (1930, 2). Like mainstream economists, Freud held that humans have a "natural" aversion to work. He could not see the positive potential of work beyond how it exists in its debased form under unfavorable social conditions.

******

In the next chapter, attention is shifted to how workers used threats of insurrection to gain formal political power during the nineteenth century. This is followed by a look at how post-World War II abundance established the conditions in which work could come to be valued as an end in itself, and thus more than merely a means to consumption.

4

Victory Over Material Scarcity

> The economic problem, the struggle for subsistence, always has been the most pressing problem of the human race... we have been expressly evolved by nature—with all our impulses and deepest instincts—for the purpose of solving the economic problem.
> —John Maynard Keynes 1930, 366

Although extreme inequality, exploitation, and debased work have characterized most of human history since the rise of the state and civilization, so too have extraordinary advances in technology and social organization. This progress has forged ahead geometrically, proceeding with ever greater speed, especially following the rise of capitalism, an economic system Joseph Schumpeter characterized as one of creative destruction. Since the mid-nineteenth century, it has brought extraordinary improvements to the material lives of practically everyone in rich countries.

Technological progress over the past few centuries is stunning and much noted. But so too is progress in social conditions. Over the past two centuries, slavery, the most abject condition for workers, has become illegal everywhere. Since World War II, the exploitative colonialism that reduced defeated and subjugated peoples to debased conditions, often approximating slavery, has practically disappeared. Polygamy and harems have virtually vanished as monogamy has become the legal norm and practice in almost all of the world's nations. Racial, ethnic, and, increasingly, gender equality are embraced as morally appropriate and necessary goals. Violence against humans continues to decline, as it has over the full course of human history (Pinker 2011). Democracy, with all adults legally enfranchised, only came forth in the twentieth century. Between 1990 and 2023, a mere 33 years, the world's infant mortality rate declined by 61% ("World Infant Mortality Rate 1950–2023," n.d.). Over the past 60 years, global life expectancy increased by 40%, from 52 to 73 years. Over this same period, global literacy doubled from 42 to 86%. Between 1914 and 2019, extreme global poverty fell by 34%. Humanity has finally arrived at the point where it is possible to envision victory over the problem of material scarcity for all humanity in the very near future, at least in the sense of ending dire material privation.

This chapter addresses the extraordinary social progress within today's wealthy societies consequent to workers gaining formal political power over the past 150 years. To keep the exposition manageable, attention is focused mainly, albeit not exclusively, on the United States. A partial reversal of these egalitarian gains over the past 50 years will be examined in the next chapter.

Workers Gain Political Muscle

> It is the credible threat of a revolution by the population that ultimately pushes the elites to democratize.
> —Political scientist Christian Houle 2009, 592

Prior to the modern era, history was not generally understood as having directionality. The idea that material and social conditions might improve in a sustainable manner into the distant future was not entertained. More common was the view that history is cyclical, more or less ever repeating itself. This is what nature suggests with its life cycles and seasons. Civilizations rise and fall, but in the very long term, everything remains essentially the same.

The idea that material and social progress are possible only dates back about 250 years, gaining momentum in the era of the French and Scottish Enlightenments, Adam Smith, Thomas Jefferson, Emmanuel Kant, and the American and French revolutions. This optimism was rooted in the fact that uniquely in Europe, a new bourgeois class gained adequate power politically to enable capitalism to sustainably flourish and generate greater productivity growth—an increase in the amount of output produced by an hour of labor—that enabled growth in output to outstrip population growth.[1] Capitalism also generated the ideals of universal humanity and equality. A religious revolution in the form of Protestantism legitimated the institutions and attitudes of capitalism, notably by ennobling work, even as its quality was being degraded.

As capitalism matured into the nineteenth century with industrialization, it drew workers into urban factories where, under the umbrella of bourgeois values, they could organize and successfully demand improved wages and working conditions and a share of political power.[2] Karl Marx, a disciple of Enlightenment optimism, believed that workers' struggles would culminate in revolutions that would replace capitalism with humane egalitarian socialism, setting the conditions eventually for communism. Workers gained the political sway to realize Marx's prediction once they acquired the franchise. Possessing the overwhelming majority of votes, they had the democratic political weight to peacefully

---

[1] "Based on data from The Maddison-Project (2013), average real income growth in Britain between 1000 and 1820 was only 0.12% per year compared with 1.28% between 1820 and 2010. While the difference may seem small, it has resulted in an 11-fold increase in real average incomes in the United Kingdom over the past 200 years compared with a less than three-fold increase over the previous 820 years" (Peterson 2017, 4).

[2] Eastern European rulers were frightened by what they viewed as the consequences of capitalist modernization. Emperor of Austria-Hungary, Francis I, for instance, opposed factories, fearing that they would fill cities with workers where they could organize and threaten the government. For the same reason he opposed railroads: "No, no, I will have nothing to do with it, lest the revolution might come into the country" (Quoted in Acemoglu and Robinson 2012, 219). Similar resistance to industrialization was expressed in Russia, especially after the worker revolutions of 1848 that convulsed Europe.

rewrite the political script, to reconfigure social institutions to their own best advantage. That they mostly failed to do so testifies to the power of the dominant command elites retained over ideology that convinced workers to bridle their struggle for control over productive wealth.

Nevertheless, workers made substantial progress. Wages rose, working conditions improved, as did living conditions, and some social support measures put a safety net, albeit a paltry one, beneath workers. Much of what had earlier been viewed as the domain of charity was taken over by the state and came to be seen as rights. The state presented itself as an agent for social solidarity, and often as paternal caretaker.

Several other reforms were especially notable. One was the democratization of education for workers' children. In England, for instance, in a mere 30 years (between 1870 and 1900), school enrollment of 10-year old children soared from 40 to 100% (Acemoglu and Robinson 2000, 1191). More striking, in the late nineteenth and early twentieth centuries, almost all advanced capitalist countries enacted progressive income and inheritance taxes. Over subsequent decades, tax rates on the income of society's richest members were as high as 50 to 90% (Piketty 2020, 559).

Yet even more remarkable was the response to the abysmal condition of workers' health. Migrants to urban areas lost the degree of economic security provided by traditional agrarian communities and came to live in severely crowded hovels without clean water or sanitary facilities, surrounded by disease, crime, and violence. The misery of those living in slums was not only more extreme generally than that which had characterized the countryside, but also more visible and shocking, evoking strong political reaction. The consequence was that by the end of the nineteenth century, with male workers in industrializing countries possessing the right to vote, substantial advances in diet and health were made for working class families. The threat of revolution by an increasingly organized working class not only increased wages and improved working conditions, but it also forced public authorities to institute improvements in sanitation and water supplies. Cleaner water and better nutrition as incomes rose enabled children to grow taller and stronger. This, combined with medical advances, allowed life expectancy at birth in England and Wales to increase from 40 in 1850 to 45 in 1900 to 70 by 1950 (Deaton 2013, 83).

The Great Depression and Unparalleled Subsequent Social Progress

Since its early beginnings, capitalist economies have periodically experienced financial crises that set off economic depressions. Economic output greatly contracted, firms went bankrupt, and workers lost their jobs. Although financial crises and depressions temporarily cost elites parts of their fortunes, the harshest suffering has been borne by workers who endured long-term unemployment, often inflicting homelessness, malnutrition, and even starvation on them and their families.

The Great Depression of the 1930s was the severest. It also stands out as unique in the extent to which it delegitimated the ideology of elites. Widespread suffering called into question the laissez-faire ideology that had justified economic policies generating explosive inequality and financial instability during the 1920s. As free-market economists Milton and Rose Friedman put it, the Depression "discredited [and] shattered the public's confidence in private enterprise" (1988, 458; 462). This economic dysfunction and the accompanying suffering also challenged the prevailing economic theory that legitimated the laissez-faire policy stance of minimal government, making way for the Keynesian revolution that justified government intervention into the workings of the economy to lessen inequality and better protect the economy from dysfunctional instability. Inequality in income, wealth, and opportunity lessened during the subsequent four decades and social reforms dramatically improved the work lives and well-being of most citizens. These reforms were guided by economic doctrines that emphasized government's responsibility for full employment at decent wages and improved working conditions. In the United States, only government could guarantee workers and citizens generally a more humane "New Deal."

Although European workers equally gained as laissez-faire was substantially delegitimated, to maintain clear focus the following discussion will primarily address the gains in the United States.

Popular support for worker militancy encouraged workers to demand improvements in work conditions as well as wages. Between 1932 and 1940, average wages increased by 46% (Olenin and Corcoran 1942, 1). The trade unions of the Congress of Industrial Organizations (CIO) fought both within firms and in the political arena to bring dignity to factory work by improving work conditions, setting limits on what could be demanded of workers, and by agitating for a shorter workweek.

As the Depression lingered on, President Franklin Delanor Roosevelt became increasingly militant in his support for workers. In his presidential campaign of 1936, he called for a wealth tax. He also advocated marginal income tax rates (tax rates on highest dollar of taxable incomes) as high as 79%, stiffer inheritance taxes, and greater taxes on corporate profits. He declared in his presidential address of 1936 that the rich "economic royalists" formed an "autocracy" that sought "power for themselves, enslavement for the public" (Quoted in Kennedy 2001, 227–28). By significantly empowering workers, his New Deal created what historian Jefferson Cowie termed the "great exception" in American political history (2017).

Among the political programs enacted over these 40 years that benefited the general population, the most consequential were workers' rights to collectively bargain, Social Security, unemployment insurance, minimum wages, the G.I. Bill, Medicare, Medicaid, Food Stamps, public housing and rent subsidies, Project Head Start, the Job Corps, the Occupational Safety and Health Administration, the Consumer Product Safety Commission, the Mine Enforcement and Safety Administration, and the Environmental Protection Agency. Public goods benefiting the working class such as schools, parks, playgrounds, and public transit were vastly expanded in quantity and quality. And the proportion of Americans living in poverty declined dramatically from about 30% in 1950 to 11% in 1973.

Three job creation programs were launched during the 1930s, employing 1.4 to 4.4 million people each month (Rose 2013, 155). There was also an unsuccessful attempt to make "Employment Assurance" a part of the Social Security Act. In 1943, a "New Bill of Rights" was proposed, but not adopted, that would have entailed the "formal *acceptance by the Federal Government of responsibility* for insuring jobs at decent pay to all those able to work regardless of whether or not they can pass a means test" (Rose 2013, 170). In his 1944 State of the Union address, Roosevelt advocated an "economic bill of rights" that would include the "right to a useful and remunerative job" and the "right to earn enough to provide adequate food and clothing, and recreation" (Rose 2013, 170). The original draft of the Full Employment bill of 1945 affirmed that "all Americans able to work and seeking work have the right to useful, remunerative, regular, and full-time employment" (cited in Rose 2013, 170), which, had it been retained, would have obliged the Federal Government to guarantee employment, serving as the employer of last resort. The Humphrey–Hawkins Full Employment Act of 1978 was the last attempt to guarantee employment, but it came forth in a political climate that was rapidly turning against labor's interests. Chapter 7 will pursue the moral and social rationality of guaranteed employment and its central importance for human flourishing.

Highly progressive income taxation also revealed the increased muscle of labor between the 1930s and 1970s. The highest marginal income tax rates were: 1929: 24%; 1936: 79%; 1942–43: 88%; 1944–45: 94%; 1946–50: 91%. Top marginal tax rates remained in the upper 80s from 1951 until 1964, and 70% from 1965 until 1981. The top marginal rate averaged 81% between 1932 and 1980 (Piketty 2020, 447). In 1940, the estate tax was raised to 70%, with a $40,000 exemption. In 1941, it was again raised to 77%.

As noted, these policies that served to substantially reduce inequality were the result of the relative delegitimation of laissez-faire ideology. Significantly freed from this ideology, workers with the majority of votes could democratically pursue their own interest in bettering their economic condition. In terms of lessened inequality, the results are striking. Whereas the top 1% of households in 1929 received 22.5% of all pre-tax income (including capital gains), their share fell to 9% by the late 1970s (Piketty and Saez 2006). Between the 1930s and mid-1970s, what economist Arthur Burns termed a "revolutionary leveling" (Williamson 1991, 11), and economists Claudia Goldin and Robert Margo called the "Great Compression" (1992), seemed to confirm economist Simon Kuznets' conjecture that inequality would decrease in the later stages of economic development (1955). Wealth distribution returned to a state that had disappeared in the decades after the Civil War.

A sense of the political pressure to create a more just society serving workers and the disadvantaged is markedly evident in Lyndon Johnson's State of the Union Address in 1964 in which he declared a war on poverty.[3] For a short while, this war appeared headed for a quick victory. Whereas in 1964, 19% of Americans were living in poverty, in a mere 7 years this had fallen to 11% (Jencks 2015, 82).

The Primordial Problem of Scarcity Conquered

If every Man and Woman would work four Hours each Day on something useful, that Labor would produce sufficient to procure all Necessaries and Comforts of Life.
— Benjamin Franklin, quoted in Suzman 2021, 229

---

[3] Johnson avowed that

This administration today, here and now, declares unconditional war on poverty in America. I urge this Congress and all Americans to join with me in that effort. It will not be a short or easy struggle, no single weapon or strategy will suffice, but we shall not rest until that war is won. The richest Nation on earth can afford to win it. We cannot afford to lose it (Quoted in Jencks 2015, 82).

The huge, prosperous, and well-integrated US economy experienced robust economic growth following World War II. Between 1946 and 1976, Gross Domestic Product grew an average of 3.8% per year and unemployment averaged 5% and remained under 4% for a third of this period. During this "Golden Age of Capitalism"[4] the United States became a more equal and just society. Inflation-adjusted per capita income increased by about 90% for the population as a whole, but only about 20% for the richest one percent. According to the US Census Bureau, between 1947 and 1968 the Gini index for income inequality fell to 0.386, the lowest ever recorded for the United States.[5] Workers held considerable political power, thanks to strong unions whose members included almost one in every three workers in 1948. The GI bill, providing benefits to World War II veterans, financed a fifth of all new homes built between the end of the war and 1966, and home ownership increased from 43.6% of households in 1940 to 64.4% in 1980. The GI Bill, also financed college educations for 2.3 million veterans, practically all being the first in their families to attend college (Sitaraman 2017, 202).

Laissez-faire doctrine had been delegitimated to such an extent that Republican Presidents Dwight Eisenhower and Richard Nixon did not seek forcefully to roll back the broadly beneficial measures that had been enacted by the Democratic Party during the New Deal between 1932 and 1940, the Fair Deal between 1945 and 1952, and the Great Society between 1963 and 1968. Indeed, Nixon was more progressive than any later Democratic president before Joe Biden.[6] The rollback in

---

[4] This dynamism also characterized Europe, where it is often called *les trente glorieuses*, the thirty glorious years.

[5] The Gini index or coefficient is an index for income distribution and varies between 0 to 1, where 0 indicates perfectly equal distribution where everyone receives exactly the same income and 1 indicates perfect inequality where one individual receives all income.

[6] Economist Michael Perelman reports that likely more new regulation was imposed on the economy during the Nixon administrations than during any other. Further, his "legacy includes the food stamp program, creation of the Environmental Protection Agency, the Occupational Safety and Health Administration, Earned Income Tax Credits, and the Equal Employment Opportunity Commission, along with passage of the Freedom of Information act and the Clean Water Act" (2007, 32). Capturing the deemphasis of a focus on generating ever-more material output, Republican President Richard Nixon's economic advisor, Herbert Stein claimed that there are more important things to do than "making larger a gross national product" (Stein

measures benefiting non-elites would only begin to occur with the resurgence of laissez-faire ideology in the late 1970s, the election of Ronald Reagan in 1980, and the increasing embrace of laissez-faire ideology by the Democratic Party.

Wealthy elites who had seen their relative share of national income, wealth, and privilege decline continually struggled against the progression of egalitarian ideals and labor-friendly social policies that had been launched in the 1930s. Their greatest success was curbing worker power with Congressional passage of the Labor Management Relations Act of 1947 (the Taft-Hartley Act), overriding President Harry Truman's veto. This act permitted states to ban union shops and prohibited unions from engaging in secondary boycotts.[7] It also prohibited unionization of foremen or low-level supervisors.

On the ideological front, a Red Scare, generated in the wake of World War II in the form of McCarthyism, demonized the political aspirations of workers. It led to the purging of Communists and other leftist activists from the United Auto Workers (UAW) and much of the broader labor movement. Legal scholar and historian Ganesh Sitaraman reports that "Between 1947 and 1956, more than five million federal employees were screened by an anticommunist loyalty program; twenty-five thousand were subjected to an FBI full field investigation; and twenty-seven hundred were dismissed" (2017, 195). It is noteworthy that a Red Scare following World War I had also helped reverse the worker progress achieved during the Progressive Era.[8]

The opportunistic Red Scares in the wake of both world wars represented an extraordinary ideological tactic to delegitimate the sense of solidarity and egalitarianism that had been generated by wartime sacrifices. The ideals of solidarity and egalitarianism were characterized as the abiding principles of the godless communism that led to people's enslavement.

2010, 87). The Council of Economic Advisors captured the optimism of the 1960s by claiming that we were on the cusp of ending recessions for good (Perelman 2007, 23).

[7] A *secondary boycott* refers to when a union's power in a dispute with its employer is extended to put pressure on another employer to not do business with the union's employer.

[8] For an analysis of the use of nationalism to quell worker militancy, see Wisman and Reksten 2024.

Unprecedented Abundance and the Surge of Nonmaterialist Values

...the Western World ... [is] capable of reducing the economic problem, which now absorbs our moral and material energies, to a position of secondary importance ... [T]he day is not far off when the Economic Problem will take the back seat where it belongs, and ... the arena of the heart and head will be occupied, or re-occupied, by our real problems – the problems of life and of human relations, of creation and behavior and religion.
— John Maynard Keynes 2009, viii

Although the ideology of a dire threat of communism served to brake and even reverse some pro-labor and egalitarian policies, the nation's temperament remained largely favorable to political measures benefiting the general population. Moreover, exceptional post war economic growth meant that children born soon after the Second World War's end—the Baby Boomers—would, on average, grow up to have a standard of living almost twice that of their parents. This robust economic growth and low unemployment, combined with labor's relatively high degree of political muscle, kept alive the egalitarian spirit awakened in the 1930s.

Born within this climate of material security and progressive policies was an extraordinary new development in the human condition: for the first time in human history, a generation came of age without fear of dire material privation. The parents of US Baby Boomers had witnessed the extreme hardship of the Great Depression, and Europeans of the same generation had known both the suffering of the Great Depression and the horrors and privations of World War II. For post-World War II Americans, and soon for Western Europeans, unparalleled material abundance meant that the most fundamental economic problem of scarcity had been overcome.[9] Rich nations' output was more than sufficient to provide their citizens with the basic necessities of life: nutritious food, health care, housing, and clothing. Between 1940 and 1960, home ownership increased from 43.6 to 61.9% and car ownership from 27 to 61 million. In the same period, the share of homes with bathtubs and showers increased from about 60% to about 88%. Yet more striking, in a mere 60 years, life expectancy rose from 47 in 1900 to 67 years in 1960. The resulting sense of security was buttressed by welfare programs that put a floor on economic hardship.

The combination of robust economic growth, labor empowerment, lessened inequality, and freedom from the fear of extreme privation set the conditions for a cultural revolution, most visibly expressed in the so-called counter-cultural or hippy movement. But this was merely the flashy tip of the iceberg. Massive cultural and socio-economic effects were to be found much deeper.

The value shift that occurred as this first generation came of age had been predicted by economist John Maynard Keynes in his essay, "Economic Possibilities for our Grandchildren" (1930), and by social psychologist Abraham Maslow's 1954 book, *Motivation and Personality*. Maslow developed a hierarchy of human needs that he presented in the form of a pyramid. In a society where material insecurity prevails, humans are first and foremost focused upon materialistic needs at the pyramid's broad base. Their concern is with physical survival itself. All other goals are secondary. Only when material security has been attained will people feel comfortable or "liberated" to actively pursue higher, nonmaterialistic goals, such as political freedom, social justice, a sense of belonging, self-esteem, or self-actualization.[10] With material security at the broad base and self-actualization at the peak, Maslow's pyramid and analysis gave theoretical expression to a potentially happier future, often

---

[9] Political economist John Kenneth Galbraith's *The Affluent Society* (1957) was the first major widely read work in economics to recognize this extraordinary achievement. It became a best seller with considerable influence on Baby Boomers. It is notable that he had recognized that the problem of scarcity had been solved in his earlier *American Capitalism* (1952).

[10] This may help explain why the United States' long and insistently expressed message of freedom and democracy to the world's poorer peoples seemingly had so little impact. Until people have the material security to feed their children, such high ideals appear as relatively unimportant.

projected by visionaries, where material needs have been satisfied and humans spend their lives creating a good and just society while becoming the most and best each one can be.[11]

Sociologist Ronald Inglehart drew upon Maslow's general framework to a study of post-World War II youth. He found that this extraordinary victory over the harshness of scarcity and the rise of a welfare state generated a shift from materialist to postmaterialist values, from "an overwhelming emphasis on material well-being and physical security toward greater emphasis on the quality of life." Postmaterialists "are likely to give top priority to nonmaterial goals such as self-expression, belonging, and intellectual or aesthetic satisfaction" (2020a, 110). They "are Postmaterialists precisely because they take economic security for granted" (1989, 5, 238).

Inglehart grounds his thesis of a shift from materialist to postmaterialist values upon two hypotheses: a scarcity hypothesis that one's priorities reflect one's socio-economic environment so that one places greatest subjective value on those things that are in relatively short supply; and a socialization hypothesis that, to a large extent, one's basic values reflect the conditions that prevailed during one's preadult years (1989, 56). The socialization hypothesis does not mean that no further value changes occur beyond adolescence. The implication is only that "human development seems to be far more rapid during preadult years than it is afterward, and the great bulk of the evidence points to the conclusion that the statistical likelihood of basic personality change

---

[11] Philosopher Herbert Marcuse, in very different terms, had also recognized and celebrated the overcoming of scarcity in his widely read and highly influential *Eros and Civilization*. He took issue with Freud who had claimed in *Civilization and Its Discontents* (1930) that civilization required a repression from which there can be no escape. Humans had traded freedom for security. Marcuse argued against the contemporary relevance of this position, claiming that the scarcity that led Freud to view the need to curtail the pleasure principle no longer prevailed in the rich countries: "The very progress of civilization under the performance principle has attained a level of productivity at which the social demands upon instinctual energy to be spent in alienated labor could be considerably reduced" (1955, 129). For Freud, civilization required that sexuality in particular must be repressed. Note that as Postmaterialist values arose, so too did popular music—rock and roll—that began removing the polite veil over sexuality in music by referring more explicitly to sex and even sex acts, to the consternation of their more Materialist parents.

declines sharply after one reaches adulthood." Consequently, "fundamental value change takes place gradually, almost invisibly; in large part, it occurs as a younger generation replaces an older one in the adult population of a society" (R. Inglehart 1989, 69).

As noted above, Inglehart defined materialist values as relating to physiological needs, specifically those having to do with physical and economic security. These values encompass the following categories: preserving a stable economy, furthering economic growth, combatting rising prices, supporting strong defense forces, fighting crime, and maintaining law and order. By contrast, the postmaterialist values relate to social and self-actualization needs and encompass belonging and esteem as well as intellectual and aesthetic values. They include the following categories: creating a less impersonal society, having more influence in their work and community, more say in government, exercising freedom of speech, recognizing that ideas count, and enjoying beautiful cities and nature.

From extensive surveys of attitudes, values, and behavior carried out over nearly two decades, Inglehart found considerable support for his thesis. Those born after World War II placed less importance upon economic and physical security than older cohorts, while giving greater importance to the environment and such nonmaterial needs as community, belongingness, and self-expression. Other postmaterialist values also appear to be associated with the coming of age of the early baby boomers, such as greater equality, racial justice, gender parity, and rejection of war and imperialism. Inglehart reports that "postmaterialists are more likely to engage in unconventional political protest than are materialists" (R. Inglehart 1989, 361), and this period witnessed a surging civil rights movement, the rise of feminism, and massive opposition to the US war in Vietnam. Further, postmaterialists "are far more favorable than materialists toward abortion, divorce, extramarital affairs, prostitution, and homosexuality." Materialists, conversely, tend to adhere to traditional societal norms that favor child rearing—"but only within the traditional survival paradigm of the two-parent heterosexual family, which is reinforced by norms that stigmatized all sexual activity outside that framework" (R. Inglehart and Welzel 2005, 126).

Inglehart and Wetzel also found that these postmaterialist values are not merely held in youth, to be abandoned with age. They found that "from 1970 to 1999, people did not become more materialistic as they aged—indeed, many of these birth cohorts were slightly *less* materialist at the end of this period than they were at the start" (2005, 101). Inglehart reports that whereas "In the USA in 1972, Materialists were three times as numerous as Postmaterialist.... By 2000 Post materialists were slightly more numerous than Materialists in Western Europe and twice as numerous as Materialist in the USA" (2020b, 29). Nevertheless, "there was a clear tendency for each cohort to dip toward the materialist pole during the recession of the mid-1970s and again during the recessions of the early 1980s and the early 1990s" (2005, 102).

Parents of earlier generations who had experienced or witnessed extreme material privation felt compelled to raise their children under the discipline of a strict regime. Failure to do so would not have adequately prepared them for a world of potentially pinching scarcity. These parent-workers have been characterized by their deference to authority, their tolerance for rules and hierarchy, and their conformity (Whyte 1956; Braverman 1998; Lewchuk 1993). But parents of post-World War II generations, raising their families in unparalleled affluence in a robust economy, were more willing to indulge their children. They were more drawn to raise their children according to the permissive codes of pediatrician Benjamin Spock, whose *Baby and Child Care* (1946) was one of America's post-World War II's best-selling books. His guide to child rearing was translated into 39 languages and sold 50 million copies by the time of Spock's death in 1998 (Hidalgo 2011).

It appeared that the highly optimistic vision which in 1930 John Maynard Keynes imagined coming to fruition in a hundred years was arriving well in advance. An American worker in 2015 could maintain the same average income level of 1930 with only a third as much work time, only 17 weeks a year (Autor 2015).[12]

---

[12] Curiously, at mid-nineteenth century, using rudimentary technology, Henry David Thoreau was able to announce: "For more than five years I maintained myself thus solely by the labor of my hands, and I found that by working about six weeks in a year, I could meet all the expenses of living. The whole of my winters, as well as most of my summers, I had free and clear for study" (1948, 56).

Because unprecedented affluence put people at ease, they could not only be less strict with their children but also "lighten up" on themselves. Yet, if Inglehart's research conclusions hold, it is especially with the post-World War II children—this first generation raised in such affluence—that the greatest impact would occur. Did this unprecedented affluence generate a discipline problem? Was this behind the decline in SAT scores between 1965 and 1981? As will be seen in the next chapter, a discipline problem did appear in some workplaces, a problem that would nourish a political backlash.

In support of his thesis, Inglehart notes studies revealing that postmaterialists are underachievers economically. As would be expected, they are typically born to richer and better educated parents. But when this advantage was factored out, Inglehart finds, "among those whose education continued beyond the age of 18, Postmaterialists earn less than Materialists." Sociologist Robert Wuthnow reported that in the early 1980s, American capitalism faced a "moral crisis" brought on by a "precipitous" decline in the willingness of workers to work hard. He found this decline to be especially pronounced among more elite, better educated workers (1982). Less motivated by income, they place greater emphasis upon "interesting, meaningful work and working with congenial people" (R. Inglehart 1989, 172, 162), suggesting they are happier.[13] Psychologists Robert Biswas-Diener, Ed Diener, and Maya Tamir report that "a growing body of research suggests that materialism can actually be toxic to happiness" (2004, 24). Economist Bruno Frey reports other research revealing that people who seek financial success as a key to the good life consistently suffer lower self-esteem, vitality, and life satisfaction (2008, 7).

---

[13] It is noteworthy that the rise of postmaterialist values occurs in a period when the nature of work is being transformed as a majority of workers become employed in the service sector. This happened first in the United States in 1956. Ronald Inglehart and Wayne Baker write that

> Less effort is focused on producing material objects, and more effort is focused on communicating and processing information. Most people spend their productive hours dealing with other people and symbols. Increasingly, one's formal education and job experience help develop the potential for autonomous decision-making. Thus, the rise of postindustrial society leads to a growing emphasis on self-expression (2000, 21; 22).

To Inglehart, these findings suggest that an engine for dynamic economic growth was lost in the shift from materialist to postmaterialist values. He states that "nations with relatively high proportions of postmaterialists show significantly lower rates of economic growth than those of nations with high proportions of Materialists" (1989, 175). But this seems wrong. Productivity growth was much stronger between 1945 and 1975, when baby boomers were maturing with postmaterialist values, than in subsequent years when later generations were experiencing greater material insecurity. Moreover, the weak productivity growth over the past 50 years may be traceable to other factors such as exploding inequality and the associated failure of education to advance adequately to meet the needs of the economy (Wisman 2022).

Postmaterialist values included decreases in conformity with the "establishment." Young people no longer felt such a strong need to adhere strictly to traditional social norms. They dressed more causally in jeans, T-shirts, sweatshirts, and sandals; young women went braless, and men grew long hair and beards and they both experimented with alternative lifestyles, Eastern religions, and narcotics. A few experimented with communal living.

Sociological and psychological treatises came forth that described the conformity of modern life and the revolt against it, notably, sociologist David Riesman's *The Lonely Crowd* (1950), urbanist William Whyte's *Organization Man* (1956), sociologist Paul Goodman's *Growing Up Absurd* (1960), and psychiatrist R. D. Laing's *The Divided Self* (1965). The wide popularity of novels such as J.D. Salinger's *The Catcher in the Rye* (1951), and Albert Camus' *The Stranger* (1942) captured in fictional form the youth's rebellion against conformity.

Philosopher Jesse Glenn Gray published an essay in *Harper Magazine* in (1965) entitled "Salvation on the campus. Why existentialism is capturing the students." He noted that students were being drawn to thinkers who addressed the need for authenticity and rejection of unjust social institutions. They were guided toward idealism and sought personal freedom. A few years later, cultural historian Theodore Roszak explored this movement in greater depth in his widely read book, *The*

Making of a Counter Culture: Reflections on the Technocratic Society and Its Youthful Opposition (1995).

******

Tragically, the Cultural Revolution unleashed by abundance and greater equality helped set the stage for a reaction that would reverse the 40-year trend toward greater equality and re-establish greater insecurity. The quasi-utopian future that visionaries had imagined and that seemed to be birthing over the three decades following World War II was smothered in early infancy by a resurgence of laissez-faire ideology. A convergence of events and forces came together to bring this about, perhaps most politically visible by the fact that a substantial portion of Americans whom President Richard Nixon rallied as "the silent majority" retained traditional materialist values. They felt strongly alienated by the flashier and (to them) degenerate cultural values espoused by postmaterialists, and they were, consequently, vulnerable to the persuasive power of laissez-faire ideology.

The intensified economic insecurity that gathered steam in the 1970s weakened postmaterialist values in the children of the Baby Boomers. The political and economic dynamics that arrested the thrust toward a more humane future is examined in detail in the next chapter.

5

What Abundance Promised Got Crushed

[D]o not let us overestimate the importance of the economic problem, or sacrifice to its supposed necessities other matters of greater or more prominent significance.
— John Maynard Keynes 2009, 373

Never before in history has humanity been better poised to realize the conditions for flourishing and happiness. The primordial problem of material scarcity that continually threatened and periodically caused mass starvation has been solved in rich countries for three quarters of a century, and this unprecedented victory will likely reach most of the world's poorer populations in the near future. Major wars might also belong to the past, none having occurred during this same period. But there is little celebration; folks are not dancing in the streets. As was seen in Chapter 4, in the three decades following World War II, there was a growing sense that a far more liberated future was in store, but that optimism got crushed.

What went wrong? Socio-economic conditions during the 1970s enabled a resurgence of laissez-faire ideology that delegitimated government policies which since the 1930s had dramatically improved worker welfare and life conditions for most Americans and Western Europeans. This sense of material security had enabled a post-World War II generation to turn attention to post-materialist values. However, this sense of security was shattered as a broad sense of unease and insecurity began to become pervasive after the mid-1970s. Belief that the future would be better weakened. Tragically, accompanying rising pessimism, stable communities—a psychologically critical prerequisite for happiness—further eroded.

It is the nature of capitalism's creative destruction that it builds upon itself such that, over the long haul, its pace accelerates.[1] During the four decades between the mid-1930s and mid-1970s, declining inequality led to public policies that steered capitalism's creative destruction to benefit the broad population. But after the mid-1970s, the resurgence of laissez-faire ideology has fueled public policies that have redirected capitalism's creative destruction to disproportionately benefit elites, generating soaring inequality. This pace of technological dynamism and the failure to channel its benefits to the broad population became especially virulent following the fall of Eastern European state socialist societies when the Soviet Union imploded in 1991. Eastern European socialism had provided an important form of military, economic, and doctrinal "friction" slowing the unbridled advance of laissez-faire capitalism. Since the disappearance of that friction, laissez-faire-driven capitalism has come to be seen as the only viable and attractive form of society, and it has penetrated into virtually every corner of the globe, altering practically all countries' political and social institutions.

This chapter examines how the promise of lessened inequality, more humanized work, richer community life, lessened insecurity, and reduced stressfulness that were beginning to be glimpsed following World War II—the dream of past visionaries—has been smothered over the past half century by resurgent laissez-faire policies that have exploded inequality and subjected most Americans to heightened insecurity and stress. The next chapter will address the urgent need for reform to reverse current trends that threaten the death of democracy and our ability to avoid

---

[1] Critical to creative destruction is technological progress which has been geometrically advancing—ever gaining greater speed—over the entire history of humanity.

ecological devastation. The subsequent two chapters outline measures that can serve as the foundation for an attractive alternative vision to laissez-faire capitalism, reawakening the postmaterialist dream and turning it into a reality.

Resurging Job Insecurity and the Re-Disciplining of Workers

> Everyone but an idiot knows that the lower classes must be kept poor or they will never be industrious.
> — Arthur Young 1771, IV:361

The postmaterialist aspirations that arose in the three decades following World War II were short-lived. As the United States entered the 1970s, deficit spending in support of the Vietnam War generated worrisome inflation. This was exacerbated by two exogenous shocks: exploding oil and food prices. Accompanying and worsening the problem of inflation, rising standards of living, along with postmaterialist values, resulted in what was believed to be a labor discipline problem. Workers faced labor markets that had become especially tight after 1965 in consequence of President Lyndon Johnson's reluctance to raise taxes to cool an economy overheated by Vietnam War expenditures. He feared that higher taxes might push parents to join their children protesting the war. With an overheated economy, wages were increasing and getting a job was relatively easy.

Consequently, when that first post-World War II generation, raised in such unprecedented affluence, entered the job market in the mid-sixties, a significant proportion of them were disinclined to work hard in uninteresting jobs where they could be bossed about merely for income with which to buy more consumer goods. They focused greater attention on the need to combat war, racism, sexism, and poverty. As noted in Chapter 4, many young people looked upon traditional materialist values with indifference, if not disdain. In their place, they focused on social justice and celebrated self-expression, richer interpersonal relations, and meaningful work. This "counter-cultural" movement drew strength from anti-war activism and the civil rights movement. Many were influenced by books such as philosopher Herbert Marcuse's *One Dimensional Man* (1964) and sociologist Philip Slater's *The Pursuit of Loneliness* (1970).

This aversion to monotonous, dangerous, or otherwise degrading work was aggravated by the fact that, by the 1960s, the labor movement had acquired sufficient political power to force the creation of a far more generous welfare system. Not only did the level of affluence dampen fear of extreme material privation, but government stood by as guarantor of basic economic security. This trend was not limited to the United States. Over the course of the twentieth century, in all wealthy countries, the costs of social welfare measures increased government taxes from about 10% of national income to between a third and a half.

Emboldened by a sense of material security, labor became militant in demanding higher wages, shorter work weeks, safer workplaces, better health and vacation benefits, and greater voice in decision-making. Labor's aggressive militancy was such that by 1969 the number of strikes in the United States was at its highest level since World War II. In 1970, there were 5716 strikes involving more than three million workers, and the number of days of labor time lost due to militancy was the highest since 1946 (Winslow 2010, 3). Many of these strikes were "wildcat," meaning they were not sanctioned by unions and were often illegal. Comparable worker militancy during this period also occurred in Europe.

Their combativeness paid off. Employers generally ceded to their demands. In the late 1960s, this militancy spread even to public-sector workers, who began striking, often in violation of legal constraints. Striking public school teachers, postal workers, garbage collectors, and city office workers generally met with success in bettering wages, benefits, and the quality of the workplace.

Labor's more privileged position was extraordinary. Since the rise of capitalism, many workers were compelled by fear of unemployment and privation to engage in unsafe and unpleasant work at subsistence wages. But if that fear were to fade, how could workers be motivated to work diligently, especially in boring and unfulfilling jobs under the control of managers who bossed them about? An attractive carrot could perhaps do the job, but the character of work had not substantially changed. Workers were free politically, and now free from the threat of dire material privation, but they were not free in the workplace. They continued to be ruled over by bosses, with no say over choosing their managers and little or no say over the work process.[2]

The accompanying labor-discipline problem was most strikingly captured in what became known as the "Lordstown syndrome." A General Motors plant in Lordstown, Ohio was staffed with mostly young workers who chafed at the mindless character of the work and believed their participation in decision-making would not only make their jobs more fulfilling but also improve operations and output quality. Their disgruntlement led to poor worker discipline, high absenteeism, and high turnover. Lordstown was an extreme instance of an increasingly pervasive problem. A young labor leader told oral labor historian Studs Turkel that Lordstown was "the Woodstock of the working man" (Winslow 2010, 10).

A strike at Lordstown in 1972 became a national news story. It exposed the dissatisfaction of a new generation of young workers, even with high wages, with the mindless drudgery of the assembly line (Loomis 2018; Wuthnow 1982). This severe labor-discipline problem has been credited as a cause of the productivity slowdown that appeared after 1966 (Bowles, Gordon, and Weisskopf 1991). The renegade strikers at Lordstown remained GM's poster children for radicalism within the union, but as the 1970s wound down, the reality became very much the opposite. Rising and persistent unemployment fueled worker insecurity. Tim O'Hara, the vice president of Local 1112 and a Lordstown worker for 41 years recalled that as bargaining power was turning against the workers, "We've kind of agreed to everything that they asked us to, to have job security." Whereas control over the workplace had been central

---

[2] This period witnessed a surge of interest in workplace democracy, whereby workers democratically elect a firm's management and the firm's assets are worker-owned or held in trust (Azzellini 2015; Wisman 1991). Political scientist Cal Winslow writes that looking back at worker post-war optimism, "The demand for 'workers control,' the ownership and control of industry and its democratic management by the workers in the interests of all the people—this must now seem utterly utopian" (2010, 32).

to labor demands following World War II, in the 1970s, these demands "faded as deindustrialization brought desperation" (Jaffe 2019, 35; 36).

The 1971 devaluation of the dollar and abandonment of its gold backing put upward pressure on prices and added to inflation as the costs of imports rose and US firms faced less intense foreign competition. Yet, despite postmaterialist behavior and rising inflationary pressures, the economy was booming in early 1973, even as poor harvests worldwide led to grain shortages and price increases. The Organization of Petroleum Exporting Countries (OPEC) began cutting output in 1974, pushing up prices for all products whose production depended upon oil. Shortages and higher prices emerged for other raw materials. A wage-price spiral was set in motion whereby workers demanded higher wages in expectation of higher prices, while businesses raised prices in anticipation of higher wages. Although the economy crashed in late 1973, the inflation rate reached 12.3% by late 1974.

The severe recession that began in late 1973 lasted until spring 1975. It was the worst downturn since the Great Depression, pushing unemployment to nine percent and rekindling worker insecurity. Six years later, the recession from mid-summer 1981 to late fall 1982 pushed unemployment to 10.8%, and re-disciplining of labor by means of job insecurity shifted into high gear. Between 1979 and 1982, weekly take-home pay fell by more than eight percent, and by 1982, 44% of new contracts required workers to accept wage freezes or cuts (Parenti 1999, 120). These recessions occurred as deindustrialization was gathering momentum. Instead of shutting plants down with strikes, workers began demonstrating to keep them open. President Ronald Reagan made a tough-on-labor message clear in 1981 when he fired illegally striking members of the Professional Air Traffic Controllers Organization. Although Reagan was the only US president to have been at the head of a union, the Screen Actors Guild, his political transformation toward the right exemplified the persuasive power of revived laissez-faire ideology.

The resurgence of laissez-faire ideology during the 1970s came dressed up with the name of "supply-side economics." It nourished a virulent strain of anti-labor ideology that laid the blame for economic dysfunction on a problem of labor discipline and government overreach. Declining sympathy for labor seeped into the Democratic Party. Historian Cal Winslow suggested that Jimmy Carter, whose election as President in 1976 led the Democrats back into power, "was, perhaps, the worst [president] for labor in the postwar period" (2010, 24). Declining sympathy for labor would continue in the Democratic Party for almost half a century until Joe Biden's election in 2020. The Democratic Party's betrayal of the interests of labor eventually led to the election of Donald Trump in 2016 and again in 2024.

The unemployed came to be increasingly seen, not as victims of macroeconomic dysfunction—conditions beyond their control—but as individuals who refused to actively seek out employment or accept available jobs. Welfare was depicted as enabling their lack of initiative and thus a cause of unemployment and the breakdown of the family, while many receiving benefits were characterized as fraudsters. President Reagan reinforced and popularized this view with his complaint of "welfare cheats" and "Cadillac welfare queens." Many workers bought into this view, helping tilt the political balance in favor of the elite owners of productive wealth.

Other events were souring the general mood. US military superiority seemed in question as troops were pulled out of Vietnam—America's first loss of a war.[3] The dollar's devaluation and loss of gold backing suggested a weakened America. The fueling of inflation by the formation of OPEC signaled a decline in US influence abroad. Annual productivity growth in the United States between 1973 and 1979 was less than one percent (Lindbeck 1983, 14). Stagflation—the simultaneous occurrence of high unemployment and high inflation—characterized an unwell economy where Keynesian macroeconomic stabilization policies no longer worked. Between 1979 and 1981, Iranian militants held 52 Americans hostages,

---

[3] Political scientist Sheldon Wolin writes that "Vietnam marked a crucial turning point. A fitful, stupid imperial war remarkable not only for the American defeat but for the fact that, unlike earlier imperial ventures, it was vigorously and successfully opposed at home. The reassertion of constitutional limits on executive power and the successful mobilization of a demotic protest movement meant that military defeat was actually a democratic victory—over its imperial power" (2010, 190).

and US attempts to free them failed. The United States and its people seemed less like masters of the universe.

The news media were filled with essays bearing titles such as "the fall of the American Empire" and "the end of the American century."[4] And although any number of culprits were found responsible for the seeming decline in American power and world prestige, a continuing claim was that the United States had gone soft, if not degenerate. Widespread reporting on the hippies' use of drugs convinced many that degeneracy was indeed metastasizing in the land. Inglehart notes that "To some extent, post materialism was its own grave digger. From the start, the emergence of radical cultural change provoked a reaction amongst older and less secure strata who felt threatened by the erosion of familiar values" (2020b, 175).

Labor's relaxed sense of security was shattered. Students became more focused on preparing for high paying jobs. During the 1960s and early 1970s, when unemployment was low and wages were rising, a college student could major in practically any subject and expect to land a high paying job. By the mid-1970s, this confidence in an easy prosperous future disappeared. Between 1968 and 1996, the percent of American college freshmen who viewed the "development of a philosophy of life" as an important undertaking fell from 82 to 42%, while the percent seeking to "be well off financially" rose from 40 to 74%. Students fled the liberal arts to major in more specific career oriented subjects. Young people became jaded concerning the potential for making the world more humane, and those believing that "keeping up with political affairs" was important fell from 52 to 30% (Macionis 1999).

Continuing Erosion of the Conditions for Flourishing

---

[4] A notable proponent of this view is Samuel Huntington, who in a bestselling book, *The Clash of Civilizations and the Remaking of World Order*, held that "the hegemonic power of 'the West' and of the United States is in decline" (1996, 306–7, 310).

5 What Abundance Promised Got Crushed   103

Work, in its best sense, the healthy energetic exercise of faculties, is the aim of life, is life itself.
— Alfred Marshall 1873, 115

Although rich nations have overcome humanity's primordial threat of material privation, the promise of liberation this victory offered has been largely aborted. The damage has been not only to human happiness, but to the potential for avoiding ecological devastation.

This crushing of the optimism for a richer and more humane society that emerged in the 30 years following World War II is one of the great, but unrecognized, tragedies of modern history. And the elements of this tragedy—soaring inequality, widespread insecurity, malaise, and political dysfunction—have continually worsened over the almost 50 years following the resurgence of laissez-faire ideology. These disorders threaten us with a loss of democracy and the capacity for avoiding ecological ruin. It is urgent that the necessary reforms be understood and put in place while there remains adequate democracy to do so.[5]

Ironically, over this period, the growth in material output has been astounding. When measured in constant 2017 dollars, average per capita American income rose over 350%, from $19,397 in 1959 to $68,988 in 2024. This would suggest that everyone should feel far more secure, content with their lives, and optimistic concerning the future. But just the opposite appears true, reminding us that what is most important is relative as opposed to absolute standing. Thus, although absolute material standards of living have greatly improved, exploding inequality has reduced the relative standing of the bottom 90% of the population.

The fading of the optimism following the mid-1970s has, during the almost half century since, turned to a dark pessimism. In the 30 years following World War II, parents expected their children's lives to be better than their own. This is no longer true. Whereas 90% of Americans born in the 1940s in the United States could expect to make

---

[5] Political discourse typically and misleadingly depicts states as either democratic or non-democratic. But the extent to which a state is democratic is a question of degree, falling somewhere on a spectrum from none to pure. According to Freedom House, democracy has been declining worldwide. Since 2006, there has been a global democratic recession with more countries experiencing diminishing than increasing political rights and civil liberties (*The Washington Post* 2025, A16; Serhan 2022).

more than their parents, this fell to 50% for those born in the 1980s (Kahloon 2021, 69–70). In 2019, less than 30% of parents believed that life overall would be better for their children (Daniels 2021, 35). What has fueled this darkened mood is the insecurity and stress generated by public policies reflecting the political power of the wealthy.

It is worth recalling that in the first 98% of the history of our species, *Homo sapiens*, we lived as hunter-gatherers. Although, as discussed in Chapter 2, technology was rudimentary, there was little sense of material insecurity. There was confidence that nature would provide for basic needs. Indeed, it did so with relatively few hours of work. Moreover, because no elites held ownership and control of productive wealth (hunting and gathering territories), no one was deprived of access to the resources necessary for survival. There was no involuntary unemployment. They also lived in communities where, because food was shared, individual risk of starvation was minimal—no one starved unless all did.

As seen in Chapter 3, this material security disappeared with the rise of the state. Warrior elites seized ownership and control of productive wealth, forcing all others to work for them to survive. They have ever since done so as slaves, serfs, indentured servants, indebted peasants, and wage workers. The earlier sharing community also largely disappeared, meaning that some could starve while others remained well fed with surplus food left to spoil.

Chapter 4 summarized the promising three decade period following World War II when unparalleled abundance in the advanced capitalist countries greatly reduced the sense of material insecurity, and many, especially among the young, embraced postmaterialist values. However, as seen in this chapter, events in the 1970s and the resurgence of laissez-faire ideology led to public policies that have greatly increased not just material insecurity, but malaise more generally.

It is ironic that whereas over the past 70 years the primordial threat of extreme material privation has been solved for the rich countries, their citizens continue to suffer painful insecurity. For many, the principal source of this insecurity is material. But for far more, it is the difficulty of living meaningful lives that provide stable social status and self-certification of value. As will be seen below, what is foremost in generating this insecurity is to be found in the domains of work and community.

Employment and Financial Insecurity

> Jobs are not just the source of money; they are the basis for the rituals, customs, and routines of working-class life. Destroy work and, in the end, working-class life cannot survive.
> — Anne Case and Angus Deaton 2020, 8

The creative destruction of capitalism has quickened in pace since its earliest evolution. It has generated unparalleled material wealth and political freedom. It also has created an increasingly turbulent existence for workers, as new technologies and globalization continually destroy old industries and form new ones. Old jobs disappear as new ones are created. Old skills become obsolete as an increasingly sophisticated workplace puts a premium upon higher and higher levels of education.

This creative destruction weakens communities. Increased job insecurity means that workers must be more mobile, forcing them to become less attached to their communities. As firms die, decrease in importance, or relocate to where wages are lower or environmental laws less stringent, communities are devastated.

Traditional values and attitudes are also continually under attack. Old ideas and values become delegitimated and replaced with new ones more consistent with a world in which new science and technology worsen job insecurity and weaken communities. The brief survey below reveals the decline in employment and financial security over the past half century.

In the *Great Risk Shift* (2019), economist Jacob Hacker addresses how two traditional anchors of economic security, the workplace and the family, have become too weak to provide the financial security and community support they once offered. This weakening has left families more vulnerable to unanticipated economic shocks. Central to this erosion of support have been public policies, driven by laissez-faire doctrine, that have prompted government and corporations to reduce resources spent on job and income security, health care, and retirement.

A measure of this heightened insecurity is a 2017 Chapman University poll that found half of Americans identified "not having enough money for the future" as one of their greatest fears (2017). And this apprehension appears well grounded: A Federal Reserve survey reveals that about 40% of Americans would face difficulty paying for an unexpected emergency expense of $400 (Nova 2019). The negative consequences of this insecurity extend well beyond its financial impact. It has been found that suffering financial strain consumes cognitive 'bandwidth' and results in less self-control, leading to more unhealthy behavior over all income groups (Beenackers et al. 2016). The obesity epidemic which began about 1980 is one of the most visible consequences (Wisman and Capehart 2010).

Labor markets radically changed between the periods 1940–1980 and 1980–2010. Labor economist David Autor submits that "a partial list would include changes in the relative supply of college and noncollege labor, rising trade penetration, offshoring, and globalization of production chains, declines in labor union penetration, the changing 'bite' of the minimum wage, and certain shifts in tax policy" (2015, 10).

Through their economic and political power, labor unions played critical roles in raising wages, improving the quality of the workplace and the general welfare of most Americans between the 1930s and 1970s. Much of the subsequent stagnation of wages, degradation of workers, and decline in general well-being is substantially traceable to the waning of union power.

Union membership in the United States reached its peak in the early 1950s at approximately 33% of the workforce. By 2024, this membership had fallen to 9.9%, with only 5.9% in the private sector (BLS 2025). Although the cause of the decline of unions in the United States is often credited to the decline of the manufacturing sector, it should be noted that in Canada, where manufacturing has equally weakened, unions remain strong.

Attention instead should be focused on political forces. Among the causes, about one-third of private-sector employers illegally fire workers for efforts to unionize their workers, while half of employers threaten to close the worksite if the workers unionize. Further, twenty-seven states have "right to work" laws that undermine the finances of private-sector unions (McNicholas, Sanders, and Shierholz 2019, 6; 8). As the percent of unionized workers has dramatically declined, workers have had fewer organizations to look out for their interests, and thus their influence on public policy has dramatically declined. For instance, it is noteworthy that corporations spend $34 on lobbying for every dollar spent by labor unions and public-interest groups combined (Drutman 2015). In 1978, bankruptcy laws were revised by Congress to permit corporations to restructure more quickly, abrogating union contracts and other worker protections in the process.

Unions brought far more to workers than greater job security, higher wages, and a degree of political power. They also brought, as economists Anne Case and Angus Deaton note, "some democratic control to workers, at work and more broadly in society, and were often a key part of local social life" (2020, 164). Perhaps surprisingly, although unions have dramatically declined to account for only 9.9 percent of wage and salary workers, in 2024 the Pew Research Center found that a majority of Americans view unions favorably (Cerda 2024).

To make ends meet in 2019, 29 percent of US workers took on work beyond their primary jobs, with 36% of these participating in the gig economy (Gallup 2019). Gig workers are frequently depicted as entrepreneurs. But they typically work for a single firm that sets the conditions of work and pay. Thus, their gig entrepreneurial status essentially hides the authority of their employers. They lack the right to join or form unions. They are not covered by minimum wage legislation. They are not provided with benefits.

An increasing proportion of jobs are less than full-time. Since 2010, over half of new jobs have been temporary contracts, and 40% of young workers have short-term jobs without benefits (West 2018, 81). Case and Deaton address their insecurity, noting that these workers no longer "have a long-term commitment to an employer who, in turn, was once committed to them, a relationship that, for many, conferred status and was one of the foundations of a meaningful life" (2020, 4). They go on to point out:

Cleaners, janitors, drivers, and customer service representatives "belonged" when they were directly employed by a large company, but they do not "belong" when the large company outsources to a business-service firm that offers low wages and little prospect of promotion. Even when workers are doing the same jobs that they did before they were outsourced, they are no longer part of the marquee corporation. As economist Nicholas Bloom memorably puts it, "they are no longer invited to the holiday party" (2020, 7).

Research finds that temporary workers suffer much greater anxiety and unhappiness with their jobs than do full-time employees. Their fear of unemployment substantially impairs their mental health (Reichert and Tauchmann 2011) and augments the incidence of physical pain (Chou, Parmar, and Galinsky 2016).

The changing character of work has also reduced vacation time. According to the Bureau of Labor Statistics, the vacation rate (percent of total work hours taken for vacation) fell from 3.3% of worktime in 1980 to 1.7% in 2022. Two new forces lie behind the decline in full-week vacations. One is that new technology makes it easier to have workers connected to work even while on vacation, reducing the attractiveness of "getting away." Second, the expansion of paid time off plans (PTO) lumps sick days, personal days, and vacation time into a single unit of time available to workers. These plans were extended from 35% of workers in 1995 to 67% in 2022. Economist Elise Gould suggests, "Workers may be reluctant to use PTO because they felt that they have to save it for health or personal days" (Van Dam 2023, 1; 4).

As wealthy elites have gained substantially greater shares of wealth, income, and political power, so too has their power increased as stockholders, as owners of corporate America. This ownership is extremely concentrated. In 2020, according to Federal Reserve data, the wealthiest one percent of Americans owned 51.8% of stocks and mutual funds, and the richest 10% of the population owned 87.2%, leaving the bottom 90% in possession of only 12.8% (Pisani 2020). Of financial bonds, 60.6% are owned by the richest 1%, and 98.5% by the top 10%, leaving only 1.5% for the bottom 90% (Koechlin 2013). The Tillman Act of

1907 outlawed financial contributions to federal candidates by corporations and nationally chartered banks. However, on January 21, 2010, in "Citizens v. Federal Election Commission," the Supreme Court ruled that corporations have the same First Amendment free speech rights as individuals and thus can spend as much money as they wish to support or oppose political candidates. This has dramatically increased the political power of the corporation-owning elites. Due to concentrated ownership, firms' managers direct their attention ever more to serving the interests of capital owners as opposed to the earlier mission of also serving their other stakeholders (employees, customers, and communities). The dominant view has become that the management's sole obligation is to the shareholders. And those at the head of management have been richly rewarded. Between 1978 and 2023, top CEO compensation increased by 1085%, compared to a 24% increase for average workers. Whereas in 1965 CEOs gained 21 times as much as a typical worker, this rose to 290 times in 2023 (Bivens, Gould, and Kandra 2024) Many contemporary CEOs have risen to the heights of society's richest.

Malaise: Lives and Deaths of Despair

> I confess I am not charmed with the ideal of life held out by those who think that the normal state of human beings is that of struggling to get on; that the trampling, crushing, elbowing, and treading on each other's heels, which form the existing type of social life, are the most desirable lot of humankind, or anything but the disagreeable symptoms of one of the phases of industrial progress.
> — John Stuart Mill 1909, 748

As noted earlier, despite a 350% increase in output per capita between 1959 and 2024, optimism has dramatically faded. Given the explosion of inequality and the rise of job insecurity, it is not surprising that the least well off have become less optimistic. But the sense of malaise extends even to those much better off.

An Economic Security Index has been created that "incorporates into a single integrated measure three core influences on economic security: (1) income loss, (2) medical spending shocks, and (3) the buffering effects of financial wealth" (Hacker et al. 2014, S6; S28). This index shows that, even before the financial crisis of 2008 and the ensuing Great Recession, Americans were facing the greatest insecurity and heightened risk within a generation. It further reveals that this insecurity had been rising since 1985.

Gallup annually interviews Americans asking question relating to their financial security, health, sense of purpose, social relationships, and community life. Unexpectedly, 2017 turned out to be the worst year for well-being on record. Indeed, the overall index score was lower than it was during the Great Recession. But whereas financial worries dominated gloomy moods during the crisis years, in 2017, emotional and psychological factors dominated. There was less satisfaction in work and social relationships. Diagnoses of depression reached an all-time high (Long 2018). A more recent 2025 Gallup poll finds that Americans' assessment of their personal finances finds a record-high 53% believing it is worsening (Powel 2025).

Whereas life expectancy continued to increase in other countries prior to the covid pandemic, life expectancy in the United States declined for 3 years beginning in 2014. Leading causes have been identified as drug overdoses, alcohol abuse, suicides, and cardiometabolic diseases such as obesity, diabetes, and hypertensive heart disease (Harris, Majmundar, and Becker 2021). All of these causes would appear to be linked to despair.[6] The probability that children and adolescents in the United States will live to age 20 is decreasing for the first time in a century (Woolf et al. 2023). By way of international comparison, whereas life expectancy in the United States is 77.2, in Japan it is 84.8 years, and the average in other high income countries is 82.5 years (Woolf and Aron 2023, A17).

The US suicide rate has been steadily increasing since 1999, climbing by 33% over the subsequent 20 years. This represents more than 47,000

---

[6] Case and Deaton cite the unravelling of the Soviet Union as evidence of the effect of despair on longevity. Life expectancy fell between 1987 and 1994 by 7.3 years for men and 3.3 years for women (2020, 107).

people every year. More than a million attempt to take their own lives. Those most at risk are middle-aged men with relatively little education. While fatalities have decreased in the workplace, workplace suicides have increased (Wan 2020).

More alarming, suicide among teenagers and young adults has risen by more than seen in any other age group. It is the second cause of death for those between 10 and 14 years of age and exceeds their deaths from homicide. Between 2007 and 2017, their rate of suicide increased 56%, from 6.8 to 10.6 deaths per 100,000 people. Over the same period, this group's first cause of death, accidents, declined substantially (Bilsen 2018). Young males commit suicide in greater number than young females, although the latter make more attempts. Relative to the total population, young men are four times as likely to die from suicide (Kahloon 2023, 64). Yet, while suicide rates have been increasing in the US, since 2000 they have been falling in the rest of the world (Case and Deaton 2020, 98). Case and Deaton find that "the increase in pain among less educated Americans can be traced back to the slow disintegration of their social and economic lives, and the pain is, in turn, one of the links through which disintegration leads to suicide and addiction. The story of the deaths of despair often passes through pain" (Case and Deaton 2020, 83–84).

In their book, *Deaths of Despair*, Case and Deaton find the rise of malaise in American society most acute among those of the white working class lacking college educations. They write, "Our main argument in this book is that the deaths of despair reflect a long term and slowly unfolding loss of a way of life for the white, less educated, working class" (2020, 146). The fastest-rising death rates among this population have been from suicides, drug overdoses, and alcoholic liver disease.[7] However, "the widening gap between those with and without a bachelors degree is not only in death but also in quality of life; those without a degree are seeing increases in their levels of pain, ill health, and serious mental distress, and declines in their ability to work and to socialize"

---

[7] A Gallop poll asked, "Has drinking ever been a cause of trouble in your family?" In 1948, the answer was 15%, falling to 12% by 1970, and soaring to 33% by 2018. Ninety percent of drug overdose deaths are among those without a bachelor's degree (Case and Deaton 2020, 105–6; 121).

(2020, 2, 3). Case and Deaton report that "In 1993...at age 40, those without a bachelor's degree were almost three times more likely to report poor health than those with a 4 years degree (8% versus 3%).... [For the former, this rate] doubled between 1993 and 2017 (from 8 to 16%)" (2020, 76).[8]

Marriage rates are declining among those without a bachelor's degree, while incidences of cohabitation and children born out of wedlock are rising (Case and Deaton 2020, 4).[9] Although there is little risk of acute starvation in industrialized modern societies, food insecurity plagues the least privileged in the United States. In 2021, 10.2% (13.5 million) of US households were food insecure at some time during the year (USDA 2023).

While the skill needs in the US economy continue to increase rapidly, due to soaring inequality and declining public support for education, the fraction of the population receiving bachelor's degrees has stagnated since the 1990s. The fraction holding a bachelor's degree rose from a quarter of those born in 1945 to a third of those born in 1970. But for those born after 1970 and completing the bachelor's after 1990, the rate has barely increased (Case and Deaton 2020, 50). This failure of the supply of educated labor to keep pace with demand is evidenced by the earnings premium accruing to the more highly educated (Katz and Goldin 2010). Among nations, the United States has the highest wage returns to cognitive skills, a sign that such skills are scarce and a cause of inequality (Autor 2014, 845). It is this premium that has devalued the relative status of those lacking this education.

---

[8] Case and Deaton report that

> The fraction of whites without a bachelor's degree who expressed difficulty in going out to do things like shop or go to the movies and the fraction finding it hard to relax at home have increased by 50% for those aged 25 to 54, and the fraction finding it difficult to socialize with friends has nearly doubled in this twenty-year period [1997–2017]. The inability to socialize with friends not only removes one of life's most pleasurable and important activities but also puts people at risk for suicide (2020, 79).

[9] Economist and Happiness researcher Bruno Frey reports that "cohabitation does not provide the same benefits as marriage, perhaps because of the lesser degree of certainty" (2008, 152). But this could be due to a need for greater security in an overly insecure environment.

This shortage of those earning bachelor's degrees is evident in the fact that although the United States long led the world in the percent of 25 to 34-year-olds holding college degrees, by 2023 it had fallen to 152th place (OECD 2023). The Programme for International Student Assessment (PISA) found in 2015 that the United States ranked 38th out of 71 countries in math and 24th in science (Pew Research Center 2017). Almost half of all science graduates in the United States are foreign born. In the rising concern with economic stagnation, economist Robert J. Gordon has argued that the declining quality of education in the United States stands as a principle "headwind" to economic dynamism and growth (2016, 624–27). It may also forbode ill for the future of democracy. Political scientist Sheldon Wolin claims that "For its part, democracy is ultimately dependent on the quality and accessibility of public education, especially of public universities" (2010, 161).

As noted above, even those earning degrees appear more driven to do so for employment security and income than for intellectual development and self-fulfillment. Ironically, as Americans continued becoming collectively wealthier, an economy driven by rising inequality left them less secure, more stressed, and more focused on vocational or "careerist" education that is presumed to better ensure jobs.[10] Research finds that where inequality is high, parents spend more time instilling a need to compete for achievement in their children so they can outpace their peers and become successful (Doepke and Zilibotti 2019). The dreams of the visionaries and the expectations generated by Maslow's pyramid of needs have been quashed, or, more optimistically, put on hold. Higher education has traded off "culture" or knowledge for the public good and self-fulfillment for vocational training (Wisman and Duroy 2020).[11] Not

---

[10] The explosion in tuition has heightened the need for a careerist education among students and parents alike so as to get their money's worth. Unbeknownst perhaps to both parents and students, "studies have found that in the corporate world, liberal arts graduates were more likely than others to rise to senior management positions" (Ginsberg 2013, 176).

[11] Laissez-faire doctrine and a surge in inequality have produced a decline in political support for federal and state funding for higher education. According to a 2019 poll, only 33% of Republicans judged colleges and universities as positive. For the US President Donald Trump's son Donald Jr. said of universities, "[They will] take $200,000 of your money; in exchange [they will] train your children to hate our country" (Daniels 2021, 7; 5). Promotion of a careerist reorientation in higher education comes from surprising quarters. Political scientist David Kirp reported that

surprisingly, psychologist Jean M. Twenge finds that, "having grown up immersed in social media, the generation of students entering college around 2013, the 'iGen,' were less mature and more prone to anxiety disorders. They were concerned with safety, especially from ideas they disagreed with" (2017, 146–61).

Over the past half century, communities have greatly weakened, resulting in a decline in social capital. Social capital is a term used to describe the quality of relationships among people who belong to communities in work, where they live, and in general social interaction. A high level of social capital enriches the experience of being a member of a community while enabling both the member and community to function more effectively.

Much of this decline in social capital is due to exploding inequality. One of the reasons, economist George Irvin reports, is that "poorer people are more likely to feel out of place participating in community groups, more likely to feel ill at ease and to think that they will make fools of themselves and be looked down upon" (2007, 15). This retreat from social participation not only reduces social capital and thus community wellbeing, but it also inflicts pain on those who feel excluded. "Brain scans reveal that the pain of feeling excluded by others stimulates the same areas of the brain as does physical pain" (Wilkinson and Pickett 2019, 57).

Single-person households in the United States have increased from 6.9% of total households in 1960 to 37.9% in 2022 (Statista 2022), and those suffering loneliness constitute a growing proportion of the population. According to AARP, in 2018, forty percent of US adults declare they are lonely, double the number in the 1980s (Long 2018). Loneliness is associated with adverse outcomes such as anxiety, depression, and higher mortality and morbidity risk (Lim et al. 2016).

The Obama administration hopes to advance the goal of equal opportunity in higher education by adopting a market-driven rating system designed to give students a clearer picture of colleges' costs and outcomes....The message is plain—the dollar-and-cents return on investment is what counts....Market values trump everything, including learning how to think...[To] Washington policymakers, a university is little more than a vocational training ground (2015, 120).

An important component of social capital is trust. Sociologists Richard Wilkinson and Kate Pickett explain, "High levels of trust mean that people feel secure, they have less to worry about, they see others as co-operative rather than competitive" (2011, 57). But trust has been dramatically declining, principally due to soaring inequality. In their survey of studies on trust, they find that "With greater inequality, people are less caring of one another, there is less mutuality in relationships, people have to fend for themselves and get what they can—so, inevitably, there is less trust" (2011, 56).

The European and World Values Survey has found that trust is higher in countries with less inequality. The *General Social Survey* conducted by the US government has also determined that trust is higher in US states with less inequality (Wilkinson and Pickett 2011, 53–54). Wilkinson and Pickett relate that on a scale of 100, as inequality increased, trust in other people and social institutions in the United States fell from 60% in 1960 to less than 40% in 2004 (2011, 54). More recently, the Pew Research Center reports that whereas in 1964, 77% of Americans trusted the Federal Government, by 2019, this proportion had fallen to 17% (Bell 2022).

As trust has fallen, sales of home security systems have soared as has the demand for gated communities. Even the young people's adventurous practice of hitchhiking that was common from World War II until the late 1970s has disappeared. As people of different classes interact less, they become more dissimilar, see themselves as such, and reveal less trust in those of other classes and races, and often in those of their own class.

Political scientist Robert Putnam describes in *Bowling Alone* (2000) how Americans began to participate less and less in a wide range of social activities involving other people following the 1970s—family dinners, evenings at home with friends, and events hosted by institutions like churches, unions, and clubs.[12]

---

[12] There has been a rapid rise in those who report themselves to be unaffiliated with any religion. From the mid-1970s until 1990, only seven or eight percent were "nones." In 2016 almost 25% of the population was unaffiliated, and among young working class whites aged 18–29 the percentage rises to nearly 50 (Case and Deaton 2020, 176).

The Challenge

> [Economists'] obsession with GDP shift[s] the emphasis from the worker to the product of work. From a Buddhist point of view, this is standing the truth on its head by considering goods as more important than people and consumption as more important than creative activity.
> — E. F. Schumacher 1979, 34

Since the rise of the state, ideology serving the interests of elites has almost always been adequately persuasive to pacify the exploited workforce, enabling the extraction of the "surplus" output that exceeds their bare subsistence needs. Although severe crises have at times partially delegitimated the elite's ideology, recovery was generally quick. The elite's wealth gave them adequate sway over religious doctrines that legitimated their status. In modern times, their wealth disproportionately enables them to influence the secular domains where socio-economic thought is created and dissimulated, such as in the media, think tanks, and educational institutions.

Only once has the prevailing ideology been delegitimated sufficiently that public policies could be explicitly undertaken to redistributed wealth, income, and privilege to the broader population to such an extent that inequality decreased. This occurred when the hardship of the Great Depression of the 1930s undermined the persuasiveness of laissez-faire ideology. The consequence was that during the 40 years between the mid-1930s and the mid-1970s public policies substantially improved economic and social conditions for most of the population. Greater economic and social security set the conditions in which postmaterialist values could come forth as the more-widely shared abundance during the decades following World War II freed ever more of the population from fear of material privation.

However, as addressed above, economic and social conditions of the 1970s created an opening into which laissez-faire ideology resurged in what came to be called supply-side economics.[13] The consequence is that over the past half century, elites have gained greater control over the political realm and public policies have been put in place that have dramatically increased inequality.

What has enabled this ideology to be adequately convincing is the lack of an alternative vision that would serve the interests of the greater population by reducing inequality and insecurity while expanding the domains of freedom. The nature and urgency of an attractive alternative vision to laissez-faire capitalism are addressed in the next chapter.

---

[13] Supply-side economics was a revolt of the rich against policies that had been reducing their relative status. As journalist Louis Menard writes, "Government spending more than doubled between 1950 and 1962. Meanwhile, the top marginal tax rate in the United States and the United Kingdom was close to ninety per cent. It was a neoliberal's nightmare." And this was despite the fact that

> between 1950 and 1973 the world G.D.P. grew at the fastest rate in history. The United States and Western Europe experienced remarkably high rates of growth and low levels of wealth inequality—in fact, the lowest anywhere at any time. In 1959, the poverty rate in the United States was twenty-two per cent; in 1973, it was eleven per cent. It was also a period of 'liberation.' People felt free, acted out their freedom, and wanted more of it. They weren't supposed to feel that way. They were supposed to be passive and dependent (2023, 70).

6

The Urgent Need to Humanize Work and Recover Community

The dogmas of the quiet past are inadequate to the stormy present. The occasion is piled high with difficulty, and we must rise with the occasion. As our case is new, so we must think anew and act anew.
— Abraham Lincoln 1862

Extensive studies have found that pursuing consumption as a major source of personal meaning and social and self-respect does not advance human happiness. This pursuit also threatens ecological devastation and our species' future well-being, if not our very existence. Studies have found that it is in work, not in consumption, that the greatest potential for human flourishing is to be found, and that our focus should be on improving the quality of work experience. Happily, the task of implementing institutional changes to improve work life and ennoble work is made easier by the fact that, in rich countries, the basic economic problem of scarcity has been solved. Unhappily, the dominance of laissez-faire ideology hides the need for these reforms from view.

This chapter addresses the urgent need to replace the laissez-faire ideology that justifies extreme inequality and presents consumption as the goal to be pursued with a superior vision that promises freedom from unemployment, democratic freedom in the workplace, and richer community life, while preserving capitalism's two principal institutions of private property and free markets.

The urgency of corrective action stems from disturbing evidence that humanity appears headed toward the death of democracy and, consequently, toward impotence to avoid ecological Armageddon, arguably the greatest challenge humanity has ever faced. Laissez-faire ideology and the vision of material progress it nourishes are grounded in the belief that economic growth should be society's foremost goal and the corollary presumption that ever-increasing consumption is the key to a happier future. Growth-oriented public policies validated by laissez-faire thinking have differentially directed the fruit of economic dynamism to wealthy elites. Measures to address ecological degradation are hampered because they would not be in the short-run interests of wealthy elites. Consequently, they use their disproportionate political power to stymy implementation of the necessary ecological measures to preserve our habitat.

Elites are also using their political muscle to erode democracy and head off public policies that would reduce their wealth, income, and privileges, as had happened between the mid-1930s and mid-1970s. With democracy eliminated, or even greatly weakened, arguably the necessary ecological measures cannot be enacted.

What is necessary, then, is an attractive alternative vision that, if embraced by a majority of the electorate, could reverse the decline in democracy and enable implementation of appropriate ecological measures. The prospect that is proposed in this chapter, and greatly elaborated in Chapters 7 and 8, repudiates the view that economic growth should be relentlessly pursued and proposes that our hope lies in employment security, the democratic enrichment of work experience, and its consequent enrichment of community life.

The Rise of the Material Progress Vision and the Growth Trap

> Modern capitalism inflames, through every sense and pore, the hunger for consumption. Satisfying that hunger has become the great palliative of modern society, our counterfeit reward for working irrational hours. Advertisers proclaim a single message: your soul is to be discovered in your shopping.
> — Robert Skidelsky 2012

It is often taken for granted that humans have always striven to accumulate material possessions. However, as noted in Chapter 2, prior to the adoption of agriculture about 10,000 years ago, almost all humans were nomadic, precluding any significant accumulation of material wealth beyond a few primitive weapons, tools, clothing, and jewelry. But there was a force beyond their nomadism precluding the individual accumulation of wealth. These early societies held private accumulation to be selfish, unfair, and destructive of community. Consequently, it was subject to ridicule or even punishment.[1] Competition for status and mates had to be expressed through other forms of behavior such as being courageous warriors, good hunters or gatherers, being cooperative, generous, good storytellers, artistic, or just fun to be with. These behaviors contributed to community well-being and were thus highly valued. It is only in the last two percent of the human story, accompanying the rise of states and civilization about 5500 years ago, that accumulation of substantial personal material wealth even became possible. It proved achievable when the stronger gained the power to dominate and exploit the weaker.

In state society, a thin elite lived in relative luxury while the masses lived at subsistence with barely enough to survived. Where productivity

---

[1] Biologists Charles Lumsden and Edward O. Wilson point out that "In hunter–gatherer societies such as the !Kung of the Kalahari, conspicuous attempts to improve personal status and to accumulate large quantities of personal goods are met with ridicule and hostility" (1983, 150–151). Even in early agricultural societies, where wealth was sought, it was not to become ever wealthier, but to give it away in community feasts, a generous act that brought approbation and status to its sponsors.

increased and surplus was not wholly expropriated by elites, population growth generally followed, leaving standards of living for the masses relatively stagnant near the subsistence level. Warrior elites might increase their own affluence through intensified exploitation of workers or plunder of other societies, but these actions did not augment wealth, they merely reallocated what already existed. Consequently, sustainable economic growth was not imagined. There could be good years and bad, but history was generally viewed as cyclical. Even rising empires would peak and fall. Such cycles were often understood in religious and moral terms. Good times were rewards for appropriate moral behavior, while bad times were punishment for sinfulness (e.g., the biblical flood). Historian Richard Tawney notes, for instance, that even as late as the early eighteenth century in England, "The idea of economic progress as an end to be consciously sought… had been unfamiliar to most earlier generations of Englishmen, in which the theme of moralists had been the danger of unbridled cupidity, and the main aim of public policy had been the stability of traditional relationships" (1926, 206–7).

It is only in the last few centuries that productivity growth and the resulting expansion of output began to sustainably outpace increases in population, and it slowly came to be seen that growth is possible, that someone's increase in wealth did not have to mean someone else's decrease, and that with appropriate institutions, everyone could become wealthier. The project of deliberately and fundamentally altering societies' institutions to promote economic dynamism and political freedom only began to be a political focus in the eighteenth century. This was the intent of Adam Smith's advocacy of laissez-faire. From the rise of Mercantilism in the sixteenth century, governments had greatly intervened in regulating economic activities. Smith argued that freeing the economy from these strictures and leaving markets free from government interference would promise increased freedom, economic dynamism, and lessened inequality.

Yet the idea that economic growth was possible spread slowly. While Smith was envisioning rising living standards, Edward Gibbon, famous for his treatise on the fall of the Roman Empire, claimed that there was an upper limit to economic output, which could be attained during peaceful and favorable climatic times, such that only a small surplus would be available to a few (2010). And even Adam Smith and subsequent members of the classical school of political economy believed that economic growth would eventually run its course and end in stagnation. Nevertheless, against a background of widespread poverty, it is understandable that the idea that economic growth (the expansion of material output) would become society's primary focus.

The view that greater wealth was possible generated a "material progress vision," according to which it is economic growth that will generate progress and make possible the good and just society (Wisman 2003). Therefore, society should consider economic growth as its highest priority. This has promoted a preoccupation with greater material output as the key to improved human welfare. Largely neglected have been such essential components of human well-being as more creative and fulfilling work, greater equality in the distribution of opportunity, income and wealth, richer community life, a sustainable environment, and more time for family, friends, and reflection. Rather, maximum material output is held to be the key to a better future. For the sake of utmost economic growth and the greatest potential for augmenting everyone's consumption, capitalism's creative destruction must be fully unleashed, even at the cost of ever more intense competition, inequality, insecurity, stress, and environmental destruction.

Since the rise of the state and extreme inequality, elites have competed through conspicuous consumption for the pinnacle of status. Only they could participate in this competition as all below were left without means beyond those necessary for bare subsistence. This began changing in industrial economies in the second half of the nineteenth century when, through strikes and the threat of insurrection, workers gained the political power to hold onto a part of their surplus output. As wages rose above subsistence, workers began spending their surpluses, imitating elites in seeking status through conspicuous consumption, famously analyzed by Thorstein Veblen in *The Theory of the Leisure Class* (1899). A consumption arms race was launched in which workers struggled for status and social and self-respect through greater consumption. Rising inequality forced them to work long hours, frequently in unfulfilling work, to maintain their relative consumption status, as elites, always in competition among themselves for highest status, raised the bar ever higher.[2]

It is important to note that workers were driven toward seeking social status through consumption by the fact that they became less capable of achieving social and self-respect through work and community. Prior to industrialization, most worked in agriculture, where, even when extremely exploited, workers, excepting with gang slavery and *corvée* labor (unpaid forced labor), had a significant degree of control over the work process. How well and hard they worked could be seen and appreciated within their communities, providing them with social merit and self-respect. When proletarianized into factories and urban areas, workers lost control of the work process as work was debased by the division of labor, machine regularity, rigid hours, and strict supervision. Urbanization accompanying industrialization diminished workers' potential for acquiring certification of value through participation in their communities. Moreover, although having a job continued to provide a degree of social and self-respect within factories, how hard and how well one worked was no longer visible to others and could no longer serve as readily as a source of pride and status.

Inequality makes it harder for work to serve as a means for achieving fulfillment. Because inequality propels households toward greater consumption to maintain relative social standing, inequality encourages workers to choose income over work quality. The labor market reinforces this tendency.[3] As political scientist Robert Lane points out, "In the labor market where workers are free to choose, there is

---

[2] Keynes predicted that by 2030, productivity gains would result in a workweek of about 15 hours (1930). Had he read Veblen, or done so carefully, he would have noted that, instead of reduced hours, future surplus might be absorbed in conspicuous consumption. Veblen wrote: "As increased industrial efficiency makes it possible to procure the means of livelihood with less labor, the energies of the industrious members of the community are bent to the compassing of a higher result in conspicuous expenditure, rather than slackened to a more comfortable pace" (1899, 111). Indeed, an "emulation in expenditure stands ever ready to absorb any margin of income that remains after ordinary physical wants and comforts have been provided for" (1919, 394). Since 1900 in the United States labor productivity has increased almost nine-fold. Since Keynes' 1930 essay "Economics for Our Grandchildren," productivity has increased fivefold, while leisure has grown by a mere three percent (C. B. Frey 2019, 334).

[3] So too does mainstream economics. Economist Tibor Scitovsky, notes that the "effects of work are completely missing from the economist's numerical index of economic welfare…work which produces market goods may be an economic activity, but the satisfaction the worker

poor information on quality of work life, the default values of money are strong, family benefits flow from money but not from intrinsic [work] satisfaction" (1991, 406). Consequently, work becomes a means to greater consumption, as opposed to an outlet for self-expression, creativity, and community.[4]

The material progress vision is not merely in people's heads. It is also embedded in society's social institutions. For instance, economic growth lowers unemployment and puts upward pressure on wages. Thus, understandably, second only to addressing foreign aggressors, unemployment poses the greatest challenge to political incumbents. Their success in dealing with unemployment significantly determines their ability to stay in power. In democracies, political parties across the spectrum, striving to hold onto or acquire office, struggle to convince the electorate that their candidacy and the policies they advocate hold the greatest promise of stimulating economic dynamism and thereby benefiting the working class. This frequently, if not usually, entails sacrificing other social goals, such as defending the environment, to protect or generate employment. A contemporary example is that despite the huge ecological cost of using coal for energy, the closure of coal mines is opposed because coal workers would lose their jobs and their communities would wither.

Happiness research reveals the material progress vision to be a mistake. It finds that, above a fairly low threshold, greater subjective well-being does not result from higher incomes and higher levels of consumption. Although average levels of satisfaction are considerably lower in very poor countries than in rich ones, after a certain income level has been attained, further increases do not raise subjective well-being (Diener et al. 1995; Veenhoven 1993; Easterlin 2001, 2002, 2019; B. S. Frey 2008).[5] Psychologists Robert Biswas-Diener, Ed Diener, and Maya Tamir report

---

himself gets out of his work is not an economic good because it does not go through the market and its value is not measurable" (1976, 17).

[4] Two centuries ago, well before any realization of the disastrous environmental consequences of runaway consumption, philosopher Friedrich Hegel pointed to the central importance of rewarding work for a full life, contending that "recognition from his professional peers... would save the individual from the temptation to seek recognition through the display of wealth, and from the 'bad infinity' of unlimited wants" (1821, para 250–255).

[5] Economist Richard Easterlin, for example, writes, "In the United States happiness today is no greater than 70 years ago when real GDP per capita was one-third of its current level;

that "a growing body of research suggests that materialism can actually be toxic to happiness" (2004, 24).

In terms of income and consumption, what appears to be important is one's relative as opposed to absolute position. A notable study by economists Sara Solnick and David Hemenway (1998) finds that when presented with the question of whether they would prefer to live less-well-off in a rich society or near the top in a poorer society, fifty percent claimed they would give up half their real income to live in a society where they were better off than most others. In terms of evolutionary biology, this makes sense. What counts in determining the probability of attracting sexual partners and thus sending one's unique set of genes into future generations is relative status.

Humans are biologically driven to compete for status. But how this drive is socially channeled is determined by a society's institutions. Today's social institutions direct behavior toward earning high incomes to be successful in competing for status through consumption. This deflects from view the two interrelated domains of work and community in which fulfillment and self-esteem are more richly nourished.[6] As noted above, this is the lesson of our evolution and confirmed by anthropological studies and happiness research. Nevertheless, despite the commanding influence of the material progress vision, people continue to recognize that work and community are critically important for their well-being. And they are highly interrelated.

Research finds that although the unemployed have a great deal of free time, their demoralization leads them be "even less involved in their communities than those with jobs" (Kahloon 2023, 66). Work and community are critically important to people. In their extensive interviews, sociologist Robert Bellah and his associates found "Americans in agreement that two of the most basic components of a good

---

in China, life satisfaction in 2015 was about the same as in 1990 despite a roughly fivefold multiplication of real GDP per capita" (2019, 7).

[6] The American Time Use Survey and the UK Annual Population Survey find that "work is reported to be more meaningful than consumer purchase, socializing, relaxing, or leisure. Jobs that are both high on personal autonomy and direct pro-social impact are rated as the most meaningful, including the jobs of health professionals, therapists, nurses, midwives, teachers, lecturers, and social workers" (Cassar and Meier 2018, 217).

life are success in one's work and the joy that comes from serving one's community" (2007, 196).

Ecological Devastation

> To make men industrious—to make them shake off that lethargy which is natural to them, they must be inspired with a taste for the luxuries and enjoyments of civilized life. When this is done, their artificial wants will become equally clamorous with those that are strictly necessary… In highly civilized societies, new products and new modes of enjoyment are constantly presenting themselves as motives to exertion, and as means of rewarding it. Perseverance is, in consequence, given to all the operations of industry; and idleness, and its attendant train of evils, almost entirely disappear.
> — John Ramsey McCulloch 1825, 209)

Few days go by without news reports about the increasing difficulty of avoiding ecological devastation. This holds true despite a long series of international accords dating back to the 1987 Montreal Protocol when all 197 members of the United Nations agreed to regulate nearly 100 chemicals known as ozone-depleting substances. In Rio de Janeiro 5 years later, 154 states signed the United Nations Framework Convention on Climate Change (UNFCCC), agreeing to combat "dangerous human interference with the climate system" (Puko 2023a). In all, 29 United Nations climate summits have produced accords to halt further ecological devastation.

Although these accords have stimulated positive environmental measures, they have not reversed, stopped, or even substantially slowed ecological degradation. According to the World Meteorological Organization, concentrations of carbon dioxide are growing more rapidly than at any time since our species evolved and demands for fossil fuels continue to grow (2024). Only one percent of increased greenhouse gas emissions projected for 2030 has been trimmed. On September 8, 2023, the UNFCCC concluded that "there is a rapidly narrowing window" for avoiding increasingly severe disasters (Dennis 2023). Even if nations fulfill existing pledges, warming is expected to rise by 2.4 degrees Celsius (4.3 degrees Fahrenheit) by century's end with catastrophic consequences. On September 20, 2023, U.N. Secretary General António Guterres lamented that "Humanity has opened the gates of hell. We must make up time lost to foot-dragging, arm-twisting and the naked greed of entrenched interests raking in billions from fossil fuels" (Puko 2023a).

The summers of 2023, 2024, and 2025 were the hottest recorded in human history. They were accompanied by massive heat waves, wildfires, and flooding that resulted in enormous loss of life, impaired health, and economic losses. The level of carbon dioxide in the atmosphere has risen to levels above those of the past few million years. The atmosphere has already warmed about 1.2 degrees Celsius (2.16 Fahrenheit) (Dennis 2023). About two-thirds of mammals, fish, reptiles, and amphibians have gone extinct in the last 50 years (Mellon 2022, A13). Invasive species, hitching rides on ships and planes, have been credited with about 60% of animal and plant extinctions. The other principal causes of extinction are habitat destruction, climate change, pollution, and over-exploitation of species (Grandoni 2023).

If this destruction of the human habitat were to end our planet's ability to support human life, it would be our species' suicide. Extreme ecological devastation joins nuclear weapons as human created Frankensteinian monsters threatening the end of the human adventure.

Why, given the continual barrage of dire news on this environmental threat, are appropriate actions not taken? The proximate answer is that humanity has embraced a material progress vision that has captured us attitudinally and institutionally in a growth trap. Yet there is a deeper reason. As will be addressed below, wealthy elites, whose interests would be most harmed by measures to halt, or even reduce, environmental degradation, use their wealth to influence political policy makers to block or slow their implementation.[7]

The ecological challenge is a global challenge, requiring that the world's nations successfully coordinate to address a free-rider problem.

---

[7] As this book goes to press, President Donald Trump and a Republican controlled Congress are rolling back earlier enacted environmental measures.

Reducing emissions of CO_2 and other pollutants is a global public good, which means that the benefits to any country of curbing its emissions is only a fraction of the costs it would bear in doing so alone, and thus national self-interest militates against undertaking such reductions unless all or most others do so as well.

The free-rider problem is widely recognized among the world's nations, and strategies for dealing with it are not lacking. For instance, an especially promising one is offered by economist William Nordhaus (2015), who proposes a climate club, the members of which would agree to cut their emissions by the required amount. Non-members and member-cheaters would suffer punitive tariffs on their exports to member countries. Setting these penalties at the right level would encourage worldwide compliance by making it in each nation's self-interest to do so. Penalties could be adjusted for poorer nations less capable of meeting the set environmental standards.

But why, when nations have met on the climate issue, have they not adopted Nordhaus' proposal or some equally promising strategy? The reason is the even more daunting second stumbling block mentioned above: high levels of inequality provide wealthy elites with widely disproportionate political power to oppose environmental measures to protect their own interests.

Beyond providing elites with disproportionate political power, inequality, and especially *rising* inequality, generate other forces resulting in environmental degradation. As the ever-richer wealthy raise their own consumption expenditures, lower income households, to maintain their relative status, imitate the higher spending of those above them. Inequality encourages households to seek social certification and status through consumption because splurging serves as a proxy for how rich they are and, therefore, how hard they work. Rising inequality strengthens this dynamic as does the degree to which people believe that their status is dependent upon their own efforts. The attitudes, institutions, and behavior generated by this focus on consumption reduce the potential for people to achieve status or validation through environmentally friendlier domains such as work and community.

Second, wealthy elites enjoy a short-run economic benefit because the cost of pollution—taken in the broadest sense of damaging the environment—is not included in the price of their much greater consumption. The United Nations Environment Program reports that the world's wealthiest one percent account for twice the emissions of the poorest 50% (Dennis et al. 2020). The richest 10% create 40–50% of global carbon emissions (Starr et al. 2023). An average American's annual carbon footprint is about 17.6 tons of carbon dioxide equivalents a year, which is about twice that of a citizen of the European Union and almost 10 times that of the average Indian citizen (Dennis et al. 2020). According to another estimate, the consumption by the richest seven percent of the world's population produces 50% of the world's greenhouse gas emissions (Sayer 2015, 323). Global Footprint Network reports that "if everyone in the world consumed at the level of US citizens, it would require five earths to support them sustainably, or three earths at European levels of consumption" (quoted in Sayer 2015, 315). The wealthiest one percent of households in the United States with 16% of national income accounted for 17% of greenhouse emissions; the top 10% for 43% of these emissions.

Third, elites overwhelming own the means of production. Weak controls on polluting activities and governmental subsidies for fossil fuel production mean their assets yield higher profits. Note, for instance, that among the G-20 Cooperation Forum, fossil fuel subsidies surpassed one trillion dollars in 2022, four times higher than they were in 2010. And these G-20 member states produce 78% of the world's planet-warming emissions (Puko 2023b).

Fourth, elites also have the wealth, connections, and information to live in places and in ways that shield them from pollution's most harmful consequences. As political economist James Boyce has put it, "The global environment is our common home, but not everyone lives in the same room" (2007, 314). The poor occupy by far the most polluted rooms—a form of climate apartheid.

Optimism is hard to muster when global emissions are 62% higher than they were when international negotiations began over three decades ago (Dennis et al. 2020). Success depends upon delegitimating the laissez-faire ideology that hoodwinks enough voters in believing that policies that in fact disproportionately benefit elites are in everyone's interests.

An international study has found that, controlling for per capita income, a more equal distribution of political power, as gauged by degree of political democracy, civil rights, and literacy, correlates with stronger environmental quality (Boyce 2007). This result is supported by a study of the 50 American states that reveals a correlation between more equal distribution of political power and stronger environmental policies (Boyce et al. 1999). According to a survey by the Pew Research Center, whereas 88% of Democrats view climate change as a very serious threat, only 31% of Republicans share this view (Dennis 2020). Republican President Donald Trump, has significantly rolled back the environmental measures put in place by his predecessors, and Congressional Republicans continue to attempt to do so. Trump, running for President in 2024, claimed that the science of climate change is a "hoax" (Shimron 2023). And now, again President, he has set in motion the process to again exit the Paris Accords and "drill baby drill!".

But might not wealthy elites come to realize that if our habitat is destroyed, their privileges or even their own survival would come to an end? Anthropologist and historian Jared Diamond has found that elites in past civilizations pursued their own immediate self-interest in competitive consumption for status even when they had before them the evidence of severe environmental decline, their civilization's decay, and, thus, the long-run ruin of the foundations upon which their own privileges and livelihoods depended (2006). These collapses of civilizations were local; the threat today is that collapse will be global and total.

Laissez-faire ideology is currently threatening the survival of democracy, which if lost, will make it highly unlikely that the measures necessary to successfully address the challenge of avoiding ecological disaster can be implemented. In the next section, attention turns to the rapidly rising current threat to democracy.

Loss of Faith in Democracy and Threat of Its Death

> We can either have democracy in this country or we can have great wealth concentrated in the hands of a few, but we can't have both.
> — Louis Brandeis, U.S. Supreme Court Justice, 1916–1939
> We support the election process, we support democracy, but that doesn't mean we have to support governments that get elected as a result of democracy.
> — Republican President George W. Bush, 2001–2009, cited in Bumiller 2006

Although humanity lived in democratic political conditions for the first 98% of its history, it became extremely rare and fragile following the rise of the state. It existed in classical Athens between roughly 450 to 322 B.C., but in a minority form that constituted only about 14% of the population, excluding women, foreigners, and slaves (Wolin 2010, 243).[8] Democracy did not reappear for the next 2000 years. When defined in terms of universal adult suffrage, it only emerges in the twentieth century when the franchise was extended to women. Thus, it is necessary to note that the common tendency to label nations democratic or non-democratic is highly misleading. No society is ever purely democratic or fully absent of any democracy. Democracy always exists in degree.

The extreme fragility of democracy is captured by the fact that it was destroyed in France during the 40 years following the French Revolution. Universal male suffrage accompanied the Revolution of 1789. But following the 1830 revolution, the Orleanist monarchy set forth a number of decrees—the July Ordinances—one of which excluded even the commercial middle-class from elections in its attempt to re-establish

---

[8] Political leaders were selected by lottery, as was later the case in Renaissance Florence and Republican Venice (Sitaraman 2017, 28). The great virtue of lottery democracy is that since any citizen could be selected to rule, there is an interest in all being well educated, promising a more equal society.

the *Ancien Régime*, limiting the franchise to a mere 0.75% of the population, mostly landowning aristocrats (Acemoglu and Robinson 2000, 1184), demonstrating that democracy can be substantially eliminated. In many nations since, democracy has been continually crushed, typically in military coups d'état serving the interests of wealthy elites.

It is understandable that elites always oppose democracy. In principle, democracy empowers non-elites to peacefully use the political process to better their condition, or even dramatically reduce or more extremely eliminate inequality in wealth, income, and privilege. For this reason, as inequality has exploded worldwide over the past 50 years and provided elites with greater political power and interests to protect, more nations have experienced weakening than strengthening democracy (Herre and Roser 2023). The Swedish-based International Institute for Democracy and Electoral Assistance reports, "across every region of the world, democracy has continued to contract," with 2022 marking the sixth consecutive year in which more countries experienced democratic declines than increases. Freedom House reports that globally, democracy declined for the 18th consecutive year in 2024 (*The Washington Post* 2025, A16). Many have lost confidence that democracy is in their best interests. Legal scholar Ronald Daniels reports that "in the United States, the fraction of citizens who report being dissatisfied with democracy now stands at a record high of 55%" (2021, 94).

Although democracy has been more enduring in the United States than in any other major nation, this is not because of support from wealthy elites, who have always feared democracy and continually acted to restrain if not eliminate it.[9] This was even true of the founders of the American Republic. Their thin ideological argument was that the masses are driven by passion as opposed to reason. Democracy, as James

---

[9] The title of de Tocqueville's celebrated work on America, *Democracy in America,* understandably created a view of him as one of democracies great champions. To the contrary, as an aristocrat, he was fearful of democracy and believed the franchise should be limited to property owners who pay taxes: "any power of voting" by those who do not pay taxes is "a violation of the fundamental principle of free government" and "amounts to allowing [the poor] to put their hands into other people's pockets for the purpose which they think fit to call a public one" (quoted in Losurdo 2014, 254).

Madison put it in *The Federalist Papers*, represents the "wishes of an unjust and interested majority" (Cooke 1961, nos. 10, 64).[10]

When elites felt their wealth, income, and privilege were especially under threat in the 1930s, they attempted to overthrow democracy in a coup. When Franklin Delano Roosevelt launched his New Deal as the Great Depression deepened in the early 1930s, he was labeled a "traitor to his class." Journalist and historian Sally Denton writes that "there is much evidence that the nation's wealthiest men—Republicans and Democrats alike—were so threatened by FDR's policies that they conspired with antigovernment paramilitarism to stage a coup" (2022).

Since the 1970s, Republicans have succeeded in reducing democracy through gerrymandering, making voting difficult (especially for those unlikely to vote for Republican Party candidates), and packing the judiciary with conservative judges (Richardson 2023). As noted in Chapter 5, in 2010 the Supreme Court in *Citizens v. Federal Election Commission* overturned two precedent decisions, providing corporations with the same First Amendment free speech rights as individuals and permitting them to spend without limit to support or oppose political candidates.[11] Because corporations are overwhelmingly owned by the very rich, their political muscle was greatly magnified. In 2013 the Supreme Court gutted the Voting Rights Act of 1965, stripping the Justice Department's

---

[10] Economist Gerald Friedman writes:

> Democracy, which antedated the development of capitalism in the United States, became by the late nineteenth century a threat to the power of American businessmen. Their property, as one employer said, was put 'at the mercy of the ignorant, idle, and vicious' in a 'democratic country where every man is allowed to vote.' Restrictions on popular participation in government began to be enacted in many American states to protect property against democracy (1988, 24–25).

[11] "In 1912, Louis Brandeis told a congressional hearing, 'We cannot maintain democratic conditions in America if we allow organizations to arise in our midst with the power of the steel corporation.' He called it the 'curse of bigness'—the threat from concentrated power to individual character, to the capacities which we need to govern ourselves. The answer was to break up monopolies and give workers the chance to develop the art of self-government in their own organizations. 'Our objective is the making of men and women who shall be free—self-respecting members of a democracy—and who shall be worthy of respect,' Brandeis wrote. But democracy in any sphere is a serious undertaking, it substitutes self-restraint for external restraint" (Packer 2021, 202).

ability to screen voting laws in nine states, most in the South, with histories of racial discrimination.

More recently, first term President Donald Trump, having lost his bid for reelection in 2020, illegally attempted to coax voting stations to do the necessary for him to win. He provoked his supporters to stage an assault on the US Capital to persuade senators to not verify the election victory of his opponent. His instructions to his white-nationalist supporters was: "Proud Boys, stand back and stand by." Representing the interests of the rich, the Republican Party overwhelmingly supported Trump for reelection as president in 2024, despite his authoritarian pronouncements and his May 2024 felony conviction. Trump and his supporters, including prominent Republican leaders, depict the felony conviction as due to partisan politics, thereby putting into question the nation's judicial system—the bedrock of democracy. Upon retaking office in 2025, he immediately pardoned almost all of those convicted of assaulting the Capitol.

It should be noted that wealthy German elites supported the authoritarianism of Hitler in the 1930s, fearing dispossession by the left. A report by the American Political Science Association (APSA) in partnership with the organization Protect Democracy claims that the Republican Party has become open to authoritarian and anti-democratic impulses (APSA 2023).

As noted earlier, laissez-faire ideology was sufficiently delegitimated during the Great Depression of the 1930s to enable the passage of measures that reduced inequality and greatly improved living conditions for most people. However, expressed as supply-side economics, this ideology resurged to dominance during the 1970s. It aided wealthy elites in influencing public policy that has led to an explosion in inequality to such an extent that, as discussed in Chapter 5, a sense of despair prevails among society's least privileged.[12]

---

[12] This explosion in inequality is captured by how the benefits of productivity growth have been shared. Between 1948 and 1979, productivity grew by 118.4% and worker compensation 107.5%. Between 1979 and 2021, productivity grew by 64.6% and worker compensation by 17.3% (Economic Policy Institute 2022). It is noteworthy that productivity grew by almost twice as much during the three decades of declining inequality than during the subsequent four decades of dramatically rising inequality.

Prior to the expansion of democracy in the nineteenth century, elites disproportionately controlled states. Well before Karl Marx claimed government to be the executive committee of the ruling class, the same point was made by Adam Smith, the alleged author of laissez-faire doctrine:

> Laws and government may be considered in this and indeed in every case as a combination of the rich to oppress the poor, and preserve to themselves the inequality of the goods which would otherwise be soon destroyed by the attacks of the poor, who if not hindered by the government would soon reduce the others to an equality with themselves by open violence (1763, 208).[13]

What Smith understood was that throughout history, governments were the handmaidens of the rich and enemies of the poor. But with the rise of democracy this relationship was potentially reversed. With the democratized franchise, non-elites can, in principle, use government to improve their well-being at the expense of the wealthy elites, just what they did between the 1930s and 1970s. Only highly democratic government and a weakening of the elite's ideology can lead to improvements in the conditions of non-elites.

Because democratic government has always been potentially the enemy of the wealthy, politicians who represent the elites' interest have embraced the laissez-faire ideology that government is corrupt and incompetent and therefore must be severely limited. In his first inaugural presidential address in 1981, Republican Ronald Reagan made this strikingly clear, declaring that "Government is not the solution to our problem; government is the problem." Grover Norquist, a leading Reagan supporter and head of Americans for Tax Reform, declared the goal to be "to cut government in half in twenty-five years, to get it down to the size where we can drown it in the bathtub" (Dreyfuss 2001). The new rallying cry became cutting taxes to "starve the beast." Large budget deficits played a useful role in justifying the necessity of cuts in programs benefiting the less well off. For instance, the "Big Beautiful Bill" that

---

[13] He also wrote: "Till there be property there can be no government, the very end of which is to secure wealth and to defend the rich from the poor" (1763, 404).

Trump signed into law on July 5, 2025 will greatly increase the federal debt with tax cuts especially benefitting the rich while justifying cutting food assistance for the poorest household and eliminating health care offered by Medicaid for about 16 million poor citizens.

Given their embrace of political programs that manifestly are to their own benefit, how do political candidates representing the interests of wealth elites get elected when these wealthy elites constitute only a very small fraction of the voting public?

The wealthy elites' politicians succeed because their laissez-faire ideology convinces an adequate portion of the electorate that redistributive measures would not be in their interests. For instance, elites have long demonized the least privileged, and especially the unemployed, as lazy ne'er-do-wells handicapped by dependency on welfare (Wisman and Cauvel 2021). They should show initiative *as earlier Americans always did.* American society is presented as providing exceptional opportunity for vertical mobility such that everyone gets their just deserts. The rich worked hard to gain their wealth, and everyone else could, and should, do the same. Governmental welfare programs that shield people from the need to take responsibility for their lives must be eliminated.

Tax cuts for the rich and for the corporations they overwhelming own plus deregulation are presented as generating economic dynamism, increasing employment, and raising wages. Thus, everyone wins. However, since World War Two, economic dynamism was considerably more robust when inequality was declining than when it was increasing.

These arguments for laissez-faire ideology may not alone be sufficient to convince an adequate portion of the electorate to vote for the rich's political candidates. But greater shares of the electorate are drawn in to support the elite's candidates by piggy-backing their economic arguments onto hot populist cultural issues such as abortion, gay rights, race issues, immigration, gun control, creationism, and a desire to ban books found offensive. Moreover, these cultural issues are laden with an emotional energy that economic issues lack.[14] And some issues, such as racism and immigration, are both cultural and economic.

---

[14] Behavioral economists find that people systematically make decisions that are against their own interests, driven more by emotions than economic reason. In *What's the Matter with Kansas?* (2005), Thomas Frank provides wide-ranging evidence for this view.

Further, many Americans, and especially the least privileged, have been depoliticized and fail to vote.[15] They are preoccupied by the difficulties of getting by from week to week, facing long workdays, job insecurity, soaring health costs, and poor education for their children. Voting in the United States is held on Tuesdays, a workday, unlike Sundays in most countries, leading many financially challenged workers to conclude that a vote that counts for so little is not worth the lost income.[16]

How, then, might laissez-faire ideology be delegitimated? This is the critical question. Only once has the ideology of elites been adequately challenged such that peaceful political measures could be enacted that reduced inequality and substantially improved the welfare of the greater population. This occurred due to the extreme hardship accompanying the Great Depression of the 1930s. An equally severe crisis could conceivably occur. However, the response following the financial meltdown of 2008 and the subsequent Great Recession suggests that the suffering during such crises can be limited. Lessons have been learned. This may mean that the hardship from future crises may be sufficiently limited to preclude delegitimating laissez-faire ideology. In this light, the delegitimation of the elites' ideology in the 1930s and the consequent

---

[15] Daniels reports that today "Americans are… less disposed to democratic involvement than previous generations. The number who deem it 'very important' to stay informed about current affairs in public issues dropped from 56 to 37% between 1984 and 2014, with 20% saying that being informed is 'not an obligation' that a citizen owes to the country, up from 6% in 1984" (2021, 95). Economics journalist Indress Kahloon writes: "Democracy's most basic currency is trust, and, to judge by the usual indicators, we seem to be running out of it. Back in 1964, more than 3/4 of Americans said they trusted the federal government; Today, according to the Pew Research Center only a quarter of Americans do. In the 1970s, Gallup found that around 70% of people trusted the media; today, about 40% do. Even worse, trust in the media has become polarized along party lines….Half of registered voters think that the opposing party is not just bad but downright evil" (2021, 67). This dramatic decline in trust is found to be a consequence of the exploding inequality over the past 50 years (Wilkinson and Pickett 2011; 2019).

[16] Case and Deaton report that "Working-class whites do not believe that democracy can help them; in 2016, more than 2/3 of white-working class Americans believed that elections are controlled by the rich and by big corporations, so that it does not matter if they vote….Analysis by political scientists of voting patterns and Congress supports their skepticism; both democratic and republican lawmakers consistently vote for the interests of their more prosperous constituents with little attention to the interest of others" (2020, 13).

sustained 40-year decline in inequality appears as a historical singularity (Wisman 2020).

Lacking an attractive alternative economic vision, there are powerful reasons why laissez-faire ideology is so persuasive. The capitalism it extolls, but misrepresents, has produced unparalleled prosperity and freedom. It claims that unfettered markets channel human competitiveness into beneficial social outcomes (Adam Smith's invisible hand). It celebrates individual initiative and views outcomes as the responsibility of individuals. It presumes fluid social mobility such that the rich deserve their wealth and the poor their poverty.[17] And, if many view the system as unfair or even cruel, they have not been presented with an attractive alternative. But an alternative vision is available. It is summarized below and elaborated in Chapters 7 and 8.

The Needed Reforms of a New Vision

[I]t may be a banality that we need others for many things, but we need them far more than we realize, particularly for dignity and respect.
— Nassim Nicholas Taleb 2010, 94

As discussed in Chapter 5, over the past 50 years, a prolonged period of relative wage stagnation, a dramatic increase in inequality, and the dislocation brought on by an increasingly robust pace of creative destruction have generated a widespread sense of malaise. It has also generated a great deal of pessimism about our future.

This pessimism is in part due to a belief that no routes other than the current path proposed by laissez-faire capitalism are available to us. The collapse of state socialism in Eastern Europe over three decades ago is widely viewed as proof of this.[18] Because capitalism has won its battle

---

[17] Although the US was long the nation of opportunity and vertical mobility, this is no longer true. It is easier today to rise from poverty in Western European countries (Sandel 2018, 4).

[18] Throughout the twentieth century, socialism was viewed by many on the left as an alternative to laissez-faire capitalism. Today, however, as sociologist Eric Olin Wright notes, "even for most critics on the left, socialism as a future to capitalism no longer has much credibility" (2013, 2).

with socialism, it has definitively proven its superiority and should be accepted as-is. Even arguments for the need to sand off its jagged edges receive relatively little support. After all, if laissez-faire capitalism has outlasted its competition and has proven the economic arrangement that permits the most sustainable growth in wealth, would it not be best to let it do its full force unimpeded?

But the capitalist vision as expressed by its dominant laissez-faire ideology threatens the future of democracy and environmental sustainability. In response, this book addresses a causal chain that must be broken if democracy is to be preserved, if ecological devastation is to be averted, and human flourishing advanced. The chain begins with the power of laissez-faire ideology to persuade an adequate portion of the electorate that contemporary capitalism with its extreme inequality is the best that can be done. Adherence to this ideology locks us onto a disastrous trajectory.

But there is an alternative vision that better concords with our evolutionary heritage and contemporary values. The key reforms advanced by this vision provide for basic job security and extension of freedom into the workplace,[19] while preserving the two most fundamental social institutions of capitalism—private property and markets—that have delivered unparalleled wealth and freedom. It is important to note that there is nothing inherent in capitalism as an economic system of private property and markets that requires great inequality, worker insecurity, and that workers be separated from ownership and control of productive wealth.

This alternative vision gains attractiveness by being constructed on only two straightforward measures: guaranteed employment and workplace democracy. The simplicity of these measures matches that of the prevailing laissez-faire vision. This is important because for an alternative vision of our social future to be convincing, attractive, and embraced,

---

Political scientist Francis Fukuyama wrote while Eastern Europe's state socialism was imploding: "Today...we have trouble imagining a world that is radically better than our own, or a future that is not essentially democratic and capitalist....Moreover, the logic of modern natural science would seem to dictate a universal evolution in the direction of capitalism" (1989, 46; xv).

[19] Philosopher Elizabeth Anderson explores the manner in which wage work has become a form of tyranny where employers have powers over workers that would never be tolerated on the part of government (2017). Employers are able to exercise this power with little oversight.

simplicity is critical. Too frequently, progressive proposals for reform consist of long laundry lists of measures, expressed in complex terms.

Support for the reforms proposed in this book is found in how we evolved as a species when work was selected to be pleasurable to channel energies to its performance, and thereby better assure our species' survival. Work was not forced upon some by unequal social status. Productive resources (hunting and gathering grounds) were freely and equally available to everyone and therefore unemployment was nonexistent. Where work was undertaken with others, it was democratic, enabling all to participate in decision-making. There were no bosses. As seen in Chapter 2, this evolutionary claim finds extensive empirical support in anthropological and happiness research.

Of course, few would wish to return to a foraging mode of subsistence and there is no need to do so. Society can restructure the world of work to recapture the basic aspects of the primordial work experience that promoted flourishing, and in doing so augment economic dynamism. The proposed reforms replicate the core characteristics that were selected in human evolution to make work pleasurable. Not only would these reforms provide employment security and expand democratic freedom into the workplace, but also enable society to best take advantage of capitalism's creative destruction.

Both of these reform measures—guaranteed employment and workplace democracy—would substantially reduce the threat of ecological devastation. Guaranteed employment would do so by eliminating the need for economic growth to generate employment. Workplace democracy, by ennobling work and community, would reduce the reliance upon consumption as the principal means of seeking status.

Unemployment and its threat are the most powerful and cruel coercive tool that the owners of productive wealth have over their workforce. Yet second only to addressing foreign aggressors, unemployment poses the greatest challenge to politicians in power. Their success in dealing with unemployment significantly determines their ability to stay in power. In democracies, political parties across the spectrum, striving to win or hang onto office, struggle to convince the electorate that their advocated policies hold the greatest promise of stimulating economic growth and thus reducing unemployment. This frequently, if not usually, entails sacrificing the environment to generate employment. Guaranteeing employment would eliminate this trade-off.

Workplace democracy would provide an important source for pride and the respect and appreciation of others. The quality of output could be credited to workers as opposed to bosses. The individual worker's hard and high-quality work would benefit and be appreciated by co-workers and the community. Worker owned and controlled firms would have no incentive to relocate to where labor is cheaper, whether domestically or abroad, providing communities with greater stability. With less threat of being geographically uprooted, workers would have greater incentive to invest in their communities and their environmental quality. Note also that whereas stockholders of polluting firms do not generally live near the firms, their workers do and if they controlled these firms they would have a decided interest that they not pollute their local environment.

The goal, of course, is to institutionally structure society in such a manner as to enable the greatest human flourishing, where humans stand the greatest potential for attaining status and self-respect in a manner consistent with other social goals such as freedom, democracy, material provisioning, equity, community, and environmental sustainability. The central argument of this book is that it is through altering the conditions of work that this goal can be attained. The next two chapters will sequentially address how work can be guaranteed and workplace democracy implemented.

7

Creative Destruction and Security with Guaranteed Employment

[The] real problem, fundamental yet essentially simple [is] to provide employment for everyone.
—John Maynard Keynes 1930: 267

[If] a man does not have a job or income, he has neither life or liberty nor the possibility of the pursuit of happiness. He merely exists.
—Martin Luther King, cited by Carl Herman

The great art then to make a nation happy and what we call flourishing, consists in giving everybody an opportunity of being employ'd.
—Bernard de Mandeville 1714, 197

As discussed in Chapter 2, during the first 98% of human history, private property in resources did not exist and consequently, unemployment did not exist. All of societies' members had equal access to productive wealth, essentially the hunting and gathering grounds necessary for their provisioning. Typically, in community with others, they freely worked to meet their needs. During this early history, humans evolved to experience work to be fulfilling and pleasurable to encourage its performance and thus enhance the potential for survival.

As seen in Chapter 3, this changed with the rise of the state when warrior elites seized possession and control of productive wealth, mostly in the form of land. To survive, all others had to work on the elites' land or with their capital and give up their surplus for the privilege of doing so. Workers have done so ever since as slaves, serfs, indebted peasants, and wage workers. Although most workers in rich capitalist countries today retain some of their surplus, the overwhelming majority must still locate and contract with owners of productive wealth or their agents (e.g., corporations) to provide them with employment. However, some percent of workers are unsuccessful in arranging these contracts to work. They are unemployed. Capitalism is the only system in which any sizable portion of the workforce suffers unemployment.

Since the late eighteenth century, laissez-faire ideology has insisted that, due to the dynamics of labor markets, jobs are always available and thus involuntary unemployment cannot exist within capitalist economies. The reasoning is that should the supply of workers exceed the demand, competition among workers for jobs will push down the wage level until it is profitable for employers to hire all available workers. Therefore, except for the "frictionally" unemployed—workers seeking and changing jobs—the unemployed clearly are not willing to seek out and accept the available jobs. They are voluntarily unemployed. Societies need feel no guilt for the self-inflicted condition of the voluntarily unemployed.

This understanding serves as ideology because it justifies subjecting the unemployed (typically the least privileged members of society) to suffer the hardship of joblessness and hides the fact that maintaining a pool of unemployed workers—what Marx called the reserve army of the unemployed—serves the profit interest of the owners of the means of production by helping hold down wages and disciplining workers. If workers are not content with their wages or working conditions, there are the unemployed outside the gate who would eagerly replace them. If for any reason employers are unhappy with specific workers, they can be fired and replaced by jobless workers. For these reasons, a supply of unemployed workers has always existed within capitalist economies.

Economists have added to the ideology legitimating unemployment by dressing it up in a naturalistic and scientific sounding concept:

the so-called "natural rate of unemployment," more technically called the non-accelerating inflation rate of unemployment (NAIRU). This concept claims that there is a level of unemployment below which inflation can be expected to rise as workers are empowered to demand higher wages and increase the costs of production. The policy prescription is that, in order to avoid the burden to society of rising inflation, some percent of the workforce must be condemned to joblessness. Since World War II in the United States, NAIRU has generally been estimated to be between 3.5 and 6%. The very concept, especially when expressed as a natural rate of unemployment, suggests that this is what nature mandates.[1] Some must suffer being unemployed so that the economy not suffer inflation.[2] This ideology well serves the interests of the owners of productive wealth in two ways. First, as noted above, a reserve army of the unemployed serves to hold down wages and discipline workers to tolerate their low wages and debased work conditions. Second, inflation, if not avoided, erodes the value of the wealthy's assets, especially those held in long-term bonds.

But unemployment is not natural and exists only due to the political power of the owners of productive wealth, backed by their self-serving ideology. Unemployment can be eliminated. Indeed, in times of war, it usually has been. During World War II, for instance, the US government essentially guaranteed employment, albeit without this as the goal. Employment rose by 17 million (Vatter 1985, 16–17), increasing the total labor force by 18%. In so doing, it drew minorities and women into the active workforce, breaking through barriers that had traditionally excluded them.

But the deaths, maiming, destruction, and horror of war are not necessary to achieve full employment. It can be guaranteed by society in peacetime to all willing and able workers. Those who fail to locate employment in the regular labor market can be given government or government-approved jobs, and, where necessary, the appropriate reskilling to prepare

---

[1] Nobel Laureate economist William Vickrey aptly called this "one of the most vicious euphemisms ever coined" (1992, 341).
[2] Note that inflation of asset values such as stocks and real estate does not bring a similar response, although booming asset inflations can lead to financial crises with dire consequences far surpassing all but extreme inflation.

them for employment in the regular economy. Anyone refusing such employment would be on their own. Welfare can be reserved for those unable to work.

The idea of guaranteeing employment is not new to American political discourse.[3] It was advocated by President Franklin Delanor Roosevelt in the 1930s and 1940s, and it figured in an early draft of both the Social Security Act of 1935 and the original draft of the Full Employment bill of 1945. It remained part of political discourse following World War II and was last proposed in legislation in the Humphrey-Hawkins Full Employment Act of 1978. But since the resurgence of laissez-faire ideology in the late 1970s and its embrace even by most political leaders in the Democratic Party, guaranteeing employment has fallen from sight.

However, guaranteed employment has again begun to draw attention. The Center for American Progress has endorsed it for hard-hit regions. It has been embraced by progressive American politicians Bernie Sanders, Cory Booker, Kirsten Gillibrand, Jeff Merkley, Alexandria Ocasio-Cortez, and Richard Winfield. It also has substantial support among Americans. In a 2019 Hill-Harris poll, a job guarantee was supported by 78% of the electorate, including 87% of Democrats, 71% of Republicans, and 81% of Independents (Tcherneva 2020, 114). That it is not public policy reveals the extent to which elected political officials often do not represent the will of their constituents.

There are compelling reasons why society should implement guaranteed employment. First, tolerating involuntary unemployment is morally wrong. Second, unemployment inflicts major costs on society. Third, combined with reskilling, guaranteeing employment is essential to meet the challenges of an ever-quickening pace of creative destruction in the forms of technological advances and globalization. Fourth, it will improve work quality. Fifth, it eliminates poverty. And sixth, it eliminates the need for economic growth to generate employment at any cost,

---

[3] Nor was it absent from international discourse. Article 23 of the Universal Declaration of Human Rights of 1948 proclaims a universal right to work: "Everyone has the right to work, to free choice of employment, to just and favorable conditions of work and to protection against unemployment." The American representative to the United Nations led the fight for its adoption.

even ecological devastation. These compelling reasons for the adoption of guaranteed employment will be examined in turn.

The Inhumane Personal Cost of Unemployment

> A man willing to work, and unable to find work, is perhaps the saddest sight that fortune's inequality exhibits under this sun.
> — Thomas Carlyle 1840, Chap. 4

It is the cruel personal costs borne by the unemployed that make the claim of a moral obligation to provide socially guaranteed employment especially compelling.

The costs to workers of being unemployed are usually expressed by economists in material terms of lost income, lowered consumption, depreciation or erosion of skills (human capital), loss of health insurance, and decreased networking opportunities. Although these costs are substantial, there are many other costs that receive less attention but carry more weight in terms of happiness. They include mental distress, low levels of personal fulfillment and self-esteem, diminished social status, social isolation, marital instability, poorer health, alcohol and substance abuse, increased vulnerability to suicide, proneness to violence and crime, and loss of personal security as human capital deteriorates. All of these costs fuel insecurity, stress, and malaise, robbing the unemployed of the requisites for flourishing. These costs are briefly examined below.

Psychologist David Dooley reports that "A century of research on the mental health impact of employment status has documented the generally adverse effects of job loss" (2003, 9). Arguably, the greatest cost suffered by the unemployed is the mental distress unemployment generates. Fear of unemployment also substantially reduces the mental health of employees (Reichert and Tauchmann 2011). Case and Deaton suggest that fear of becoming unemployed may also predict suicide (2020, 102).

Those losing their jobs appear to suffer a sort of psychological scarring such that not only do they report low happiness scores while out of work (Clark and Oswald 1994; Winkelmann and Winkelmann 1998; Argyle 2001), but these lower levels of happiness persist even after reemployment: their lives after reemployment work are less happy than the lives of those who never endured unemployment (Clark, Georgellis, and Sanfey 2001; Lucas et al. 2004, 11). This is striking in that people are surprisingly resilient in adapting to severe conditions. Even long-term paraplegics do not attest to being unhappy (Oswald and Powdhavee 2005). But people do not adapt well to chronic pain and unemployment (Lucas et al. 2004). People suffer more from unemployment than from impaired health (Winkelmann and Winkelmann 1998, 1) or divorce or marital separation (Clark and Oswald 1994, 658). Economist Avner Offer finds that "The strongest determinant of low life satisfaction is absence of social connection, particularly unemployment and separation…" (2007, 7).

The unemployed suffer greater social isolation and participate in fewer social leisure activities than do their employed counterparts. The Pew Research Center reports that 43% of those unemployed for more than six months report that it has strained their friendships, resulting in less social contact (Morin and Kochhar 2015). For young workers, unemployment hinders their integration into society (Kieselbach 2003, 74).

Job loss results in poorer health outcomes, especially those related to elevated stress and anxiety such as heart attacks, strokes, and obesity (Burgard et al. 2009; Wisman and Capehart 2010). The unemployed experience higher mortality rates, with those displaced by age 40 suffering a fall in life expectancy of 1–1.5 years (Sullivan and Wachter 2009). Higher mortality is experienced by workers even 20 years after suffering long-term unemployed (Couch et al. 2013).

The stress suffered by the unemployed is contagiously suffered by others in the household, especially spouses (Rook, Dooley, and Catalano 1991; Hansen 2005). The result is greater incidence of divorce. Men suffer on average more intensely from unemployment than do women. This concords with Darwin's theory of sexual selection because joblessness would make men less attractive as mates and potential fathers.[4]

---

[4] In a survey of 10,000 women in 37 different world cultures, evolutionary psychologist David Buss found that women put more value on a partner's financial prospects than did men, and

Fifty-four percent of the unemployed lack romantic partners versus 32% of the employed (Ingraham 2019).

Unemployment has been associated with increased sexual dysfunction, especially male impotence (May and Bobele 1988). It also can increase domestic violence, perhaps because, as sociologists Ross Macmillan and Rosemary Gartner note, "It signifies a challenge to the culturally prescribed norm of male dominance and female dependence. Where a man lacks this sign of dominance, violence may be a means of reinstating his authority over his wife" (1999, 949).

A study of data from 63 countries found that one of five suicides is due to unemployment (Nordt et al. 2015). The unemployed suffer feelings of worthlessness and being unwanted (Sen 1997, 167). Social exclusion, spatial isolation, decreased self-esteem, alcohol and narcotics abuse, lack of independence and decreased income all play a part in mental illness and suicide.

Not unexpectedly, the psychological distress caused by unemployment is in substantial part a function of social norms. It depends upon whether the unemployed are socially viewed as personally inadequate or as victims of an economy unable to provide jobs for all. Accordingly, the higher the level of unemployment, the less likely the unemployed feel their condition to be a personal failing (Clark and Oswald 1994, 658).

A recent study finds that even working only one day a week in a paid job provides significant improvement in self-esteem, social networking, and life satisfaction. This held for both the otherwise unemployed and stay-at-home parents. Extending worktime did not appear to add significantly to well-being. This suggests that robotization can dramatically shrink worktime without negatively affecting psychological welfare (Kamerāde et al. 2019).

In terms of material insecurity, the average duration of an unemployment spell in the United States has doubled from 11.4 weeks in December 1960 to 22.3 weeks in December 2023 (St. Louis Fed 2024). Job insecurity almost always means income insecurity. The average unemployment insurance replacement ratio in the United States in 2018

---

that "Ambition and industriousness, cues to resource acquisition, also tend to be valued more heavily by females than by males" (2011, 112).

for qualifying workers was about 45%, and, strikingly, only 26% of those unemployed who had worked in the prior 12 months and qualified for relief applied for unemployment insurance benefits (Bureau of Labor Statistics 2019).

The least well-off of the unemployed lack access to institutions such as banks and insurance companies that are available to help the more fortunate with life's uncertainties. Instead, they must look to relatives and state services that serve marginalized persons. As noted in Chapter 5, about 40% of Americans would face difficulty paying for an unexpected emergency expense of $400 (Nova 2019).

In addition to psychological scarring, the unemployed suffer reputation scarring in the form of the negative judgment of potential employers. Economists Stefan Eriksson and Dan-Olof Rooth report that employers view nine months of unemployment as equivalent to four years of lost work experience, with the attendant loss of skills (2014). Only one in four workers returns to pre-layoff earning levels after five years (Mauldin 2016), and for most, a period of unemployment results in a permanent loss of earnings over a lifetime (Abraham et al. 2019; Couch et al. 2013).

Human capital—the full complement of skills and capabilities a worker brings to the labor market—generally depreciates during periods of unemployment. This may even generate, as economist Amartya Sen puts it, in "a loss of cognitive abilities as a result of the unemployed person's loss of confidence and sense of control." Further, "The discouragement that is induced by unemployment can lead to a weakening of motivation and make the long-term unemployed more resigned and passive….This can yield a hardening of future poverty and further unemployment" (1997, 162; 162–63).

Sen's analysis is supported by economist William Darity's research: "We observed that since spells of unemployment and even underemployment produce learned helplessness, low self-esteem, and depression, those spells can lead to reduced intensity and persistence of search, reduced cognitive efficiency, and reduced motivation to acquire skills that might improve prospects for re-employment" (1999, 495).

Because of these personal costs, it is morally wrong for an overwhelming majority of the population to condemn even a small portion of society to unemployment. The personal costs that these unfortunates must suffer are far too high. This tyranny of the majority sacrifices those who are usually society's least privileged to what is perceived—mistakenly, as will be seen in the next section—to be in the best interests of the society.[5]

The Heavy Social Costs of Unemployment

> Though ... People are the wealth of a Nation, yet it can only be so, where we find Employment for them, otherwise, they must be a burden.
> — John Cary 1719 (2010),48

Many of the personal costs of unemployment have a public dimension, negatively affecting others in society. The most obvious social costs of unemployment include the loss of output, lower consumption, reduced tax revenues, greater inequality, higher government expenditures on income assistance and social support programs, increases in the expenses of taxpayer-sponsored health care, and diminished human capital and economic dynamism as the skills of the unemployed deteriorate from disuse. Sen also notes how high unemployment, such as that in Western Europe, can lead to conservatism toward labor-saving technological progress and resistance to raising the retirement age. These attitudes tend not only to impair economic dynamism and constrict potential output but also to impede an easing of the retirement cost burden facing future generations (1997, 165).

---

[5] The social conditions and social choice that condemn some to unemployment has a parallel in Shirley Jackson's classic macabre short story, "The Lottery." It is the story of an annual ceremony during which a fictional town's citizens draw lots, and then the "winner" is stoned to death. Presumably this is natural and good, in the interest of the broader community. As old man Warner puts it, "Lottery in June, corn be heavy soon." The difference is that in Shirley Jackson's town lottery, all citizens had equal chances of "winning," whereas in the job lottery the chances—as determined by social background, race and sex—vary greatly. Although those who draw unemployment are not literally stoned to death, most suffer immensely and some even death.

Increased unemployment also leads to increased criminal activity. For instance, Stephen Raphael and Rudolf Winter-Edmer find a "positive and highly significant effect of unemployment on property crimes" (2001, 274). Studies by Jeff Grogger (1998) and Eric Gould, Bruce Weinberg, and David Mustard (2002) reveal that youth criminal activity positively correlates with the unemployment rate. Youth unemployment has also been found to correlate with right-wing extremist crime (Falk, Kuhn, and Zweimüller 2011). Prisons to house convicted criminals are expensive. In 2022, the US prison population was 1.8 million (Prison Inside 2023), costing over $80 billion per year.

Unemployment fuels prejudice against immigrants and minorities. This has become especially true for immigrants in the United States and Europe. They are seen as competing for employment and taking away jobs from citizens. In a similar manner, Sen reports, "unemployment feeds the politics of intolerance and racism…." Gender relations might also be harmed, since gender conflict arises "because the entry of women into the labor force is often particularly hindered in times of general unemployment" (1997, 163; 164).

Unemployment of parents has lasting negative effects on their children, the future workforce. Children of the unemployed are more likely to suffer malnutrition and growth stunting, as well as poorer mental health (Lindo 2011; Bubonya et al. 2014). They also suffer poorer educational attainment, job prospects, and social mobility (Reeves and Howard 2013). Adolescent boys with unemployed parents are less likely to be confident about the future or to be independent and hopeful as well as more likely to attempt suicide (Strom 2003, 399; 401). Eighty percent of children living below the poverty threshold in the United States live in families without a working parent (Tcherneva 2020, 37).

Unemployment degrades neighborhoods. Although the unemployed have a great deal of free time, their demoralization and sense of shame leads them be "even less involved in their communities than those with jobs" (Kahloon 2023, 66). Neighborhoods in which the unemployed are concentrated become unsafe, ridden with crime and substance abuse.

Benefits of Guaranteed Employment

The first and foremost achievement of the social sciences has been to establish widespread public recognition that circumstances like unemployment, poor health, and poverty are the result chiefly of forces beyond an individual's control, and that collective action is required to help those suffering from such circumstances. Prior to the twentieth century, the common belief was that these problems were the result of an individual's character flaws –laziness, failure to save, dirtiness, drunkenness, gambling, and the like. Economics, the first of the social sciences to develop, initially supported such beliefs through its advocacy of laissez-faire, that government should be small and that to intervene in people's lives would only promote dependency. The laissez-faire conception was increasingly undermined, however, by the persistence of grinding poverty and the emergence of severe financial crises and major depressions.
— Richard Easterlin 2019, 5

Since the resurgence of laissez-faire ideology in the late 1970s, discussion of guaranteeing employment has disappeared from public discourse. Yet the benefits of this policy are striking and extensive. In addition to alleviating the personal and social costs noted above, they include eliminating poverty, reducing inequality, improving the quality of work, ending the political need for growth to create employment at any cost, stimulating entrepreneurship, better enabling society to meet the challenges of increasingly fast-paced technological change and globalization, and providing a powerful automatic stabilizer to reduce macroeconomic instability. These benefits are addressed below.

Poverty Eliminated, Reduced Inequality, and Higher Quality Work

Guaranteeing employment at a living wage with benefits virtually eliminates poverty, and the horrible stigma attached to it overnight. The formerly impoverished would gain the dignity and self-respect that comes from being productive members of society. Inequality would also be reduced because guaranteed employment would put a living wage floor on incomes. This means that the quality of work would improve as firms are forced to offer wages and work conditions equal to those of the program. Providing appropriate reskilling to enable successful entry into the regular workforce would essentially increase beneficiaries' wealth in the form of human capital.[6] Many crimes or debased work conditions such as prostitution would no longer be compelled by necessity.

Eliminating the Political Need for Growth at Any Cost to Generate Employment

The legitimacy of governments in all countries critically depends upon maintaining employment and reducing unemployment. Although politicians sometimes promise to do so by limiting immigration or foreign trade, the most widely embraced strategy is to induce more robust economic growth. Political pressure to stimulate growth at practically any cost is especially strong when economic crises send unemployment soaring. Tragically, this relentless pursuit of growth often entails the sacrifice of other social goals, especially protection of the environment. Guaranteeing employment, and reskilling where necessary, offers an escape from this growth trap. Indeed, "green jobs" could be made an important focus for guaranteed jobs and training.

States and localities would also be substantially liberated from the fiscally damaging competition to attract industry to generate employment. Currently, corporations extract tax breaks and infrastructure spending commitments from states competitively struggling to attract employment-generating economic activity. In this competition, states are at times tempted to relax ecological standards as well. Guaranteeing employment would free states to pursue more socially fruitful fiscal policies.

---

[6] Economists Claudia Goldin and Lawrence Katz find solid evidence that "the ups and downs in wage inequality across the century can be explained almost entirely by what amounts to a race between technological change and educational attainment" (2008, 26–28). High skilled workers have seen wage increases while the less skilled and less educated have fallen behind.

Stimulating Entrepreneurship

Starting a new business typically means quitting a job to devote full time to the endeavor. Those with entrepreneurial interests commonly hesitate to give up their employer's health insurance and fear that, should their venture fail, finding another job might be very difficult. They can understandably be discouraged from taking the risk, especially given the high failure rate of new businesses.[7] Guaranteed employment would put a safety net beneath entrepreneurs, ensuring them of a living wage job with benefits should their start-ups fail. Incidentally, start-ups account for a good deal of both job creation and innovation.

Meeting the Challenges of Robotization and Globalization

Employment insecurity and stagnant wages have provoked widespread fear of technological change and globalization, especially in the form of AI, robotization, and free trade. These fears generate support for politicians opposing innovation, globalization, or both.[8] Driving this backlash is the fact that the benefits and costs have been very unevenly shared, with corporate owners, consumers, and some workers winning while many workers suffer lost jobs and downward pressure on wages.

Throughout most of history, skills provided by on-the-job learning and education were sufficient for a lifetime. But this has become progressively less true. For instance, a century ago, the half-life of an engineer's special knowledge—the timespan over which half of his expertise became obsolete—was 35 years. By the 1960s, it was down to 10 years, and

---

[7] The U.S. Bureau of Labor Statistics (BLS) reports that approximately 20% of new businesses fail during their first two years, 45% during the first five years, and 65% during the first 10 years (BLS 2016).

[8] According to a 2017 Pew Research survey, 85% of Americans favor government measures to limit job and wage losses due to automation (Gramlich 2017). During the American 2020 presidential campaign, candidate Andrew Yang proposed a special value-added tax on firms using automation (Merchant 2018). As this book goes to press, President Donald Trump is slapping steep tariffs on multiple trade partners.

more recently, it fell to only three years (Friend 2017). For more and more jobs, the pace of technological change requires continual reskilling. Although much if not most of this updating is still provided on the job, some firms will go bankrupt, leaving their employees with skill sets that are not in demand. Thus, as labor scholar David Autor puts it, "human capital investment must be at the heart of any long-term strategy for producing skills that are complemented by rather than substituted for by technological change" (2015, 27).

It should be noted that government participation in providing the skills necessary for an increasingly dynamic economy is neither new nor radical. It began with primary schooling at the outstart of industrialization, and the years of schooling progressively increased to keep pace with the needs of the economy. Now, with an ever increasing rate of creative destruction, the availability of continual lifelong instruction becomes necessary. What private firms can be expected to provide is limited by the uncertainty of recapturing the cost of reskilling their employees. Other firms, including direct competitors, that have not borne the reskilling costs, may bid away these "higher value" workers.

Globalization also threatens skill obsolescence and unemployment. The dominant view since David Ricardo in the early nineteenth century has been that free trade benefits all countries. However, not all economists are convinced that the gains from trade are worth the harm they inflict on some workers in terms of unemployment, obsolescent skills, and lower wages. Economist Dani Rodrik writes, "The truth is that economists are pretty bad at measuring the gains from trade." Further, "most standard and accepted models of trade yield relatively small net gains from trade," implying that protectionism would not lead to significant losses. Rodrik continues, "It's surprising how much of the agenda of trade negotiations has been driven by business and how much of the existing trade rules reflect the interests of business as opposed to labor or consumer or environmental interests." However, "free trade is such a sacrosanct subject among economists, and among trade economists in particular," that it is seldom put in question (1998, 90; 94; 81).

Economist Paul Davidson claims that "maintaining full employment will require a huge overhaul of the economy and labor market that rivals or exceeds the nation's massive shifts from agriculture- and manufacturing-dominated societies over the past 165 years" (2017). But such a "huge overhaul" is not necessary. The problem has a relatively simple solution. Guaranteeing jobs at living wages and reskilling where appropriate could make everyone a winner from technological innovation and free trade. Workers would be guaranteed living wages and necessary skill upgrading, thus remaining productive members of society. Guaranteeing employment is society's best response to creative destruction's dislocations accompanying AI, robotization, and foreign trade.

In the next chapter, the issue of free trade will again be addressed, but in a different context of a tradeoff between whatever the gains it offers on one hand, and community well-being and the quality of work among democratically free workers, on the other.

Creating a Powerful Automatic Stabilizer

A guaranteed employment program would be countercyclical, moderating booms and busts. When a downturn begins, firms lay off workers, resulting in a reduction in aggregate demand that prompts other firms also to lay off workers, setting in motion a downward spiral in economic activity. A guaranteed employment program would absorb those laid-off workers, keeping them employed, thereby helping to maintain aggregate demand. In effect, the program creates a "buffer stock" into which laid-off workers are absorbed in downturns and then released back into the regular workforce during expansions. Currently unemployment insurance provides this sort of strategic reserve of workers, albeit with the disadvantages of considerably lowering incomes and without the benefits of maintaining worker skills and discipline. With guaranteed employment during expansions, employers could hire from the ranks of the government's buffer stock of workers with greater confidence that they possess the appropriate work habits and skills than if it drew from a stock of unemployed workers.

When workers are drawn from the buffer stock during economic expansions, government spending decreases, countering inflationary tendencies. The reserve army of the unemployed is replaced by the reserve army of fully-employed-buffer-stock employees.

A guaranteed employment approach contrasts radically with the Keynesian approach of attempting to increase employment by raising aggregate demand. Of course, as noted above, full employment is never attained in the Keynesian model because, to avoid the inflation monster, an economic expansion must be curtailed when the natural rate of unemployment is reached. In contrast to the indirect Keynesian strategy of managing aggregate demand, guaranteed employment would go straight to the problem by providing all willing and able unemployed workers with jobs. Full employment is maintained whatever the level of aggregate demand. It is a supply-side rather than a demand-side solution to the problem of unemployment.

The greatest burden of recessions is carried by those who lose their jobs. Unemployment frequently surpasses 10% during these downturns. Guaranteed employment would end this social cruelty.

A Universal Basic Income versus Guaranteed Employment

> We are being afflicted with a new disease of which some readers may not yet have heard the name, but of which they will hear a great deal in the years to come – namely, technological unemployment. This means unemployment due to our discovery of means of economizing the use of labour outrunning the pace at which we can find new uses for labour.
> — John Maynard Keynes 1930, 360

Joseph Schumpeter characterized capitalism as a dynamic process of creative destruction. Today this is markedly manifested in AI, robotization, and globalization. Whether they permanently reduce the need for labor or merely make learned skills obsolete and create increased churn in labor markets, a social response is widely recognized as necessary.[9] Two options have received recent attention. The most widely promoted is a guaranteed or universal basic income (UBI). The second, the subject of this chapter, is guaranteed employment. These are examined in turn.

Universal Basic Income

A policy proposal to grant everyone a basic income regardless of whether they work has been gaining traction across the political spectrum, from labor leaders on the left to libertarians on the right in the United States as well as on the political left and right in Europe. It has far broader political support than does guaranteed employment. In the United States, among liberals, it has been supported by former labor secretary Robert Reich, labor leader Andrew Stern, and 2020 Democratic presidential candidate Andrew Yang, who advocates a UBI as the means to a "humane capitalism" (2018). It has also been supported on the right by Charles Murray at the American Enterprise Institute and Michael Tanner of the Cato Institute. Additional advocates include high-tech entrepreneurs Elon Musk and Richard Branson. In France, Benoît Hamon, the socialist candidate for the 2017 presidential elections, ran with a guaranteed basic income as the centerpiece of his platform. Finland launched a pilot version in 2017, although it has been discontinued. Other pilot programs have run in Canada, the Netherlands, Scotland, and Iran (Heller 2018, 66). Firms would prefer UBI over guaranteed employment since it does not directly threaten their control over labor and may in fact permit wages to decline.

---

[9] Economists Carl Benedikt Frey and Michael Osborne estimate that 47% of American jobs are vulnerable to replacement by automation. These jobs share in common low levels of education and low pay (2019, 320). A study by economists Katherine Abraham and Melissa Kearney has found that globalization and robotization play an important role in explaining why since 2000 fewer men between the ages of 25 and 54 have been working (2018). In 2016, the Council of Economic Advisors estimated that 83% of workers earning less than $20 an hour are at risk of being displaced by automation, compared with only four percent of those making more than $40 an hour (CEA 2016, Chap. 5).

A universal basic income, although exceedingly expensive, is viewed as a clear and administratively efficient means of dealing with unemployment, poverty, and low incomes resulting from technological dynamism and globalization.

Economic journalist Annie Lowrey (2018) proposes a US UBI per person of $1000 monthly, for a total cost of about $3.9 trillion a year, which at that time would have approximately doubled US Federal taxes and government expenditures (Case and Deaton 2020, 253). Although $12,000 a year would leave an individual in poverty, it would lift a family of 2 or more above the poverty threshold.

But would working-age people be fulfilled without holding jobs? Retirees typically do not work, but their social and self-respect is grounded in the perception that they earned their right to post-work leisure. In earlier times, a wealthy leisure class did not work, its members believing themselves to be above debased labor. But such a leisure class is no longer positively viewed, and even jetsetters of 60 years ago would today likely be viewed as flawed if not debauched. Indeed, today's super wealthy not only typically work, but many put in long hours doing so. Although they might, of course, do so for yet more income, it has been found that "These mega wealthy professionals... see work as an essential part of their lives. They don't ever envision a time when they would leave it behind" (Faw 2021).

Would those recipients of the basic income who continue working not command greater status as more worthy citizens for contributing to society's economic wealth as opposed to being merely its beneficiaries? Over time, a UBI might come to be seen as a right, but so too are food stamps and they are degrading to their recipients, as is welfare generally. Because those continuing to work would have higher total incomes, would they not constitute a higher productive class, looking down upon the unemployed basic income recipients as defective social parasites? Would not this judgment be internalized into the unemployed UBI recipients?[10] Would they not feel worthless as do the non-working masses replaced by automation in Kurt Vonnegut's first novel, the 1952

---

[10] A study by economists Steven Platt and John C. Duffy found that the availability of welfare payments did not seem to reduce the higher incidence of depression among the unemployed (reported in Kates, Greiff, and Hagan 1990, 31). In Europe, benefits for the unemployed

dystopia, *Player Piano*? As Vonnegut put it in a later novel, the problem is "How to love people who have no use" (1970, 183).

Another major problem with a guaranteed income appeared long ago with the English Speenhamland welfare measure (1795–1834) that was intended to top up incomes to cover the cost of living. It effectively served as a subsidy to employers who could then pay lower wages (Spencer 2022, 137). The huge cost of a UBI might also result in cutbacks in other social support programs. Further, over time, calls for fiscal discipline could lead to cuts in the UBI, pushing the least well-off back into the poverty the program was meant to eliminate.

Finally, although the idea of a universal basic income has attracted considerable attention, would it be accepted in countries with a historically entrenched work ethic, such as the United States? North America was colonized first by Protestants who saw work as necessary to God's continuing creation. It is through hard work that social and self-respect are attained. Arguably, having a job remains a foremost means to status and self-respect in the United States, even if consumption serves as an indicator of diligent work.

Guaranteed Employment

A far superior option to a UBI is guaranteed employment at a living wage with retraining where necessary. This option is superior on several grounds. First, work is essential for social and self-respect, and should AI and robotization reduce the overall need for labor, this happy result can be shared by progressively reducing the workweek for all workers. It will be recalled from Chapter 2 that our species—Homo sapiens—evolved and existed for 98% of our history as hunter-gatherers by working 12 to 20 hours a week. Might such a shortened workweek be the human ideal that we will be poised to recover? Tax incentives could be used to

---

increased between 1975 and 1992, but the happiness gap between the employed and unemployed did not narrow (Tella et al. 2003). A sample study of American workers during the Great Depression revealed that WPA workers had significantly higher morale, general adjustment, social participation, and social status than did unemployed workers receiving direct-relief support (Chapin and Jahn 1940, 13).

nudge firms to reduce work hours (Spencer 2022, 141). Second, the prejudice against those who do not work will not dissipate quickly, readily, or even ever. Third, guaranteed employment, even with reskilling where necessary, would be far less expensive.

A guaranteed employment program might work as follows. Federal funds would be allocated to Federal projects and given to local governments that then distribute resources as needed to dispersed employment centers which would help preserve communities by tailoring employment opportunities to local needs. Employment is then offered to anyone without work who seeks a job.

Guaranteed employment would invalidate the claim that the minimum wage cannot be raised without causing further unemployment. Those losing jobs would be drawn into the guaranteed jobs sector where training would raise their skill level and productivity, making it profitable for their future employers to pay them living wages. This point merits emphasis. A guaranteed job program is not meant to simply "make work" but instead to provide the unemployed with the training and skills necessary to return as productive participants to the regular workforce.[11]

As to what would constitute a living wage, sociologist Christopher Jencks writes that "There is quite a bit of evidence that Americans need an income at least half that of families near the middle of the income distribution in order to buy the things they need to hold up their heads in public" (2015, 84). This would conform to the claim made by Adam Smith, the intellectual hero of laissez-faire economists, that workers should be able to afford "not only the commodities which are indispensably necessary for the support of life, but whatever the custom of

---

[11] Critics of the New Deal of the 1930s claim that it created useless make-work projects. However, economist Helen Ginsburg points out that workers in the Works Project Administration (WPA)

> not only built or reconstructed 617,000 miles of roads, 124,000 bridges and viaducts, and 120,000 public buildings; they also left the nation with thousands of new parks, playgrounds, and athletic fields. Moreover, they drained malarial swamps, exterminated rats in slums, organized nursery schools, and taught illiterate adults to read and write. Unemployed actors set up theaters throughout the land, often performing in remote towns and backwoods areas. WPA orchestras gave 6,000 live concerts. WPA artists produced murals, sculptures, and paintings that still adorn our public buildings (1983, 11).

the country renders it indecent for creditable people, even of the lowest order, to be without" (1776, 821).

Upon losing a job, unemployment insurance could cover a set number of weeks for the individual's job search, at the end of which, should a job not be located, the individual would join the guaranteed employment program. This program could also be crafted to provide part-time work for those who cannot work full-time due to family responsibilities. No other form of public support need be available to unemployed but "work-able" workers. Those choosing not to accept such employment would be voluntarily unemployed and thus not eligible for assistance. Welfare would be restricted to those who are unable to work.

Entering the guaranteed employment program would entail working in a government-created or -approved job structured to prepare them for quick return to the regular work world. A job placement component, working in conjunction with private employers, could facilitate this re-entry. The goal, then, would be that government employment be temporary. The government catches the unemployed as they lose their jobs and releases them as soon as possible to employment in the regular economy.

Because technological dynamism renders many jobs obsolete, the reskilling component of guaranteed employment is critical and can be predicted to become more so as the pace of creative destruction continually gains momentum. This might be in the form of apprenticeships whereby on-the-job training could be paired with more formal education in local colleges or universities. A goal of the program would be to structure reskilling to take account of the fact that people differ in their learning styles, some doing better in work-based "learning by doing." For these reasons, the OECD has made apprenticeships a central jobs strategy (Lerman 2016, 373).

It should be noted that learning as apprentices may be the most natural way of acquiring knowledge and skills. Foraging was the human mode of survival for 98% of history, and these hunter-gatherers are believed to have possessed more knowledge than workers in subsequent social formations.[12] They acquired their vast stores of knowledge through play and as apprentices to their elders, learning through practice. Indeed, until recent times, almost all productive knowledge was acquired in this manner.

Finally, created in the United States in 1933, the Civil Works Administration found jobs for four million people within two months, suggesting that a program of guaranteed employment could be implemented fairly quickly.

The Costs of Guaranteed Employment

Economists Randall Wray, Flavia Dantas, Scott Fullwiler, Pavlina R. Tcherneva, and Stephanie A. Kelton (2018) propose a guaranteed employment plan for the United States that would engage about 15 million workers at an estimated cost range between 0.98 and 1.33% of GDP, offering 32 hours a week at $15 an hour with health benefits and child care.[13] They estimate that this program would add nearly half a trillion dollars, or two percent to GDP without generating inflation, while stimulating the private sector to create an additional three to four million jobs. It would lift 83% of poor children out of poverty. Guaranteed employment would appear to be a social investment with an extraordinary rate of return.

Several other economists have also estimated the likely cost of a guaranteed employment program and found similar results (e.g., Aja, Darity, and Bustillo 2013, Attali and Champain 2005, Kaboub 2012). Forecasting the full long-run costs and benefits of guaranteed employment,

---

[12] Harari further adds that

...at the individual level, ancient foragers were the most knowledgeable and skillful people in history. There is some evidence that the size of the average brain has actually *decreased* since the age of foraging. Survival in that era required superb mental abilities from everyone. When agriculture and industry came along people could increasingly rely on the skills of others for survival, and new 'niches for imbeciles' were opened up (2015, 49).

[13] By contrast, the annual cost of child poverty in the U.S. was estimated at $500 billion a year in 2007, or close to four percent of GDP, due to the fact that child poverty leads to lower productivity growth, higher health costs, and crime (Holzer et al. 2008).

especially one with a sophisticated reskilling component, would be difficult and lies beyond the scope of this book. It should be noted that huge current government expenses would be lowered and, in some cases eliminated, and these savings would substantially reduce the net cost to society of a guaranteed job program. For instance, unemployment benefits beyond a brief period following job loss to enable a new job search would disappear and other income-support program costs would be restricted to those unable to work. Unemployment-generated health costs borne by Medicaid would be practically eliminated. And to these savings must be added the increased output, higher tax revenues, and more robust economy resulting from a fully employed and better trained workforce.

Several aspects of a guaranteed employment program would reduce inflationary pressures in the economy. As participants in the program gain the skills needed in the regular job market, productivity would be enhanced, putting downward pressure on prices. Increased job turnover generally improves job fit and thus productivity, and workers who do not fear unemployment might change jobs without undue hesitation. Upward wage pressures might be lessened in an inflationary boom period as employers could readily hire high productivity workers from the buffer stock who are willing to work, disciplined, and well-trained.

In an expansion, as workers are pulled from the buffer stock into regular employment, the program's spending would decrease. Thus, even in an expansion, inflation would be milder, and labor markets would be relatively loose. The inflation that can result from government over-stimulation of the economy to create employment would end. After the introduction of a guaranteed employment program, no further demand-driven inflationary pressure should result and the natural rate of unemployment, or NAIRU, would become zero. Any political discord surrounding how to make the call on a presumed tradeoff between unemployment and inflation would come to an end.

Why Not Before?

[The] real problem, fundamental yet essentially simple, [is] to provide employment for everyone.
— John Maynard Keynes 1930: 267

Given the critical importance of employment for income security as well as for social and self-respect, why have workers, their supporters, and the political parties allegedly representing their interests only very rarely included guaranteed employment among their demands? During early capitalism, their chances of gaining this right were nil. But once the urbanization accompanying industrialization in the nineteenth century made it possible for workers to organize and win the franchise, they had the voting power to rewrite the social script to better meet their needs. To a very limited degree they did just that. Their political muscle led to impressive improvements in their quality of life, including limits on the length of the workday, restrictions on child labor, safer workplaces, state provided retirement benefits (social security), education for their children, better sanitation, and in Europe, socialized medicine. But why did they not go for more? They possessed by far the most votes. Why did they not use their democratic political power to flatten out in a more sustainable manner the huge disparities of income, wealth, and privilege? And why did they not demand guaranteed employment and thereby gain freedom from the threat of joblessness and the personal suffering and social dysfunction that accompanies it?

The most fundamental reason is that, throughout history, elites possessing ownership and control of productive wealth have successfully promulgated an ideology that adequately legitimates prevailing inequality. It legitimates an economy in which workers, without ownership, control, or ready access to the means of production, must locate owners or their agents willing to provide them with employment. This ideology claims that elites have a right to own and control the means of production, forcing all others to prostitute their labor time to survive.

Critically, this ideology blames the unemployed for their fate (Wisman and Cauvel 2021). They are held to be lazy, if not slothful. They do not diligently seek out the jobs available. As a bumper sticker in the United States puts it, "Keep Working. Millions on Welfare are Counting on You." These negative attitudes toward the unemployed are internalized by the unemployed themselves (Hobbins 2016). Tragically, as Darity's research confirms, this leads them to behave as if unmotivated to find work: "spells of unemployment and even underemployment produce learned helplessness, low self-esteem, and depression, [and] those spells can lead to reduced intensity and persistence of search, reduced cognitive efficiency, and reduced motivation to acquire skills that might improve prospects for re-employment" (1999, 495).

Writing of the jobless during the Great Depression in the north of England, George Orwell observed:

> When I first saw unemployed men at close quarters, the thing that horrified and amazed me was to find that many of them were ashamed of being unemployed…. The middle classes were still talking about 'lazy idle loafers on the dole' and saying that 'these men could all find work if they wanted to', and naturally these opinions percolated to the working class themselves (1937, Chap. 5).

Similarly, economist Peter Temin reports:

> Unemployed men in the European Great Depression were exceedingly idle; an increase of apathy reduced all forms of recreational activity. Men passed their time doing essentially nothing; when asked, they could not even recall what they had done during the day. They sat around the house, went for walks, or played cards and chess. Most men went to bed early; there simply was no reason to stay awake. They contributed less to the running of the household than before, sometimes not even turning up on time for meals (2008, 681).

The internalization of society's blame devastates the poor's sense of worthiness and self-respect. Psychologist James Gilligan claims that the inability to find a job is the foremost driver of shame and worthlessness (2011). Economist Amartya Sen concurs, observing that unemployment may generate a loss of cognitive abilities as a result of the unemployed person's loss of confidence and sense of control....The discouragement that is induced by unemployment can lead to a weakening of motivation and make the long-term unemployed more resigned and passive...There is...considerable evidence suggesting that the typical effect, especially of long-term unemployment, is one of motivational decline and resignation (1997, 161–63).

The unemployed are caught in a trap. They internalize the view that they are responsible for their fate, and the resulting psychological debility and passive behavior signal to others that, as presumed, they lack motivation. Although many employed workers might feel job-secure and thus see little need for guaranteed employment, all are vulnerable to the overpoweringly seductive dominant ideology of the poor meriting their unhappy condition. This continually expressed ideology that those who fail to find work are slothful and thus to blame for their condition has successfully worked since the early evolution of capitalism (Wisman 2025).

A large study conducted by social psychologists John Jost, Brett W. Pelham, Oliver Sheldon, and Bilian Ni Sullivan finds that, "contrary to their own self-interest, members of disadvantaged groups were more likely to provide ideological support for [the system's inequality] than were members of advantaged groups" (2003, 20). They note that this conforms to cognitive dissonance theory which finds "that people who suffer the most from a given state of affairs are paradoxically the least likely to question, challenge, reject, or change it" (2003, 13).

The extraordinary success of this ideology is that the very idea of guaranteed employment is seldom mentioned and is outlandish to most people. It is an instance of what political scientist Peter Bachrach and Morton S. Baratz call "non-decision making," by which they mean "the practice of limiting the scope of actual decision-making to 'safe' issues by manipulating the dominant community values, myths, and political institutions and procedures. To pass over this is to neglect one whole 'face' of power" (1963, 632). Not surprisingly, then, a common response to the mention of guaranteed employment is "but that's communism, that's what the Soviet Union did and look at how that turned out!" Even progressive movements and socialist parties omit it from their platforms.

Few labor economists make mention of it.[14] Yet, suggesting confusion within the thin discourse on the topic, the poll results mentioned above show overwhelming support within the US population for guaranteed employment.

Some hope for guaranteed employment can be found in the French pilot projects *Territoires Zéro Chômeur de Longue Durée*. These initiatives were launched in 2016 to meet local needs in 10 communities (later expanded to 60). The experiment is proving to be successful and other European nations are taking notice (European Commission 2023). Another experiment, Gramatneusiedl, an Austrian village, instituted a job-guarantee problem in 2020, paying living wages with full benefits. Although it costs no more per person than unemployment benefits (about 30,000 Euros vs. 29,841.39), an Oxford study finds that people are doing better on both objective and subjective measures of well-being (Romeo 2022).

The Moral Imperative

> Work gives structure and meaning to lives; it confers status, which is not the same as earnings. It supports marriage and child rearing.
> — Case and Deaton 2020, 148

For 98% of human history, unemployment did not exist because everyone had access to productive wealth—the resources with which to work. It is only since the rise of the state 5500 years ago that unemployment became possible. Elites took control of productive wealth,

---

[14] In his comprehensive book on the challenges societies face as automation accelerates, *The Technology Trap,* Frey notes, "No single government policy can address the full spectrum of societal challenges brought by automation" (2019, 366). Accordingly, he offers an extensive menu of measures that might be taken to better address the dislocations caused by technological progress. Yet the measure he omits is guaranteed employment, which might come close to the single government policy that *could* meet most of automation's challenges. This omission indicates the extent to which the possibility of guaranteed employment has fallen not just from mainstream political discourse but also from innovative thinking. Curiously, although he ignores the possibility of guaranteed employment, he notes the central importance of work for well-being in his critique of a universal basic income (2019, 356–57).

principally land, and to survive all others have had to work with the elites' resources and provide them with their surpluses, the output above what has been necessary for workers' bare subsistence. Workers have done so as slaves, serfs, indentured workers, and wage workers. Guaranteeing employment is one of the critical measures necessary to overcome this history of exploitation and reestablish a desirable condition of life to which our species evolved.

As noted earlier, there is something morally amiss in a society that leaves a portion of its workforce unemployed and without adequate skills to find employment.[15] To condemn a portion of the population, even if only a small percentage, to remain unemployed is morally wrong. It sacrifices those who are generally the least privileged to what is mistakenly perceived to be in the best interests of society.

Unemployment is both the largest market failure and a political dereliction. Economic, social, and psychological well-being are tied to having a job. The personal costs that these unfortunates must suffer are inhumane. Equality of opportunity, just outcomes, and ecological survival constitute a moral, social, and economic imperative to offer guarantee employment and retraining to the full workforce.

---

[15] It should be noted that even if unemployment were good for the economy generally, social tolerance of unemployment violates political philosopher John Rawls's "difference principle," according to which "inequalities must contribute effectively to the benefit of the least advantaged" (Rawls and Kelly 2001, 64).

8

Creating Democracy, Freedom, and Community in the Workplace

I cannot think that [workers] will be permanently contented with the condition of labouring for wages as their ultimate state. To work at the bidding and for the profit of another, without any interest in the work—the price of their labour being adjusted by hostile competition, one side demanding as much and the other paying as little as possible—is not, even when wages are high, a satisfactory state to human beings of educated intelligence, who have ceased to think themselves naturally inferior to those whom they serve.
—John Stuart Mill 1909, 760–61
Democracy is at root a revolt against the rank ordering of society....The leveling instinct of democracy is principally directed against the arrogance of inherited or entrenched power.
—John Kane and Haig Patapan 2012, 32–33

Most workers today possess no ownership, control, or ready access to the means of production—the tools and resources with which they can work. Consequently, they must locate the owners or their agents willing to provide them with jobs. The fact that not all workers are able to do so is useful to the owners. If the supply of labor exceeds its demand, competition pushes down wages and enforces worker discipline. Thus, if workers are not content with their wages or the conditions of their work, there are the unemployed outside who can take their place. This unemployment constitutes immoral social exploitation of a portion of society's workers, typically the least privileged. Because it generates poverty, wastes economic resources, and causes collateral damage in the form of crime and degraded neighborhoods, it is also socially irrational.

Guaranteed employment at a living wage with retraining when appropriate would eliminate the immorality and social irrationality of unemployment, as was seen in Chapter 7. It would constitute the most progressive gain possible for workers within a society where they neither own nor control productive wealth. But why should workers be separated from ownership and control of the productive wealth with which they work? And why should they suffer being bossed about by the owners or their agents? This chapter argues that they should not be subjected to such treatment, and proposes how they can be reunited with productive wealth in a manner that not only expands human freedom but also enhances community.

During the first 98% of human history, workers were free in two critically important economic ways: first, they had free and equal access to the resources—hunting and gathering territories—with which to mix their labor to meet their needs. Private ownership and control of productive wealth did not exist. Second, no bosses told workers what to do. When working with others—the usual case—they did so democratically, each free to participate in-group decision-making. The major exception had to do with mounting a defense when war threatened, where success depends upon decisive leadership and rapid coordination. But these wartime leaders would give up their command and fold back into the egalitarian decision-making community when the threat abated.

As discussed in Chapter 2, it was during the first 98% of human history that our species evolved to possess essentially its current genetic makeup. During this evolution, humans were selected to experience those tastes and practices to be pleasurable that motivate them, like all animals, to behave in manners that best enable survival and reproduction. The two freedoms mentioned above—freedom of access to productive wealth and freedom from being bossed about—were the work conditions to which our species adapted.[1] Thus these freedoms can be expected to be prerequisites not just for flourishing but also for happiness.

However, these freedoms were severely compromised and frequently eliminated for most non-craft workers after the rise of the state and civilization 5500 years ago. Free access to productive wealth ended as state power came to protect ownership and control by elites. Within civilized societies, all others would subsequently have to become subservient and suffer exploitation to gain access to productive wealth. They have done so as slaves, serfs, indebted peasants, and wage workers.

It is a mere intellectual exercise to speculate whether humanity might have become as wealthy and free as we are in the rich nations today without oppression and exploitation. But, clearly, for post-scarcity societies this exploitation is no longer functional. Employment security can be assured, and the workplace can be democratized not only to free workers from exploitation but also to enable them to flourish in their work and live in richer community with others.

Most definitions of community have emphasized three elements: area, common ties, and social interaction (Lyon 1999, 5). Worker ownership and control of their firms provide all three. The workplace is a geographic site. Robust common ties exist in that all workers have very strong interests in the viability and profitability of their enterprise. Finally, the process of production, and perhaps especially the process of democratically managing the firm, provides for continuing, if not vibrant, social interaction. This sense of community is much needed in modern society. Psychologists Robert Waldinger and Marc Schultz report that "In the United States, a 2018 study suggested that three out of four adults felt moderate to high levels of loneliness… [and that] "Loneliness is more pervasive than ever before, and our ancient brains, designed to seek the

---

[1] The process called gene-culture co-evolution was discussed in Chapter 2. If a cultural practice provides survival advantage to the group and its members over a long period, the genes that privilege this cultural expression are carried into future generations. It is a process whereby, over time, cultural changes have changed humans biologically. This suggests the possibility that, similar to a supposedly innate instinct for religious belief (Wade 2009), the work conditions of our forager past may have become embedded in our genetic makeup.

safety of groups, experience those negative feelings as life-threatening, which leads to stress and sickness" (2023, 93; 29).

Humans are by nature social beings, and institutions are essential to coordinate their activities. This is as true in the modern workplace as in the polity, and, in both instances, hierarchy may be necessary. Even among the fully free, some must be entrusted to oversee coordination.

It is widely believed that worker owned and controlled firms could not capture the efficiency benefits of hierarchy within the firm. Workers would waste endless hours deciding on all firm activities. But this is not true, although a flattening of hierarchy might be expected. Instead of disappearing, the nature and purpose of hierarchy would change from "control" to "coordination" and from "power" to "efficiency" (Horvat 1982: 189–90). In the first instance, the managers have great control over the workers; in the latter, they are responsible and answerable to the workers.

The argument made here is that, just as political democracy is the ideal means of political governance, so too is workplace democracy the ideal means of governance in the realm of work. Both are grounded in the principle that no one's actions should be directed by anyone whom they have not participated in democratically selecting. The coordinators must be accountable to the coordinated.

This chapter addresses the ideal of workplace democracy and how it can become reality.

Work, Freedom, and Community

> The form of association… which, if mankind continues to improve, must be expected in the end to predominate, is not that which can exist between a capitalist as a chief, and work people without a voice in the management, but the association of the laborers themselves in terms of equality, collectively owning the capital by which they carry on their operations, and working under managers elected and removable by themselves.
> — John Stuart Mill 1909, 772–73

Today's advanced capitalist societies depict themselves as grounded in human freedom. However, in discourses on freedom, the focus is typically restricted to the political sphere: freedom from state tyranny, freedom to participate actively and equally in the governance of what is held in common. Leaders are democratically chosen and understood to be servants of the electorate. Discourse on economic freedom, by contrast, is limited to market freedom—the freedom of market participants to agree to contractual arrangements. However, this limited understanding hides from view the domain where most people are unfree—their workplaces—despite the fact that workers typically spend one-half of the time they are awake at work and preparing for and getting to and from work. They typically spend more of their waking time at their workplaces than with their own families.[2] Nor does the discourse on freedom include freedom from the scourge of unemployment. The elite's self-serving ideology of laissez-faire has successfully kept these freedoms out of public discourse to such an extent that they are rarely even mentioned. No contemporary political party or even labor movement expresses substantial support for either guaranteed employment or workplace democracy. Guaranteed employment and workplace democracy are also substantially ignored by social scientists.

Just how unfree is the workplace for most workers? Historian Miya Tokumitsu writes:

> As corporations have worked methodically to amass sweeping powers over their employees, they have held aloft the beguiling principle of individual freedom, claiming that only unregulated markets can guarantee personal liberty. Instead, operating under relatively few regulations themselves, these companies have succeeded at imposing all manner of regulation on their employees. That is to say, they use the language of individual liberty to claim that *corporations* require freedom to treat workers as they like. (2017, 54)

---

[2] Anthropologist James Suzman reports that "most of us spend considerably more time in the company of colleagues than our families, and structure our daily routines around work obligations, the work we do often becomes a social focal point, which in turn shapes our ambitions, values, and political affiliations" (2021, 373).

Philosopher Elizabeth Anderson claims that under the regime of capitalism, workers are subjects of their corporate dictators—a form of tyranny of private governments (2017). She points out that if the state held such sweeping powers, we would certainly not consider ourselves free men and women.[3]

The United States long stood as a beacon of freedom for the world. But its original concept of freedom, which predated nationhood and prevailed between the Declaration of Independence and the Civil War, viewed it as depending upon participation in the public sphere by citizens who governed themselves individually and collectively in work as well as in politics. In 1850, about 70% of the non-slave work force was self-employed (Lebergott 1964, 139). A sense of civic virtue was cultivated by the economic independence of small farmers and artisans. The freedom they celebrated depended upon "free labor," not in the capitalist sense of being free to sell labor time to the employer of choice, but instead, being free from economic dependency, free from being bossed about, not separated from ownership and control over the tools and resources with which they worked.[4]

Prior to the vigorous industrialization of the US economy following the Civil War, wage labor was viewed negatively. The ideal was that citizens should be economically independent. For instance, the yeoman farmer was Thomas Jefferson's paragon. He held that the unemployed should be granted 50 acres of land to be independent (Sitaraman 2017, 73). The prevailing American view was that wage labor should merely be a short-term means to amass savings with which to purchase tools and

---

[3] Further,

> Although they exercise their power to varying degrees and through both direct and "soft" means, employers can dictate how we dress and style our hair, when we eat, when (and if) we may use the toilet, with whom we may partner and under what arrangements. Employers may subject our bodies to drug tests; monitor our speech both on and off the job; require us to answer questionnaires about our exercise habits, off-hours alcohol consumption, and childbearing intentions; and rifle through our belongings (Quoted in Tokumitsu 2017, 54).

[4] It is noteworthy that whereas contemporary champions of laissez-faire ideology seek justification in the work of Adam Smith, the economy Smith celebrated was one of independent actors who were self-employed such as butchers, bakers, and candlestick makers. His pin factory, famous for the division of labor, employed only 10 workers.

resources and become one's own boss. In an address, Abraham Lincoln expressed this as follows: "The prudent, penniless beginner in the world labors for wages awhile, saves a surplus with which to buy tools or land for himself, then labors on his own account another while, and at length hires another new beginner to help him" (National Agricultural Library 1859).

The end of the frontier and cheap land, combined with the coming of industrialization and soaring inequality, began to massively proletarianize American workers, eroding the practice and authentic ideal of economic freedom.[5] Historian Eric Foner reports that, for many late nineteenth century Republicans, "A man who remained all his life dependent on wages for his livelihood appeared almost as unfree as a southern slave" (1995, 17).

What earlier American social thought had recognized is that freedom in workplaces nourishes political freedom. Unfree labor cultivates unfree political attitudes. Modern research supports this understanding. In his classic study of worker motivation, psychologist Frederick Herzberg found that intrinsic aspects of the workplace contribute most to job satisfaction, and these pertinently involve lack of overbearing supervision, absence of repetitive or routine tasks, and substantial complexity in work (1973). Political psychologist Robert Lane concurs, reporting research that finds "self-directedness in work is associated with nonauthoritarianism, assumption of moral responsibility for one's own acts, trust in others, self-esteem, and lower anxiety" (1991, 242). Workers with jobs that afford them a significant degree of autonomy also tend to be culturally liberal, whereas those who are bossed about and micromanaged tend to be more authoritarian (Kitschelt 1994, 12–18). Political scientists Gabriel Almond and Sidney Verba have found that across five countries and all occupational categories, workers whose thoughts on the job were sought scored significantly higher on a measure of civic competence in dealing with local and national government bodies (1989, 180ff,

---

[5] Theodore Roosevelt held that factory labor robbed workers of the physical rigors of agriculture and that doctors reported increased cases of "nervous exhaustion and irritable weakness." He believed that industrialization was making men soft, effeminate, and unfit for defending the country (Swanson 2019).

364ff). Professor of work environment Robert Karasek and psychologist Tores Theorell report that "workers whose jobs had become more passive also became passive in their leisure and political participation and workers with more active jobs became more active. These findings were significant in eight out of nine sub-populations controlled for education and family class background" (1990, 53–54).

Anthropologist Mary Douglas (1996) finds that parents who work in authoritarian workplaces, where they must take orders, pass on authoritarian attitudes to their children. They raise their children in the same way that they experience their working lives. These children are generally told what to do but are not given reasons why. By contrast, the children of professionals who have control over their work tend to encourage their children to inquire and understand why certain behaviors are appropriate. These children grow to expect a high degree of say not just over their work but also over their lives generally.This relationship between freedom in work and broader freedoms is supported by surveys of employees in the United States, Japan, and Poland during the 1960s and 1970s that found that people who exercise self-direction on the job, also value self-direction more in other realms of their life such as child-rearing and leisure. They are less likely to exhibit the nexus of traits termed the authoritarian personality (Kohn and Schooler 1983, 142).

Workers within authoritarian workplaces also suffer poorer physical and psychological health.[6] A national survey taken in 2012 revealed that British workers were significantly happier if they had "more responsibility and control over their work… [and that] employees with little control in the workplace have a 23% higher risk of heart attacks" (Priestland 2012,

---

[6] Political scientist Tom Malleson writes of the debased and servile status of contemporary workers in the following terms:

> The average worker is, in a functional sense, essentially a servant because a central duty, regardless of the particular job, is general obedience. I use the charged word "servant" here purposefully in order to highlight the heteronomy or subservience of work for the average worker. Since work tasks can never be definitively adumbrated in all their specificity, a central element of every non-professional in a hierarchical workplace is obedience to whatever the boss or manager (within, of course, legally defined boundaries) wants. In most cases, average workers are tools whose hands and brains are directed by others, for projects determined by others, and towards goals selected by others (2013, 617).

271). Psychological well-being depends upon people feeling in control of their lives (Antonovsky 1979).

What if workplaces were democratically owned and controlled? Social capital would be increased, enhancing community both at work and where workers live. These communities would be more stable, especially since they would be less threatened by profit-driven firm relocation, and workers would have less incentive to move away. Where workers participate in decision-making, their quit rate falls by a third (Moen et al. 2017).[7] Because mobility increases criminality and family break-up (Layard 2006, 179), their incidence can be expected to decrease. Economists George Akerlof and Rachel Kranton report that workers who find common cause with co-workers in pursuing the goals of their organization provide more effort and are more productive, contribute more to public goods, and coordinate more efficiently with colleagues (2005).

Although reduced labor mobility would favor stronger communities, mainstream economists generally view greater labor mobility in search of higher pay as positive since it moves workers to where their labor is more productive, thereby fueling growth. However, as noted continually within this book, given modern abundance in highly developed economies, it is not rational to continue to sacrifice all social ends to maximize production efficiency and economic growth. Moreover, worker owned and managed firms would have greater incentive that all co-worker owners be highly educated, boosting productivity.

Workplace democracy would meet what economist Bruno Frey reports psychologists identifying as three essential psychological needs:

> autonomy, relatedness, and competence. The desire for autonomy encompasses the experience of organizing one's own actions or experience of being causal. The need for relatedness refers to the desire to feel connected to others in love and care, and to be treated as a respected member of

---

[7] Economist Bruno Frey reports that "Democratic institutions increase people's well-being considerably. An increase in the extent of democracy by one mark on the ten-point Polity IV Index increases self-reported happiness to an extent similar to an increase of $4,500 per year in an individual's income" (2008, 64).

social groups. Lastly the need for competence refers to one's predisposition to control the environment and to experience oneself as capable and effective. (2008, 109)

Evolution of the Ideal of Workplace Democracy

> Any compelling argument for democratic governance of the state entails democratic governance of firms as well; and arguments that deny the legitimacy of democratic governance of firms equally oppose democratic governance of the state.
> — Samuel Bowles and Herbert Gintis 1993, 8

As was seen in Chapter 3, harsh and often cruel work conditions accompanied the spread of factories, famously branded by William Blake as "dark satanic mills" (2015). Industrialization also relocated workers from their traditional communities to live in crowded, unsanitary, and crime-ridden urban slums. A strong reaction arose among critics of these debased work and living conditions. Many of them proposed alternatives that would restore community, usually to be organized in autonomous self-governing communities of 500–2000. Within these communities, workers would be reunited with control of the tools and resources with which they labored. Experiments based on these visions spread widely, especially in the land-abundant United States.

Among the opponents of capitalism's factory conditions, Karl Marx was to have the most lasting impact. Although Marx claimed that most other critics were utopianists whose work failed the test of science, he, too, wrote of the centrality of work to human fulfillment and envisioned a future of humanized work.

Among the nineteenth-century advocates of workplace democracy, John Stuart Mill stands out by remaining within the tradition of the mainstream economics of his time. Like other advocates, he saw the benefits of worker self-management, including the healing of the standing feud between capital and labour; the transformation of human life, from a conflict of classes struggling for opposite interests, to a friendly rivalry in the pursuit of a good common to all; the elevation of the dignity of labour; a new sense of security and independence in the labouring class; and the conversion of each human being's daily occupation into a school of the social sympathies and practical intelligence. (1909, 789–780).[8]

Early workers' movements and labor unions seldom put workplace democracy on their lists of demands. In the United States, however, the Knights of Labor in the late nineteenth century included among their stated aims "To establish co-operative institutions such as will tend to supersede the wage-system, by the introduction of a co-operative industrial system." In the twentieth century, John Dewey advocated for industrial democracy. He claimed that so long as production, commerce, transportation, and the media are not under the workers' democratic control, "politics [will be] the shadow cast on society by big business" (cited in Chomsky 2014, 4–5).

Since the collapse of Eastern European state socialism, most contemporary advocates of workplace democracy no longer propose that productive wealth be owned by the state. Instead, they embrace models that preserve capitalism's two principal institutions of private property and markets. Rather than reserving productive property for a small wealthy elite, who are often absentee owners with no active engagement in the firm's decision-making, they advocate that ownership be held in common by workers who democratically elect their managers. As noted above, just as political democracy makes leaders servants of the electors, so too workplace democracy would make the elected managers servants of the workers.

To bring forth a viable form of workplace democracy, public policies (which will be discussed below) would need to privilege its existence. This does not mean the elimination of traditional capitalist firms. Although evidence suggests that most workers would prefer to share in the ownership and management of their workplaces, a minority may

---

[8] Yet surprisingly, he did not view work itself as rewarding: "Work, I imagine, is not a good in itself. There is nothing laudable in work for work's sake" (1984, 90).

prefer firms where they would not need to be responsible for decision-making or be invested in resources linked to the firm's future. Some may only be seeking temporary employment or the adventure of frequent job changes. Others may prefer to work alone or as entrepreneurs.

Although extensive evidence finds that workers thrive when they democratically participate in their firm's decision-making, extensive evidence also reveals the attractiveness of individual entrepreneurship. As Frey writes:

> the happiness of self-employed persons is higher than those employed by an organization .... Individuals derive utility from being self-employed because it gives them a higher measure of self-determination and freedom....The self-employed report higher job satisfaction than employees and people doing voluntary work and are more satisfied with their life than other people....Extensive theoretical research by psychologists suggests that individuals prefer independence to being subject to hierarchical decision making. (2008, 71; 59; 72)

In Western nations, about 10% of all gainfully employed individuals are self-employed, even though they typically earn less and work longer hours than employed individuals.[9]

Indeed, since the rise of agriculture, free peasant households acted as independent entrepreneurs. As noted above, the yeoman farmer was long an American ideal. The Land Ordinance of 1785 and the Homestead Act of 1862 were crafted to benefit family-sized farms. As noted above, a link between economic independence and political freedom was widely embraced.

Clearly, there is an important socio-economic role for those who choose to start and run businesses as sole decision-makers, and such businesses should be able to offer employment. Workers should be fully free to choose to work for entrepreneurs or undemocratic firms so long as guaranteed employment and worker-owned and managed firms exist as alternatives.

---

[9] Entrepreneurial small business owners in the United States earned an average of $51,816 in 2023. For those that are unincorporated, the average was $26,084 per year. The average annual salary in the United States in 2023 was $59,384 (Punjwani 2024).

The greatest barriers to entrepreneurship are licensure laws that require expensive time and money costs to enter many professions. These costs are typically prohibitive for the poor. As economist Milton Friedman pointed out over sixty years ago, whereas these laws are defended as necessary to ensure quality and protect the interest of consumers, they in fact exist to restrict entry into professions, limiting supply, inflating prices, and the incomes of current licensed practitioners (1962, 137–60).

As a consequence of rising job insecurity in recent decades, established specialists in increasing lines of work across America have successfully practiced rent-seeking by petitioning state governments to require licenses to practice their crafts or activities. The proportion of independent US workers needing to acquire licenses rose from 10% in 1970 to 26% by 2018 (Cunningham 2019). Where licensure is greater, so too is joblessness (Austin, Glaeser, and Summers 2018). This expansion of licensure may help explain why the number of startups fell for 40 years prior to the pandemic (Economic Innovation Group 2017). But difficult work conditions during the Covid pandemic led to a rebound of startups (Bhattarai 2023).[10]

Why Not Before?

> People arrive at a factory and perform a totally meaningless task from eight to five without question because the structure demands that it be that way. There's no villain no 'mean guy' who wants them to live meaningless lives, it's just that the structure, the system demands it and no one is willing to take on the formidable task of changing the structure just because it is meaningless.
> —Robert Pirsig 1974, 94

---

[10] This rebound was also boasted by government stimulus checks, increased unemployment benefits, and small-business loans. These entrepreneurial startup have been highest among African Americans with 35% of the total, Hispanics with 27%, and 15% for Whites (Bhattarai 2023). Many more might venture starting businesses but fear leaving their jobs with health benefits (Tokumitsu 2017, 54). Guaranteed employment with benefits could be predicted to increase their numbers.

If worker self-management is such a good idea, why is it not the norm?. Why have workers not more insistently demanded measures to bring it about? American workers overwhelmingly view it positively, principally "because they intrinsically value having more workplace power….because they intrinsically value having power over their economic lives," even if this would mean lower incomes, less efficiency, and a heavier workload (Mazumder and Yan 2023, 1; 12). Because they constitute the majority of the electorate, they could bring workplace democracy into reality. Why have they not done so? For the same reason that they do not use their political muscle to redistribute wealth, income, and privilege, or institute guaranteed employment. Elites, whose interests would be harmed by such measures, have dominant control over the ideology that convinces an adequate portion of the electorate that such measures would not in fact be in the workers' interests. It is the nature of ideology that it hoodwinks the losers into seeing as necessary and fair conditions that in fact are contrary to their best interests. Ideology promotes a mistaken view of key aspects of reality, most importantly social institutions and social relations. Accordingly, this ideology depicts workplace democracy as inefficient, non-viable, and thus destined to failure. It contends that workers are not competent to manage firms responsibly. This ideology parallels the dominant argument prevailing earlier that workers were not competent to participate through voting in the political realm.[11]

It is significant that workers' demands for democratic workplaces were most robust precisely when the elite's ideology was most under attack and at least partially discredited. This occurred during the Progressive Era at the beginning of the twentieth century and then again between the 1930s and 1970s.[12] In his 1919 presidential address to the American

---

[11] As noted earlier, what elites have most feared from democracy is being deprived of their wealth and privilege. Although political democracy improved the lives of workers and their households, the prevailing laissez-faire ideology helped the elite maintain their position. Inequality was only significantly reduced in the wake of the extreme hardship of the Great Depression that partially delegitimated that ideology.

[12] Malleson observes that

> at the height of workers' bargaining power (in the 1970s in social democratic countries) governance issues and economic democracy were firmly on the bargaining table. As a result, there were major moves towards economic democracy—for example, experiments

Economic Association, economist Irving Fisher claimed that the serious challenges facing America "would be relieved if we had more democracy in industry, that is, if the workman and the public felt that the great industries were partly theirs, both as to ownership and as to management" (1919, 16). But contemporary mainstream economics has not embraced Fisher's understanding. It rarely gives workplace democracy any mention whatsoever, even in textbooks on labor economics.

The effectiveness of the elite's ideology in dampening workers' demands is complemented by other forces. For instance, worker insecurity has greatly increased over the past 45 years, when stagnation in wages has forced workers to focus on getting and keeping jobs and struggling over traditional bread-and-butter issues. Unions, the organized voice for labor, have seen their political power devastated as globalization, labor-displacing technological change, and the decisions of state legislatures and courts have reduced their membership.

Second, workers are neither socialized to expect nor prepared to take an active role in workplace decision-making. Economists Samuel Bowles and Herbert Gintis call this a *democratic capacities constraint* due to an educational system and general culture that do not groom workers for democratic deliberation and decision-making in workplaces (1993, 96). Parents working under authoritarian conditions instill authoritarian values in their children. Moreover, modern culture, driven by the vision of material progress, nourishes the view that work is primarily a means to an income with which to purchase consumer goods and services. But, even if workers recognize the advantages of owning and managing their workplaces, they are not presented with the means to do so.

Implementing Workplace Democracy

---

in codetermination in Sweden and Germany, the Auroux laws facilitating autogestion in France, and Tony Benn's call for industrial democracy in the United Kingdom (2013, 625).

> Laws and government may be considered in this and indeed in every case as a combination of the rich to oppress the poor, and preserve to themselves the inequality of the goods which would otherwise be soon destroyed by the attacks of the poor, who if not hindered by the government would soon reduce the others to an equality with themselves by open violence.
> — Adam Smith 1763, 208

Gaining freedom from the dominance of laissez-faire ideology is necessary for preserving democracy and the evolution of a more humane and ecologically sustainable future. Acquiring this freedom requires a viable and attractive alternative vision that is grounded in employment security and workplace democracy. These are the two institutional changes proposed in the pages of this book. Both reforms leave in place the two central institutions of capitalism: private property and markets. Capitalism altered by these two reforms would still be capitalism.

Guaranteeing employment was addressed in Chapter 7. Measures supporting the creation of firms owned and democratically controlled by their workers are explored below.

Since its origins in the late eighteenth century, laissez-faire ideology has depicted property as sacrosanct and natural. But in fact, markets and private property can only substantially exist if they are defined and protected by government. That is, property rights are created not by gods or nature but by humans, by their political system. A bundle of rights is legislated or decreed that ideally serves the best interest of societies' members. But because historically elites have possessed disproportionate political power, property rights have been formulated to preferentially benefit them. Business firms, whether proprietorships or corporations, are fictional legal constructs granted rights to exist by government on the grounds that, in pursuing their private ends, they would serve the public good.

Laissez-faire ideology has also presented society's foremost social goal to be the maximization of economic output, what was discussed as a material progress vision in Chapter 6. In a post-scarcity world, however, the good must be defined as more than economic efficiency and growth;

it should also include the quality of work, communities, and the environment.

Private property is important both for efficiency and to avoid overly concentrating power in the state, a mistake made in Eastern Europe's state socialist societies. Markets are important as efficient instruments for generating information about demand, supply, prices, profits, and investment opportunities. Markets are also sites of competition, and it is important that productive units be in competition with each other not merely to enhance productivity, but also to enable the pleasure of team cooperation within firms.[13]

It was Darwin who identified the biological foundations of why human behave as they do. Human beings are competitive, as are all living beings, in the struggle to send their unique sets of genes into future generations—the dynamics of Darwin's sexual selection for sexually reproducing species. But, ironically, for humans, being cooperative can be a form of competition. Because cooperative behavior is socially valued, it can provide those who express it in socially beneficial ways with social status, making them attractive to potential mates.

Cooperation has been especially valued when groups are in violent competition with each other. This in-group cooperation and out-group warring are exhilaratingly pleasurable. This is not surprising in that during evolution humans were selected to find pleasurable the kinds of behavior that favor survival, whether of the individual or the group. In peacetime, group sports have assisted in the development of skills necessary for success in war, and cooperation and competition in sports are also highly pleasurable. This explains why team sports have always generated war-like behavior for players and fans alike. Fans of sports teams at times, both in planned and spontaneous manners, break into violence with fans of opposing teams when there is no reward in such behavior other than the exhilaration of warring, even at the risk of physical harm.

A worker-managed firm would elicit behavior in workers much like that displayed by players in team sports. Workers would cooperate with each other to remain competitive with other firms. This cooperation

---

[13] Not grasping the necessity of this competition and the importance of markets were critical failings of Marx's vision of state ownership and control of productive wealth (Wisman 2020). This failure stemmed significantly from his inadequate understanding of human behavior.

could be expected to be generally pleasurable, as it is in sports.[14] For this in-firm cooperation to work efficiently for the well-being of the economy, private property and markets must exist.

Bowles and Gintis contend that democratic firms have an efficiency advantage over conventional capitalist firms because they are better at solving agency problems in the labor market. Workers in a worker-owned firm have an incentive to discourage free-riding or shirking by co-workers since they have a stake in the firm's profits and net worth. As Bowles and Gintis put it, "The democratic firm could thus deploy a considerably more effective monitoring structure at less cost than the capitalist firm. We refer to this as the *mutual monitoring effect*"(1993, 93). Others have supported this claim, arguing that where workers have ownership stakes in the firm, they have added interest in maintaining a team spirit that promotes coordination and high productivity. Studies have found that, due at least in part to mutual worker monitoring, worker owned and managed firms exhibit less managerial supervision than traditional firms (Thompson 2015, 7). Labor economist Douglas Kruse reports that

> Over 100 studies across many countries indicate that employee ownership is generally linked to better productivity, pay, job stability, and firm survival—though the effects are dispersed and causation is difficult to firmly establish. Free-riding often appears to be overcome by worker co-monitoring and reciprocity. Financial risk is an important concern but is generally minimized by higher pay and job stability among employee owners (2016).

The question of whether democratic firms are more efficient in production, although important, is not critical. As earlier noted, in countries where the historical material scarcity problem has been solved, other social goals need no longer be sacrificed to maximum efficiency and economic dynamism. Efficiency always remains important, but as one goal to be balanced among others, especially strengthening community,

---

[14] Political economist and former Secretary of Labor Robert Reich has expressed this as follows: "Few incentives are more powerful than membership in a small group engaged in a common task, sharing the risks of defeat and the potential rewards of victory. Rewards are not only pecuniary. The group often shares a vision as well; they want to make their mark on the world" (2010, 90).

fostering worker fulfillment in the workplace, and ecological sustainability. Two other goals also stand out: the cultivation of a more democratic citizenry providing added strength to political democracy; and improved macroeconomic stability resulting from the fact that democratic firms tend to reduce work hours equally for all as opposed to laying off some during economic downturns thereby maintaining more stable worker consumption.

* * *

If a majority of the electorate were to embrace the desirability, if not the necessity of workplace democracy, what measures might their politically elected representatives enact to nourish its expansion? This section takes note of some of the most widely advocated proposals.

The most important impediment to establishing worker-owned and -managed firms is what Bowles and Gintis call a *wealth inequality constraint*. Workers typically do not possess adequate resources to meet firms' capital needs, and they have difficulty obtaining credit because they lack adequate collateral (1993, 96). Bowles and Gintis suggest providing subsidies to worker-owned firms. Realizing workplace democracy requires "that the arbitrary credit market disadvantages of the democratic firm stemming from the concentration of wealth be eliminated" (1993, 97; 98). One form this might take would be government-backed loans similar to those available to students. American Senator Bernie Sanders has proposed the creation of a US Employee Ownership Bank. Similarly, in the United Kingdom, the New Economics Foundation proposes a national investment bank that would offer credit to worker-owned and -managed firms (Gowen 2019, 31).

To encourage workplace democracy, worker-owned firms could be granted preferential corporate tax rates. Tax rates could be adjusted over time to better ensure the viability of worker owned and managed firms. It should be noted that subsidies are frequently given to industries to achieve social objectives or simply because corporate interests succeed in rent seeking (the political ability to increase profits by influencing government through campaign contributions or lobbying). Government subsidies to corporation have included direct grant payments, below-market price insurance, direct loans and loan guarantees, trade protection, and "tax expenditures" (subsidies delivered through the tax code as deductions, exclusions, and other tax preferences).

Peter Gowen, an associate at the Democracy Collaborative in Dublin, Ireland, proposes that the conversion of capitalist firms to worker ownership be encouraged by means of a tax exemption on the proceeds from selling a majority of shares in the company to a worker cooperative trust (2019, 26). Corporate law could also be amended to favor worker buyouts when firms face liquidation by providing workers with full information and time to prepare for a buyout.[15] Regional employee ownership centers could be established that offer legal and technical assistance to businesses and workers interested in firm conversion to worker ownership. A few of these are already in existence in some parts of the world such as in Ohio and Scotland (Gowen 2019, 26). In the United States, employee stock ownership plans (ESOPs) are frequently established to facilitate workers' ownership of their companies.

To stimulate the creation of democratic firms, Malleson proposes an "Incremental Democratization Plan." It would require all firms to put a percentage of their profits, say 20%, to purchase shares that are put into an internal fund controlled collectively by the firms' workers, each with one vote. The profits put into the fund would be tax-free, would remain within the firm, and could be used for investment, meaning that the plan would not reduce the firm's investment capital. Over time, the workers would acquire a controlling share of stock and, with financing made available, be able to purchase the remaining shares to fully convert the firm to a worker co-op. In this manner, over a relatively short period, much of the economy could be converted into worker-owned and -controlled firms (2013, 622–23).

Firms and governments of any size can be democratically controlled. Yet the larger a firm or government, the more removed are those who

---

[15] Gowen reports that in the United States "A poll commissioned by The Democracy Collaborative with YouGov Blue found overwhelming support for a policy that would give workers the right of first refusal when their workplaces were slated for sale or closure, with 69% of respondents in support and only 10% opposed… Unlike many proposals that aim at a more egalitarian distribution of wealth, our polling shows that a workers' right of first refusal is wildly popular across party lines, with 66% of Republicans in support" (2019).

select managers and leaders, and the less lively is the workers' or citizens' sense of active participation in decisions that affect them.[16] It would appear that we evolved to best thrive in small groups. Evolutionary biologist David Sloan Wilson and economist John Gowdy claim that "Small human groups are the most natural social units for self-regulation" (2015, 49). Psychologist Mihaly Csikszentmihalyi concurs: "The ideal social unit for accomplishing a task is a group small enough to allow intense face to face interaction, one in which members participate voluntarily, and in which each person can contribute to a common goal" (1993, 287). Biologist E.O. Wilson writes, "Our instincts still desire the tiny, united band-networks that prevailed during the hundreds of millennia preceding the dawn of history" (2013, 244). Studies have found that people are more satisfied in smaller firms due to flatter hierarchies and higher levels of autonomy on the job (Benz and Frey 2008).[17]

Unlike states, corporations do not grow for military reasons of defense. In many cases, their larger size might result from greater efficiency or lower costs due to technological, marketing, or financial economies of scale. Other firms become large through mergers and acquisition which, although they increase profits between 15 and 50%, have not been found to increase productivity (J. Lyon 2021, 42). Their large size might also make them more effective in rent seeking, a pattern of behavior that reduces an economy's efficiency of resource allocation while representing a clear perversion of democracy.[18] Evidence of such effective rent seeking is that large firms often pay tax rates lower than do smaller ones (Piketty 2022, 137). Even where economies of scale raise firms' productivity as well as their profitability, efficiency in wealth creation need no longer trump other social goals in today's rich countries.

---

[16] Aristotle held that the ideal size of the state should be between 500 and 1000 households.
[17] In the Mondragon complex of worker owned and controlled firms, cooperative are subdivided when they reach a certain size "to preserve an organizational culture of deep-level cooperation" (Thompson 2015, 10).
[18] In fact, huge firms can harm or even destroy local democracy. Social critic George Packer observes that "When towns lost their Main Street drug stores and restaurants to Walgreens and Wendy's in the big box mall out on the highway, they also lost their Rotary Club and newspaper—the local institutions of self-government. This hollowing out exposed them to an epidemic of aloneness, physical and psychological" (2021, 83).

The high degree of industrial concentration in the United States is shown by the fact the share of the economy dominated by the top one percent of companies stands at 90% (Jacobs 2022), and over the past two decades, 75% of US industries have become more concentrated (Lyon 2021, 36–37). In terms of the global economy, it has been estimated that 10% of the world's companies generate 80% of all profits (Djankov and Saliola 2018, 59).

Antitrust litigation is the usual strategy for breaking up firms that society considers too large. However, this slow and expensive process typically concerns one firm at a time. Progressive or graduated corporate income taxes could reduce firm size to what is deemed the social optimum by making it in their profit-maximizing interest to break into smaller units.

Preserving the option of entrepreneurship is important for innovation and personal freedom. Political economist Thomas Piketty offers a proposal that could promote workplace democracy while leaving room for individual entrepreneurship. It involves a sliding scale of owner voting rights according to firm size. For instance, in small companies of, say less than 10 employees, the entrepreneurs—the firms' creators—might have 90% of the voting rights. The entrepreneurs would, then, control the firms. Their voting power could decline as the number of employees increases. Thus, for example, their voting rights might drop to ten percent when employees rise to 90 or more. "In this way, a single stockholder [entrepreneur] who is also an employee of the company could have a majority of the votes in a very small company (in this case, as many as ten employees) but would have to rely increasingly on collective deliberation with other employees as soon as the company became significantly larger" (2022, 117).

According to the Small Business Administration, a small business is defined as having fewer than 1500 employees and a maximum of $38.5 million in average annual receipts (McIntyre 2020). By these criteria, over 99% of all US firms are small, and they accounted for almost two-thirds of newly created jobs between 1995 and 2021 (Punjwani 2024). Eight out of 10 small businesses have no employees, and 16% have between one and 19 employees. Thus only four percent have 20 or more (Forbes Advisor 2024). Under Piketty's proposal, practically all entrepreneurs would retain full control of their firms.

Cheaper goods and services imported from abroad have posed a challenge to some domestic firms and would do so to worker owned and controlled firms as well. Free trade has always been embraced in mainstream economics because, according to the theory of comparative advantage, it promises greater efficiency and therefore greater economic growth. However, freer trade has not benefited everyone equally; some have gained, while others, especially less skilled workers, have lost. But in today's rich countries, where the problem of material scarcity has been solved, other social goals need no longer be sacrificed to greater economic growth. This does not mean that efficiency is not important—it always is—but it must be valued in terms of other social goals. This also does not mean that foreign trade should be ended. Instead, it should be regulated in terms of its contribution to the flourishing of a nation's population. Such flourishing includes not just cheaper consumption goods and services but also quality of work, community, and a more sustainable environment.

Further, there is broad agreement today that there should not be free trade with nations that permit their companies to pollute, use child labor, maintain unsafe work conditions, or deny their workers' basic rights such as the right to unionize. Similarly, democratic control over the workplace may also be seen as a basic worker right, one of great importance. Thus, governments that do not enact measures encouraging workplace democracy could face protectionist actions incentivizing them to reconsider their policies. Or industries in which worker-owned and -managed firms predominate could be preferentially shielded from foreign competition. To the extent that participatory attitudes and behavior nurtured in democratic workplaces carry over into the political sphere, encouraging workplace democracy would also help advance political democracy abroad.

It should also be noted that substantial air and ocean pollution results from the transportation of international cargo (K. Gallagher 2005; 2009). From an ecological perspective, there is good reason to privilege buying local. Suzman reports that in the world, on average, "close to

660 pounds of food per person is wasted in the pipeline between field and plate every year" (2021, 308).

Democratic Decision-Making

> Democracy is first and foremost about equality: equality of power and equality of sharing in the benefits and values made possible by social cooperation.
> — Sheldon Wolin 2010, p. 61

How would decision-making occur within a worker-managed firm? Citizens in small-scale democratic governments often take part in discussion and decision-making in town halls. Likewise, where production units are relatively small, workers might assemble to discuss and decide upon important issues, delegating some to subcommittees. But where the number of workers is large, it would be inefficient for them to directly participate in most production-related decision-making. Instead, workers would elect managers entrusted to carry out the will of employee-owners. These managers would be accountable to their electors. Should they perform poorly, they would not likely be reelected. To deal with instances of malfeasance or incompetence, impeachment procedures could be written into firms' constitutions or by-laws.

Bad treatment by bosses is a common complaint and source of unhappiness in conventional capitalist firms, and workers generally have little recourse to bring about improvement. Management consultant and author Mary Abbajay reports, "A study by *Life Meets Work* found that 56% of American workers claim their boss is mildly or highly toxic. A study by the American Psychological Association found that 75% of Americans say their 'boss is the most stressful part of their workday'" (2018). Within a democratic firm, a disgruntled worker could initiate a campaign to assess managers who treat those they coordinate inappropriately, or in the extreme, petition for their removal.

Where workers would most naturally participate in day-to-day decisions would be in their actual work processes which has been found to support worker well-being. As Frey points out, "The more extensive the direct-participation possibilities of the citizens, the higher their self-reported life satisfaction.... [and research finds] that it is in fact the right to participate, rather than actual participation that affects people's happiness" (2008, 65; 66). From a study of a dataset of workers from 30 European countries, economists Milena Nikolova and Femke Cnossen "find that autonomy, competence, and relatedness are about 4.6 times more important for meaningfulness at work than compensation, benefits, career advancement, job insecurity, and working hours. Relatedness, which reflects supportive relationships with colleagues and superiors, emerges as the most important factor for work meaningfulness" (2020, 2).

Little noticed is that a substantial degree of workplace democracy exists within US higher education. In many of these institutions, professors participate democratically in determining the conditions of their work. Within academic departments (e.g., economics, psychology, history, etc.), they elect their chairs, decide upon curricula, initiate new programs, decide upon new hires, and make tenure and promotion decisions. Professors also participate in formulating policies beyond their departments. Nevertheless, universities and colleges remain some distance away from complete workplace democracy. Democratic decisions made at the department level must be approved by unelected higher-level administrators.

The fact that institutions of higher learning in the United States produce a world-class product, making for an enviable export industry, provides an impressive example of a highly dynamic industry that thrives without being profit-driven and harbors significant elements of workplace democracy. Academic institutions are highly competitive in markets for the best professors, students, and research grants. Private universities and colleges are private property, albeit held in trust. Given the level of competitiveness, there is no reason to believe that an economy of workplace democracy would be any less dynamic and self-transforming than current capitalism. Indeed, it could be expected to promise greater dynamism insofar as all members of a worker-owned and managed firm would have stronger incentives to ensure their firm's success than do wage workers in conventional capitalist firms.

Political Support for Workplace Democracy

> The country is governed for the richest, for the corporations, the bankers, the land speculators, and for the exploiters of labor. The majority of mankind are working people. So long as their fair demand—the ownership and control of their livelihoods—are set at naught, we can have neither men's rights nor women's rights. The majority of mankind is ground down by industrial oppression in order that the small remnant may live in ease.
> — Helen Keller 1911, 57

While the ideal of worker participation in firm decision-making has received scant attention since the resurgence of laissez-faire ideology in the late 1970s, there has been considerable support in the United States for increasing worker participation in the ownership of the firms in which they work. Legislation in 1974, supported by Republicans as well as Democrats, created favorable conditions for firms to introduce' employee stock ownership plans (ESOPs). This legislation enabled conservatives such as Ronald Reagan to join with labor leader John Lewis as advocates of worker ownership (Gowen 2019, 4).

As of 2021, 6460 of these plans exist in US workplaces, covering 14.2 million workers, about nine percent of the US workforce [National Center for Employee Ownership (NCEO) 2021]. Workers in ESOP firms make an average of 5 to 12% more in wages than their counterparts in comparable non-ESOP firms (Gowen 2019, 18). In 1919, in companies with employee stock ownership plans, the average worker had accumulated $134,000 in wealth just in the form of his or her stake in the business, with some owning shares worth a million dollars or more (Case 2019, 37). To provide perspective, the median household wealth of 3-person families in 2018 in the United States was $74,600, mostly in the form of home ownership. In the Great Recession, employee-owners were four times less likely to be laid off (NCEO 2021).[19]

---

[19] Publix supermarket chain is the largest ESOP worker-owned firm, with 1,239 retail outlets and 193,000 employees. Employees and former employees own 80% of Publix's stock. In 2020,

However, although ESOPs serve important functions in providing greater job security, higher morale, and in enabling workers to accumulate assets in the firms in which they work, there are no requirements for workplace democracy whereby workers participate in decision-making, much less in democratically selecting those who will be directing the firm's operations. This favoring of worker ownership participation without share-voting voices in decision-making has also been true abroad, such as with French Gaullists[20] and Conservatives in Britain. Only in Germany and Nordic countries have labor unions shown strong interest in worker participation in decision-making and been politically strong enough to require it (Piketty 2020, 502).[21]

Although there was considerable interest in workplace democracy between the 1930s and 1970s, this faded with the resurgence of laissez-faire ideology in the late 1970s and the collapse of the Soviet Union in the 1990s, when classical capitalism came to be portrayed as the "end of history" (Fukuyama 1989). However, interest revived in the wake of the financial crisis of 2008, fueled by the fact that worker-controlled firms fared better (Birchall and Ketilson 2009). Since the crisis, the manifesto of the British Labour Party states its commitment to doubling the size of the cooperative sector by establishing new public measures favorable to worker-owned enterprises. It also seeks to establish a "right to own," granting workers a "right of first refusal" with regard to conventional firms or sites being closed or sold (Gowen 2019, 22). In 2014, the UK government provided exemption from capital gains taxation for employee-owned trusts (Cumbers 2020, 68). Unions in the United States are also beginning to give more attention to workplace democracy. The United Steel Workers, for instance, signed a memorandum

---

it ranked 39 as one of *Fortune*'s 100 Best Companies in which to work. It is one of only eight companies that have made this list every year since its inception in 1998.

[20] Piketty reports that "French Socialists believed that the state and its high civil servants were perfectly capable of taking over the boards of directors of all key industries but that worker representatives had no place among them" (2020, 503).

[21] Labor parties in both the UK and France have seldom supported worker participation in decision making. When the British Labour Party took over in 1945, it nationalized many industries, bringing two million workers into publicly owned firms. Although pay and services benefitting the working class improved, participation in decision making was not extended to workers, remaining in the hands of a managerial class. This also remains true in France's state-owned firms (Cumbers 2020, 23).

with Mondragon Corporation in 2009 to explore unionized cooperatives (Kasmir 2016, 53).

Existing Workplace Democracy

> My task is to offer a definition of man's total needs, one that is consistent within the world of work....The primary functions of any organization... should be to implement the needs for man to enjoy a meaningful existence.
> — Frederick Herzberg 1973, xii)

Although limited in number for the reasons set forth above, worker cooperatives exist in many countries. The most extensive experiment in workplace democracy is the Mondragon complex in the Basque region of northwest Spain. Founded in 1956, as of 2019 it employed 81,507 worker–owners in 257 firms. It is the fourth largest industrial group in Spain ("Wayback Machine" 2020). The complex distributes output globally and operates in four areas: finance, industry, retail, and, with its cooperatively run university and R&D departments, the knowledge sector. Mondragon University grants undergraduate and postgraduate degrees in engineering, management, education, and culinary arts (Kasmir 2016, 53). The complex has its own investment bank, the Caja Laboral, which provides the group with financial independence from outside commercial banks. It also has its own social security system.

Each co-op within the complex is entirely owned by its workers as shareholders. Workers are not unionized. Firm-wide decisions are democratically decided within a general assembly. Complex-wide decisions are made within the Cooperative Congress, comprising representatives from each co-op. The ratio of managerial salaries to the compensation of the lowest paid workers ranges between 3:1 and 9:1, averaging 5:1, compared to an average CEO-to-worker ratio of 127:1 in Spain, 201:1 in the UK, and 265:1 in the United States. Surplus earnings are substantially reinvested, with the remainder deposited in members' personal capital accounts in the Caja Laboral to be made available for investment within the complex. Guaranteed employment is achieved by moving workers between coops and, when necessary, cutting salaries (Kasmir 2016, 53–54).

Workplace democracy also developed in post-World War II Yugoslavia when workers were empowered to appoint managers in state-owned firms. During the 1960s and much of the 1970s, economic growth in Yugoslavia outpaced all countries but Japan.

No aggregate data is available on the percentage of all firms in the world that are worker cooperatives. Yet the number is substantial, estimated globally at 2.94 million with 1217.5 million workers in all types of cooperatives (Eum 2017). In the United States, worker cooperatives have grown steadily in number over the past 20 years. There are currently 465 of them, employing about 7000 people and generating over $550 million in annual revenues (Democracy at Work Institute 2023). In France in 2010, worker cooperatives accounted for 3.5% of total employment (González-Ricoy 2014, 252).

9

Final Reflections

…an ideal picture of a society which may not be wholly achievable, or a guiding conception of the overall order to be aimed, is…not only the indispensable precondition of any rational policy, but also the chief contribution that science can make to the solution of the problems of practical policy.
— Friedrich von Hayek 1982, 1:65

In today's rich countries we live in an absurdist condition. We live with great and ever-growing material abundance yet suffer growing insecurity, stress, and pessimism concerning our future. In the United States, for example, although highly unequally distributed, per capita income in 2024 was $72,579, the amount each individual would receive if all income were equally divided. That's $290,316 for a family of four (St. Louis Fed 2025). Per capita wealth in the U.S. in 2020 was $505,420, or over 2 million dollars for a family of four (Buchholz 2021). Collectively, Americans are extremely wealthy.

Yet despite wealth far exceeding the imagination of past visionaries, a 2023 Pew Research poll reports that almost 60% of Americans believe that life in America is worse today than it was 50 years ago. The majority also judge that in 2050, only 25 years away, conditions will be yet worse: 66% think the economy will be weaker and 81% believe the gap between the rich and poor will be wider (Daniller 2023). This pessimism is understandable. Inequality has exploded over the past 50 years, longevity has been declining, jobs are less secure, medical expenses are soaring, incidence of depression is increasing, school quality is declining, prison populations are rising, and increasing numbers of citizens are suffering loneliness and "deaths of despair" (Case and Deaton 2020). And as if this economic dysfunction and malaise were not challenging enough, the very survival of democracy is in question. Should democracy weaken further, or even disappear, arguably there will be little hope of avoiding ecological Armageddon, potentially even ending the human story. It is urgent that we rechart our course.

What is necessary to redirect our trajectory is the same as what can promise human flourishing. It is an attractive alternative to laissez-faire ideology's vision of our future, grounded in the fact that, beyond basic material needs and security, humans flourish when living within social institutions that best enable the attainment of social and self-respect—outcomes that are most promisingly forthcoming in the realm of work. As opposed to an ineffective pursuit of fulfillment through ever greater consumption, the alternative vision set forth in this book privileges freedom, democracy, creativity, and community in work life.

However, the challenge of delegitimating and replacing laissez-faire ideology is formidable. This ideology is firmly entrenched in contemporary economic and political institutions and attitudes that benefit elites who possess extraordinary influence over the public sphere.

The Yoke of Laissez-Faire Ideology

> …it seems compelling that the costs of redistributive taxation and democratic politics to the elites and, hence, their aversion to democracy should be generally higher for the elites in a society where the difference in

incomes between the elites and the citizens is greater.... The most important implication is that as inequality increases and democracy becomes more costly for the elites, repression becomes more attractive.
— Daron Acemoglu and James Robinson 2006, 36–37

The root cause of our contemporary social dysfunction and malaise is the inequality that has been exploding over the past 50 years. But why is it tolerated? The reason is that the laissez-faire ideology that has legitimated public policies that have dramatically increased the wealth, income, and privilege of elites has been sufficiently persuasive to hoodwink enough voters into believing that such measures are in their interests as well.

Extreme inequality is not, of course, new. It dates back 5500 years to the rise of the state and civilization when warrior elites used metal weaponry, military organization, and ideology to seize ownership and control of productive resources (principally land) such that to survive all others had to work for them. They did so as slaves, serfs, indebted peasants and wage laborers. Their surplus output—that above bare subsistence—was expropriated by ruling elites.

Although force was usually necessary for setting up exploitative regimes, ideology has always been the ongoing means of its perpetuation. Using force to maintain inequality is expensive, creating resistance and potentially inciting insurrection. Far better is an ideology that convinces the exploiters and the exploited alike that the prevailing social order is as it must be, and thus is just. With the rise of the state, religion was transformed to do precisely that. Gods were depicted as creating a perfect world. As omnipotent and omniscient god-beings, they could not do otherwise. Thus, like all else, the social order was perfect. Everyone had his or her unalterable proper place and role. Contesting this order was blasphemy, a transgression often resulting in torture and death.

Religion remained the principal ideology for legitimating inequality until the late Middle Ages in Europe when a bourgeoisie emerged and Protestantism created competition as to the ultimate grounding of truth and meaning. As the previously entrenched Catholic Church lost its monopoly, it opened the gates for secular science and philosophy. Mercantilist economic thought entered the public square and argued that, because workers are slothful, they must be kept poor lest they not work. Mercantilist thinking even justified state intervention to hold down wages and inflict harsh punishment on vagrants. Workers must also be kept ignorant to avoid discontent with their abject conditions. Over subsequent centuries, economics gradually replaced religion as the dominant ideology legitimating inequality, and it continues to do so today.

Enlightenment thinkers identified the state as the protector of privileges, and thus they advocated a world freer of mercantilist government interference, a world of laissez-faire that would promise less inequality and a more dynamic economy. However, laissez-faire doctrine quickly evolved into an ideology legitimating inequality. It currently makes the following claims: government is incompetent and corrupt and must be minimized; the economy should be deregulated to let businesses and households freely pursue their own interests in unfettered markets; taxes, especially on the rich and corporations, should be cut to stimulate investment and economic growth; welfare, including unemployment benefits and Social Security, must be eliminated to force the unemployed to seek jobs and poor workers to work harder and responsibly save for retirement; in a free market economy, meritocracy rules such that all get their just rewards—the rich earn their wealth and the poor their poverty.

Advocates of laissez-faire contend that it captures what has enabled capitalism to be a dynamic generator of wealth. But they overlook the decisive role government has played beyond defining and enforcing property rights. Government has created the foundational components of economic dynamism such as infrastructure, human capital, and pathbreaking research. Laissez-faire advocates ignore that with substantial government participation, economic growth was considerably more robust during the 30 years following World War Two, when the ideology was weakened and inequality declining, than in the last 50 years of laissez-faire guided public policies and exploding inequality.[1]

Laissez-faire ideology is strongest in the United States, although it has been gaining almost equal force in Great Britain since Margaret Thatcher's time in power in the 1980s, and, although more slowly, is

---

[1] It must be noted that government participation in the economy has not declined during this reign of laissez-faire ideology. Instead, government's involvement has been reoriented to benefit rich elites (Janoff-Bulman 2023).

doing the same on the continent and around much of the world. In the late 1980s, laissez-faire ideology was expressed in the "Washington Consensus," formulated and advanced by the International Monetary Fund (IMF), the World Bank, and the US Treasury as measures to stimulate economic growth in lesser developed countries. Critics claim that its success in stimulating growth was insignificant. What it clearly did was to redistribute wealth, income, and privilege upward to elites.

Can Laissez-Faire Ideology Be Delegitimated?

> Only a crisis—actual or perceived—produces real change. When that crisis occurs, the actions that are taken depend on the ideas that are lying around. That, I believe, is our basic function: to develop alternatives to existing policies, to keep them alive and available until the politically impossible becomes the politically inevitable.
> — Milton Friedman 2002, xiv

Laissez-faire ideology was challenged during the Progressive Era in the United States at the end of the nineteenth and beginning of the twentieth centuries. This accompanied worker strikes and threats of insurrection during a period of extreme inequality when "robber barons" flaunted their wealth in "gilded age" extravagance. In this climate, and with males in possession of the franchise, laissez-faire ideology was weakened, resulting in the passage of major policy measures that substantially benefited the general population, such as graduated personal income taxes, inheritance taxes, corporate income taxes, breaking up of monopolies, prohibition of corporate campaign contributions, and women's suffrage. Although not reversed, the growth of inequality slowed. However, laissez-faire ideology resurged in the 1920s, fueled by a "Red Scare" that generated anti-labor sentiments and justified political measures that expanded inequality and set the stage for a financial crisis and the Great Depression of the 1930s (Wisman 2014).

It was the economic dysfunction and suffering of the Great Depression that sufficiently delegitimated laissez-faire ideology such that during the

40 years between the mid-1930s and mid-1970s, extensive public policies greatly diminished inequality and improved the quality of life for the greater population. This partial delegitimation of laissez-faire ideology occurred when an alternative vision of the future was visible, that of socialism, given presumed viability by the Soviet experiment.[2] The exceptionally robust productivity growth, economic dynamism, and widely shared prosperity accompanying declining inequality in the decades following World War Two were the defining improvements of what has come to be called the Golden Age of Capitalism.

Given the elite's disproportionate command of the media, think tanks, education, and politics, it was arguably a mere matter of time before their ideology of laissez-faire would resurge (Wisman 2022, 351–87). It began to do so in the mid-1970s in a climate of economic dysfunction (stagflation), labor unrest, international decline of the dollar, loss of the Vietnam War, and alleged cultural degeneracy, all blamed on the 40 years of progressive programs first launched by Franklin Delano Roosevelt's New Deal in the 1930s. Guided by laissez-faire's expression as supply-side economics, public policies have been enacted that have dramatically increased inequality in wealth, income, and privilege. The destructive social consequences of this inequality have created a political climate in which the future of democracy is imperiled. Without a significant degree of democracy, it is unlikely that the challenge of ecological disaster can be avoided.

Hope for political and ecological well-being requires an attractive and persuasive alternative vision of our future to that offered by laissez-faire ideology, one that privileges job security, fulfilling work, and enriched community life while furthering the ideals of freedom and democracy. This proposition is grounded in the fact that, once basic material needs have been met, it is in work rather than in consumption that the greatest potential for human flourishing is to be found.

---

[2] Although the Soviet Union was exceedingly poor during its first decades, even experiencing starvation, it did not suffer the collapse of output and high unemployment of the Great Depression. Over 100,000 Americans applied for immigration to the Soviet Union in the early 1930s and about 10,000 did so (Tzouliadis 2009). Leftist political parties held up socialism and communism as more rational and ethical alternatives to what they judged exploitative and dysfunctional capitalism.

Two reforms have been proposed in this book to transform work experience: guaranteed employment at living wages with benefits and reskilling where appropriate; and a set of measures designed to bring forth democracy in the workplace. Such reforms would provide basic security and expand freedom and democracy to the workplace while preserving capitalism's principal institutions of markets and private property. Democracy was the political condition of humanity for the first 98% of its history. But it has been rare and fragile since the rise of the state. To nourish and preserve it into the future, other social institutions must inculcate a mentality of autonomy and democratic freedom in decision-making. That is what democracy in the workplace would do.

If widely embraced and advocated, a political platform based on guaranteed employment and workplace democracy holds promise of being highly attractive to electorates. The curses of unemployment, poverty, and inadequate professional education would be eliminated. Democracy and freedom would be extended from the political domain to work life. Moreover, such a vision would not appear all that different from classical capitalism, retaining its two principal institutions—private property and markets—without concentrating power in the state or in a small rich class owning and controlling productive wealth. It would constitute the next major progressive step in freedom's historical unfolding.

Workers, constituting the overwhelming majority of the electorate, possess the political power to rewrite the social script and convert such a vision into social reality. The only prerequisite is workers' awareness of its desirability and feasibility.

Primordial Conditions of Work and Human Flourishing

> I think that capitalism, wisely managed, can probably be made more efficient for attaining economic ends than any alternative system yet in sight, but that in itself it is in many ways extremely objectionable. Our problem is to work out a social organization which shall be as efficient as possible without offending our notions of a satisfactory way of life.

— John Maynard Keynes 1926, 5

Although the threat of political and ecological disaster is widely recognized, social causation is of such complexity that our future resists prediction. History continually throws out surprises. Thus, even without the reforms proposed here and the delegitimation of laissez-faire ideology, such dire outcomes as the end of democracy and ecological Armageddon may *not* occur. That would be grounds for great celebration. It would not, however, alter the core argument of this book.

That argument is that our extraordinary material abundance—our victory over the primordial problem of scarcity—permits us to restructure aspects of our social existence pertaining to work to enable unparalleled human flourishing. We can take full advantage of our abundance while recapturing core aspects of the nature of the work experience to which our species adapted during our evolution. We can recapture features of the community in which that work was embedded.

To survive and reproduce, humans, like all animals, must provide themselves with food, shelter, and defense. When done by humans, we call this provisioning work. But whatever term we choose, humans were selected to experience this provisioning activity during evolution to be pleasurable to best motivate its performance, and thus our species' potential for survival. We also evolved as social beings and were selected to find coordinating and working with others to be pleasurable. There was no insecurity and stress due to a threat of unemployment. There were no bosses, and, when work was carried out with others, their coordination was democratically governed. These pleasurable conditions of work endured for the first 98% of our history but mostly ended with the inequality accompanying the spread of state societies.

Our challenge today is to recreate core aspects of primordial work to more fully enable human flourishing. This entails implementing the two reforms of the world of work advocated in this book: guaranteeing employment at living wages with reskilling where appropriate and expanding democracy to the workplace.

Neither Revolutionary Nor Utopian

> …very likely the utopian element in the human imagination is one of the driving forces of history, and humanity would be immeasurably impoverished if that element ever disappeared.
> — Sociologist Peter Berger 1986: 222

Capitalism is the economic system that has created our unparalleled abundance. If the two reforms proposed in this book were implemented, would the economic system still be capitalist? Not according to Karl Marx and many on the left, who claim that the core characteristic of capitalism is the separation of workers from ownership and control of productive wealth. But the reforms proposed here reunite workers with ownership and control of productive wealth while nonetheless preserving private property and markets, the defining social institutions of capitalism as seen by its celebrants. Leftist critics would likely accept sociologist Peter Berger's statement that "a society dominated by market mechanisms would not usefully be called socialist" (1986, 174). Political historian Jerry Muller submitted, "A working definition of capitalism is 'a system in which the production and distribution of goods is entrusted primarily to the market mechanism, based on private ownership of property, and on exchange between legally free individuals'" (2003, xvii). Libertarian economist Ludwig von Mises claimed that "The market is …the focal point of the capitalist order of society; it is the essence of capitalism" (quoted in Berger 1986, 188). Social historian Michael Merrill notes the widespread view that capitalism is "little more than a synonym for a market economy" (1995, 316) Thus, according to the understanding of these non-Marxists and staunch defenders of capitalism, capitalism does not essentially require unemployment or great inequality in the ownership and control of productive wealth. An economy with guaranteed employment and workplace democracy would still be capitalism, although clearly not classical capitalism with exploitation.

Accordingly, many critics who have flatly rejected capitalism have been misguided. Fault is not to be found with capitalism as an economic system based on private property and markets. Fault instead belongs to the extreme inequality that has accompanied capitalism's historical evolution, where workers were separated from ownership, control, or ready access to productive wealth and vulnerable to exploitation by its elite owners.

Guaranteed employment and workplace democracy are not, therefore, revolutionary. But are they utopian?

Utopian visionaries have typically supposed that, given appropriate social institutions, human competitiveness would disappear.[3] In this they are mistaken. They have confused the behavior that is determined by a society's social institutions with what humans are by nature.

As Darwin made clear, our biology condemns us to be competitive. What drives this competitiveness is that we, like all animals, compete for mates to send our unique sets of genes into the future—the genes that enable successful competition. Thus, although social institutions, attitudes, and practices have culturally evolved to significantly deflect attention from this sexual competition, it is not only innate, but that which drives all other competition.[4]

Humans principally compete for high status because it makes them attractive to the opposite sex. But what gains high status is determined by the social institutions that channel the way instincts are expressed. During the first 98% of our history, individuals acquired high status by being courageous warriors, good hunters or gatherers, good storytellers, or, more generally, cooperative and generous group members

---

[3] For instance, in the early nineteenth century, entrepreneur and utopianist Robert Owen believed that in a society of abundance without private property where everyone's needs were guaranteed, the "fatal folly of distinction" would disappear. In his proposed communitarian society, "all the natural wants of human nature may be abundantly supplied; and the principle of selfishness will cease to exist for want of an adequate motive to produce it" (quoted in Rosanvallon 2013, 125–26). William Godwin went even further, believing that in his ideal utopia, not only would self-interest disappear, but even our sex drives would wither away as we transcended our animal origins.

[4] As evolutionary psychologist Satoshi Kanazawa puts it: "The fact that many of us do not think that [reproduction] is the ultimate goal of our existence or that some of us choose not to reproduce is irrelevant. We are not privy to the evolutionary logic behind our design, and no matter what we choose to do in our own lifetimes, we are all descended from those who chose to reproduce. None of us inherited our psychological mechanism from our ancestors who remained childless. Everything else in life, even survival, is a means to reproductive success" (2009, 26).

whose behavior benefited the community. On the other hand, seeking wealth or political power was discouraged and even punished because it was perceived to be destructive of community. As was seen in Chapter 2, these evolutionary claims are supported by studies in anthropology, sociology, and what has come to be called happiness research.

With the rise of the state and extreme inequality, wealth and political power became the principal sources of status and they remain so today.

No reforms, including those recommended here can eliminate competitiveness and thus alter human nature. Social institutions may alter behavior, but not human nature. Moreover, competitiveness is by no means in itself negative. If appropriately channeled by institutions, it is beneficial to social well-being. It is necessary for innovation and economic dynamism. An element of competition makes sports and much play fun. Further, as noted above, being generous and cooperative can be forms of competition as they are socially appreciated and can earn status.

*****

A Closing Reflection on Optimism

> Almost all the revolutions which have changed the aspect of nations have been made to consolidate or to destroy social inequality. Remove the secondary causes which have produced the great convulsions of the world, and you will almost always find the principle of inequality at the bottom.
> — Alexis de Tocqueville 1835, 1: Chap. xxi

It is ironic that given our extraordinary and increasing abundance—our victory over the primordial problem of scarcity—pervasive pessimism plagues people in today's privileged societies. But this pessimism is not historically deep. It has arisen over the past 50 years with exploding inequality. Optimism reigned during the previous 30 years following World War Two, the Golden Age of Capitalism, when inequality was declining in a dynamic economy. There appear to be two lessons in this. The first is that whether pessimism or optimism prevails appears to track whether inequality is rising or falling. Second, in the grander sweep of history, the period since World War Two is merely the last one and a half percent of our past since the explosion of inequality accompanying the rise of the state 5500 years ago.

Recognition that extreme inequality might be ended only arose recently, during the last 250 years, less than the last five percent of history since the rise of the state. It was then that the ideal of equality first began drawing significant attention. This was the era of the French and Scottish Enlightenments, Jean-Jacques Rousseau, Adam Smith, Immanuel Kant, Thomas Jefferson, and the American and French revolutions. Political discourse was infused with the claim that "all men are created equal," and the ideal social condition was seen to be that of *liberté, égalité, fraternité*. This new understanding that equality is a goal to be sought paralleled the mounting recognition that sustainable social and material progress is possible.

The intellectual foundations for challenging ideology date back to the seventeenth century, most notably when the first modern philosopher, René Descartes, insisted that we must doubt everything and embrace only that which survives the scrutiny of reason. Reason, rather than faith, must guide humans. This was revolutionary. Only reason can lead to truth, and as Goethe later put it, Die Wahrheit wird euch frei machen: the truth will set you free. But a sophisticated concept of ideology, one recognizing that certain doctrines serve to justify inequality and exploitation, is as recent as Karl Marx's era in mid-nineteenth century.

Belief in a divinely prescribed natural order has declined with the weakening of religion and superstition, whereas belief in the power of reason has expanded as education has become ever more democratized and extended in years. As technology progresses ever more rapidly, it geometrically expands access to information and the means for understanding it. Might the expansion in formal education, the new technologies for acquiring and communicating knowledge, and a growing consensus that reason is the rightful arbiter for verifying truth claims be grounds for optimism concerning humanity's future?

References

APSA. 2023. *APSA Presidential Task Force on Political Parties. More Than Red and Blue: Political Parties and American Democracy*. American Political Science Association and Protect Democracy. https://protectdemocracy.org/wp-content/uploads/2023/07/APSA-PD-Political-Parties-Report-FINAL.pdf

Abbajay, Mary. 2018. What to Do When You Have a Bad Boss. *Harvard Business Review*, September 7. https://hbr.org/2018/09/what-to-do-when-you-have-a-bad-boss

Abraham, Katharine G., John Haltiwanger, Kristin Sandusky, and James R. Spletzer. 2019. The Consequences of Long-Term Unemployment: Evidence from Linked Survey and Administrative Data. *ILR Review* 72 (2): 266–299. https://doi.org/10.1177/0019793918797624.

Acemoglu, Daron, and James A. Robinson. 2000. Why Did the West Extend the Franchise? Democracy, Inequality, and Growth in Historical Perspective. *The Quarterly Journal of Economics* 115 (4): 1167–1199. https://doi.org/10.1162/003355300555042.

Acemoglu, Daron, and James A. Robinson. 2006. *Economic Origins of Dictatorship and Democracy*. Cambridge, New York: Cambridge University Press.

Acemoglu, Daron, and James A. Robinson. 2012. *Why Nations Fail: The Origins of Power, Prosperity and Poverty*, 1st ed. New York: Crown Publishers.

Aja, Alan, William Darity, and Daniel Bustillo. 2013. Jobs Instead of Austerity: A Bold Policy Proposal for Economic Justice. *Social Research: An International Quarterly* 80 (3): 781–794.

Akerlof, George A., and Rachel E. Kranton. 2005. Identity and the Economics of Organizations. *Journal of Economic Perspectives* 19 (1): 9–32. https://doi.org/10.1257/0895330053147930.

Alesina, Alberto, Edward Glaeser, and Bruce Sacerdote. 2001. Why Doesn't the United States Have a European-Style Welfare State? *Brookings Papers on Economic Activity* 32 (2): 187–278.

Allen, Robert. 2001. The Great Divergence in European Wages and Prices from the Middle Ages to the First World War. *Explorations in Economic History* 38 (October): 411–447. https://doi.org/10.1006/exeh.2001.0775.

Almond, Gabriel Abraham, and Sidney Verba, eds. 1989. *The Civic Culture: Political Attitudes and Democracy in Five Nations*. Newbury Park, CA: SAGE Publications Inc.

Anderson, Perry. 2013. *Passages from Antiquity to Feudalism*, 1st ed. New York: Verso.

Anderson, Elizabeth. 2017. Private Government*: How Employers Rule Our Lives (and Why We Don't Talk about It)*. Princeton, NJ:: Princeton University Press.

Antonovsky, Aaron. 1979. *Health, Stress and Coping*, 1st ed. San Francisco: Jossey-Bass Inc.

Applebaum, Herbert. 1992. *The Concept of Work: Ancient, Medieval and Modern*. Albany, New York: State University of New York Press.

Appleby, Joyce. 2011. *The Relentless Revolution: A History of Capitalism*. Reprint. New York: W. W. Norton & Company.

Arendt, Hannah. 1958. *The Human Condition*. Chicago: University of Chicago Press.

Argyle, Michael. 2001. *The Psychology of Happiness*. 2 edition. London; New York: Routledge.

Aristotle. 2000. *Politics*. Translated by Benjamin Jowett. New edition. Mineola, NY: Dover Publications.

Attali, Jacques, and Vincent Champain. 2005. *Changer Le Paradigme Pour Supprimer Le Chômage*. Paris: Paris: Foundation Jean-Juares. http://www.metiseurope.eu/content/pdf/n9/6_attali.pdf

Austin, Benjamin, Edward Glaeser, and Lawrence Summers. 2018. Jobs for the Heartland: Place-Based Policies in 21st-Century America. *Brookings Papers on Economic Activity* 49 (1 (Spring)): 151–255.

Autor, David H. 2014. Skills, Education, and the Rise of Earnings Inequality Among the 'Other 99 Percent.' *Science* 344 (6186): 843–851. https://doi.org/10.1126/science.1251868.
Autor, David H. 2015. Why Are There Still So Many Jobs? The History and Future of Workplace Automation. *The Journal of Economic Perspectives* 29 (3): 3–30. https://doi.org/10.2307/43550118.
Azzellini, Dario, ed. 2015. *An Alternative Labour History: Worker Control and Workplace Democracy*. Reprint. London: Zed Books.
BLS. 2016. *Entrepreneurship and the U.S. Economy*. Bureau of Labor Statistics. 2016. https://www.bls.gov/bdm/entrepreneurship/entrepreneurship.htm
BLS. 2025. Union Membership. https://www.bls.gov/news.release/pdf/union2.pdf
Bachrach, Peter, and Morton S. Baratz. 1963. Decisions and Nondecisions: An Analytical Framework. *American Political Science Review* 57 (3): 632–642. https://doi.org/10.2307/1952568.
Bailyn, Bernard. 2013. *The Barbarous Years: The Peopling of British North America-The Conflict of Civilizations, 1600–1675*. New York: Vintage.
Balcombe, Jonathan. 2009. Animal Pleasure and Its Moral Significance. *Applied Animal Behaviour Science*, Special Issue: Animal Suffering and Welfare, vol. 118 (3): 208–16.
Barash, David P. 1986. *The Hare and the Tortoise: The Conflict between Culture and Biology in Human Affairs*. New York: Viking.
Beenackers, M. A., J. Oude Groeniger, C. B. M. Kamphuis, and F. J. van Lenthe. 2016. The Role of Financial Strain and Self-Control in Explaining Income Inequalities in Health Behaviors. *European Journal of Public Health* 26 (Suppl_1): ckw166.058. https://doi.org/10.1093/eurpub/ckw166.058.
Bell, Peter. 2022. Public Trust in Government: 1958–2022. *Pew Research Center—U.S. Politics & Policy* (blog). June 6, 2022. https://www.pewresearch.org/politics/2022/06/06/public-trust-in-government-1958-2022/
Bellah, Robert N., Richard Madsen, William M. Sullivan, Ann Swidler, and Steven M. Tipton. 2007. *Habits of the Heart: Individualism and Commitment in American Life*. First Edition, with a new Preface. Berkeley: University of California Press.
Bentham, Jeremy. 1983. Deontology, A Table of Springs of Action, and Article on Utilitarianism. In *The Collected Works of Jeremy Bentham*, edited by A. Goldworth. Oxford: Clarendon Press.
Benz, Matthias, and Bruno S. Frey. 2008. Being Independent Is a Great Thing: Subjective Evaluations of Self-Employment and Hierarchy. *Economica* 75 (298): 362–383.

Berger, Peter L. 1986. *The Capitalist Revolution: Fifty Propositions About Prosperity, Equality, and Liberty*. New York: Basic Books.

Berry, John Widdup. 1976. *Human Ecology and Cognitive Style: Comparative Studies in Cultural and Psychological Adaptation*. Beverly Hills : New York: John Wiley & Sons Inc.

Betzig, Laura L. 1986. *Despotism and Differential Reproduction*. New York: Aldine.

Bhattarai, Abha. 2023. American Entrepreneurship Is on the Rise. *Washington Post*, September 18. https://www.washingtonpost.com/business/2023/09/14/small-business-entrepreneurship-gem-report/

Bilsen, Johan. 2018. Suicide and Youth: Risk Factors. *Frontiers in Psychiatry* 9 (October): 540. https://doi.org/10.3389/fpsyt.2018.00540.

Birchall, Johnston, and Lou Hammond Ketilson. 2009. *Resilience of the Cooperative Business Model in Times of Crisis*. Geneva: ILO.

Biswas-Diener, Robert, Ed Diener, and Maya Tamir. 2004. The Psychology of Subjective Well-Being. *Daedalus* 133 (2): 18–25.

Bivens, Josh, Elise Gould, and Jori Kandra. 2024. CEO Pay Declined in 2023. Economic Policy Institute. https://www.epi.org/publication/ceo-pay-in-2023/

Blackburn, Robin. 1996. Slave Exploitation and the Elementary Structure of Enslavement. In *Serfdom and Slavery: Studies in Legal Bondage*, ed. M. L. Bush, 158–180. New York: Longmans.

Blake, William. 2015. *Milton: A Poem*. Scotts Valley, CA: CreateSpace Independent Publishing Platform.

Bogaard, Amy, Mattia Fochesato, and Samuel Bowles. 2019. The Farming-Inequality Nexus: New Insights from Ancient Western Eurasia. *Antiquity* 93 (371): 1129–43. https://doi.org/10.15184/aqy.2019.105.

Boix, Carles. 2015. *Political Order and Inequality: Their Foundations and Their Consequences for Human Welfare*. New York: Cambridge University Press.

Bowles, Samuel, and Herbert Gintis. 1993. A Political and Economic Case for the Democratic Enterprise. *Economics and Philosophy* 9 (April): 75–100. https://doi.org/10.1017/S0266267100005125.

Bowles, Samuel, David Gordon, and Thomas E. Weisskopf. 1991. *After the Waste Land: A Democratic Economics for the Year 2000*. 1st Edition, 2nd Printing. Armonk, NY: M E Sharpe Inc.

Boyce, James K., Andrew R. Klemer, Paul H. Templet, and Cleve E. Willis. 1999. Power Distribution, the Environment, and Public Health: A State-Level Analysis. *Ecological Economics* 29 (1): 127–140. https://doi.org/10.1016/S0921-8009(98)00056-1.

Boyce, James K. 2007. 'Inequality and Environmental Protection,' in, *Inequality, Collective Action, and Environmental Sustainability*, Jean-Marie Baland, Pranab Bardhan, and Samuel Bowles, Eds. Princeton: Princeton University Press, 2007: 314–48.

Braverman, Harry. 1998. *Labor and Monopoly Capital: The Degradation of Work in the Twentieth Century*. Anv. New York: Monthly Review Press.

Bubonya, Melisa, Deborah A. Cobb-Clark, and Mark Wooden. 2014. *A Family Affair: Job Loss and the Mental Health of Spouses and Adolescents*. Working Paper 8588. IZA Discussion Papers. https://www.econstor.eu/handle/10419/106530

Buchholz, Katherina. 2021. *Infographic: Which Countries Are Really the Richest?* Statista Daily Data. June 29, 2021. https://www.statista.com/chart/19651/countries-with-highest-per-capita-average-and-median-wealth

Bumiller, Elisabeth. 2006. Bush Rejects Idea of Boycotting Meeting in Russia. *The New York Times*, March 30: sec. U.S. https://www.nytimes.com/2006/03/30/world/europe/bush-rejects-idea-of-boycotting-meeting-in-russia.html

Bureau of Labor Statistics. 2019. *Characteristics of Unemployment Insurance Applicants and Benefit Recipients Summary*. September 25. https://www.bls.gov/news.release/uisup.nr0.htm

Burgard, Sarah A., Jennie E. Brand, and James S. House. 2009. Perceived Job Insecurity and Worker Health in the United States. *Social Science & Medicine*, 69 (5): 777–785. https://doi.org/10.1016/j.socscimed.2009.06.029.

Buss, David M. 1994. *The Evolution of Desire: Strategies of Human Mating*, 1st ed. New York: Basic Books.

Buss, David M. 2011. *Evolutionary Psychology: The New Science of the Mind*, 4th ed. Boston: Pearson.

Byrne, Edmund. 2010. *Work, Inc.: A Philosophical Inquiry*. Temple University Press.

CEA. 2016. *Economic Report of the President 2016*. February 22. https://www.govinfo.gov/features/featured-content/ERP-2016

Camus, Albert. 1942. *The Stranger*. Translated by Matthew Ward. New York: Vintage.

Carlyle, Thomas. 1840. *Chartism*. London, J. Fraser. http://archive.org/details/chartism00carlgoog

Cary, John. 1745 (2010). *A Discourse on Trade, and Other Matters Relative to It. … Written at the Request of Several Members of Parliament*, 2nd ed. London: Gale ECCO, Print Editions.

Case, Anne, and Angus Deaton. 2020. *Deaths of Despair and the Future of Capitalism*, 1st ed. Princeton, NJ: Princeton University Press.
Case, John. 2019. An Economy in Waiting. *The New Republic*, August, 37–39.
Cassar, Lea, and Stephan Meier. 2018. Nonmonetary Incentives and the Implications of Work as a Source of Meaning. *Journal of Economic Perspectives* 32 (3): 215–238. https://doi.org/10.1257/jep.32.3.215.
Cerda, Andy. 2024. Key Facts about Union Members and the 2024 Election. *Pew Research Center* (blog). October 17, 2024. https://www.pewresearch.org/short-reads/2024/10/17/key-facts-about-union-members-and-the-2024-election/
Chapin, Stuart F., and Julius A. Jahn. 1940. The Advantages of Work Relief Over Direct Relief in Maintaining Morale in St. Paul in 1939. *The American Journal of Sociology* 46 (1): 13–22.
Chapman University. 2017. America's Top Fears 2017—Chapman University Survey of American Fears. *The Voice of Wilkinson* (blog).. https://blogs.chapman.edu/wilkinson/2017/10/11/americas-top-fears-2017/
Childe, V. Gordon. 1936. *Man Makes Himself*. Nottingham: Coronet Books.
Chomsky, Noam. 2014. Thinking Like Corporations Is Harming American Universities. *Enjeux Universitaires—des Profs Vous informent* 33 (11): 1–8.
Chou, Eileen Y., Bidhan L. Parmar, and Adam D. Galinsky. 2016. Economic Insecurity Increases Physical Pain. *Psychological Science* 27 (4): 443–454.
Cicero, Marcus Tullius. 1913. *De Officiis (On Duties)*. Translated by W. Miller. Cambridge, Mass: Harvard University Press.
Clark, Andrew E., Yannis Georgellis, and P. Sanfey. 2001. Scarring: The Psychological Impact of Past Unemployment. *Economica* 68: 221–241.
Clark, Andrew E., and Andrew J. Oswald. 1994. Unhappiness and Unemployment. *Economic Journal* 104 (424): 648–659.
Cooke, Jacob E., ed. 1961. *The Federalist*. Middletown: Wesleyan University Press.
Couch, Kenneth, Gayle Reznik, Christopher Tamborini, and Howard Iams. 2013. Economic and Health Implications of Long-Term Unemployment: Earnings, Disability Benefits, and Mortality. *Research in Labor Economics* 38 (December): 259–305. https://doi.org/10.1108/S0147-9121(2013)0000038008.
Cowie, Jefferson. 2017. *The Great Exception: The New Deal and the Limits of American Politics*. Reprint edition. Princeton N.J.: Princeton University Press.
Csikszentmihalyi, Mihaly. 1993. *The Evolving Self*. New York: Harper Collins.

Cumbers, Andrew. 2020. *The Case for Economic Democracy*. 1st edition. Cambridge, UK ; Medford, MA: Polity.
Cunningham, Evan. 2019. *Professional Certifications and Occupational Licenses: Evidence from the Current Population Survey : Monthly Labor Review: U.S. Bureau of Labor Statistics*. June. https://www.bls.gov/opub/mlr/2019/article/professional-certifications-and-occupational-licenses.htm
Curle, Adam. 1949. Incentives to Work: An Anthropological Perspective. *Human Relations* 2 (1): 41–47.
Daniels, Ronald J. 2021. *What Universities Owe Democracy*. Baltimore: Johns Hopkins University Press.
Daniller, Andrew. 2023. Americans Take a Dim View of the Nation's Future, Look More Positively at the Past. *Pew Research Center* (blog). April 24. https://www.pewresearch.org/short-reads/2023/04/24/americans-take-a-dim-view-of-the-nations-future-look-more-positively-at-the-past/
Darity, William, Jr. 1999. Who Loses from Unemployment? *Journal of Economic Issues* 33 (2): 491–96.
Darwin, Charles. 1871a. *The Descent of Man and Selection in Relation to Sex*, vol. 1. London: John Murray.
Darwin, Charles. 1871. *The Descent of Man and Selection in Relation to Sex*, vol. 1. London: John Murray.
Darwin, Charles. 1871b. *The Descent of Man and Selection in Relation to Sex*. Vol. 2. 2 vols. London: John Murray.
Davidson, Paul. 2017. *Automation Could Kill 73 Million U.S. Jobs by 2030*. USA TODAY. November 28. https://www.usatoday.com/story/money/2017/11/29/automation-could-kill-73-million-u-s-jobs-2030/899878001/
Deaton, Angus. 2013. *The Great Escape: Health, Wealth, and the Origins of Inequality*. Princeton, N.J: Princeton University Press.
Democracy at Work Institute. 2023. *What Is a Worker Cooperative?* https://institute.coop/what-worker-cooperative
Dennis, Brady. 2020. *Most Americans Believe the Government Should Do More to Combat Climate Change, Poll Finds*. Washington Post. June 23, 2020. https://www.washingtonpost.com/climate-environment/2020/06/23/climate-change-poll-pew/
Dennis, Brady. 2023. *U.N. Report Warns Nations Have 'Rapidly Narrowing Window' to Cut Emissions*. Washington Post, September 8, 2023. https://www.washingtonpost.com/climate-environment/2023/09/08/un-climate-report-cut-emissions/
Dennis, Brady, Chris Mooney, and Sarah Kaplan. 2020. The World's Rich Need to Cut Their Carbon Footprint by a Factor of 30

to Slow Climate Change, U.N. Warns. *Washington Post*, December 9. https://www.washingtonpost.com/climate-environment/2020/12/09/carbon-footprints-climate-change-rich-one-percent/

Denton, Sally. 2022. Why Is so Little Known about the 1930s Coup Attempt against FDR? *The Guardian*, January 11: sec. Opinion. https://www.theguardian.com/commentisfree/2022/jan/11/trump-fdr-roosevelt-coup-attempt-1930s

Diamond, Jared. 1987. The Worst Mistake in the History Of The Human Race. *Discover Magazine*, May, 64–66.

Diamond, Jared. 2006. *Collapse: How Societies Choose to Fail or Succeed*. New York: Viking.

Diamond, Jared. 2012. *The World Until Yesterday: What Can We Learn from Traditional Societies?* New York: Viking Adult.

Diener, E., M. Diener, and C. Diener. 1995. Factors Predicting the Subjective Well-Being of Nations. *Journal of Personality and Social Psychology* 69 (5): 851–864.

Diener, Ed, and Martin Seligman. 2004. Beyond Money. Toward an Economy of Well-Being. *Psychological Science in the Public Interest* 5 (1): 1–31.

Djankov, Simeon, and Federica Saliola. 2018. The Changing Nature of Work. *Journal of International Affairs* 72 (1): 57–74.

Doepke, Matthias, and Fabrizio Zilibotti. 2019. How Economic Inequality Gives Rise to Hyper-Parenting—The Washington Post. February 24, 2019. https://www.washingtonpost.com/news/posteverything/wp/2019/02/22/feature/how-economic-inequality-gives-rise-to-hyper-parenting/?utm_term=.1b86826c9228

Dooley, David. 2003. Unemployment, Underemployment, and Mental Health: Conceptualizing Employment Status as a Continuum. *American Journal of Community Psychology* 32 (1–2): 9–20.

Douglas, Mary. 1996. *Natural Symbols: Explorations in Cosmology*. 2nd edition. London ; New York: Routledge.

Dower, John W. 2010. *Cultures of War*. New York: W. W. Norton & Company.

Dreyfuss, Bob. 2001. Grover Norquist: 'Field Marshal' of the Bush Plan. *The Nation*, April 26. https://www.thenation.com/article/grover-norquist-field-marshal-bush-plan/

Drutman, Lee. 2015. How Corporate Lobbyists Conquered American Democracy. *The Atlantic*, April 20. http://www.theatlantic.com/business/archive/2015/04/how-corporate-lobbyists-conquered-american-democracy/390822/

Dutton, Denis. 2010. *The Art Instinct: Beauty, Pleasure, and Human Evolution*. First Edition. New York: Bloomsbury Press.

Easterlin, Richard A. 2001. Income and Happiness: Toward a Unified Theory. *Economic Journal* 111 (473): 465–484.
Easterlin, Richard A. 2002. *Happiness in Economics*. Cheltenham: Edward Elgar. Cheltenham, UK: Edward Elgar.
Easterlin, Richard A. 2019. *Three Revolutions of the Modern Era*. 12435. IZA Discussion Papers. Institute of Labor Economics. https://ideas.repec.org/p/iza/izadps/dp12435.html
Economic Innovation Group. 2017. Dynamism in Retreat. *Economic Innovation Group* (blog). February https://eig.org/dynamism
Economic Policy Institute. 2022. *The Productivity–Pay Gap*. October. https://www.epi.org/productivity-pay-gap/
Eriksson, Stefan, and Dan-Olof. Rooth. 2014. Do Employers Use Unemployment as a Sorting Criterion When Hiring? Evidence from a Field Experiment. *American Economic Review* 104 (3): 1014–1039. https://doi.org/10.1257/aer.104.3.1014.
Eum, Hyung-Sik. 2017. Cooperatives and Employment. Second Global Report. CICOPA. https://ica.coop/sites/default/files/2021-11/Cooperatives%20and%20Employment%20Second%20Global%20Report.pdf
European Commission. 2023. *Territoires Zéro Chômeur de Longue Durée*. https://european-social-fund-plus.ec.europa.eu/en/projects/transforming-lives-and-communities-french-territoires-zero-chomeur-de-longue-duree
Evergreen Garden Care. 2020. *Gardening popularity—Is it growing or declining?* lovethegarden. 2020. https://www.lovethegarden.com/uk-en/article/gardening-popularity-it-growing-or-declining
Falk, Armin, Andreas Kuhn, and Josef Zweimüller. 2011. Unemployment and Right-Wing Extremist Crime. *The Scandinavian Journal of Economics* 113 (2): 260–285.
Faw, Larissa. 2021. *Why Do The Mega Rich Continue To Work?* Forbes. January 11. https://www.forbes.com/sites/larissafaw/2013/01/29/why-do-the-mega-rich-continue-to-work/
Feltman, Rachel. 2014. Switch to Farming Weakened Skeletons: Human Bones Became Less Dense as Ancestors Settled, Studies Show. *The Washington Post*, December 24, 2014, A3.
Fisher, Irving. 1919. Economists in Public Service: Annual Address of the President. *The American Economic Review* 9 (1): 5–21.
Flannery, Kent, and Joyce Marcus. 2012. *The Creation of Inequality: How Our Prehistoric Ancestors Set the Stage for Monarchy, Slavery, and Empire*. Cambridge: Harvard University Press.

Foner, Eric. 1995. *Free Soil, Free Labor, Free Men: The Ideology of the Republican Party before the Civil War*. Oxford: Oxford University Press.
Forbes Advisor. 2024. *Small Business Statistics of 2024*. https://www.forbes.com/advisor/business/small-business-statistics/
Frank, Thomas. 2005. *What's the Matter with Kansas? How Conservatives Won the Heart of America*. Reprint. New York: Holt Paperbacks.
Frank, Robert H. 2005. Positional Externalities Cause Large and Preventable Welfare Losses. *American Economic Review* 95 (2): 137–141.
Frank, Robert H. 2011. *The Darwin Economy: Liberty, Competition, and the Common Good*. First Edition. Princeton N.J.: Princeton University Press.
Freud, Sigmund. 1930. *Civilization and Its Discontents*. New York: Dover Publications.
Frey, Bruno S. 2008. *Happiness: A Revolution in Economics*, 1st ed. Cambridge, MA: The MIT Press.
Frey, Carl Benedikt. 2019. *The Technology Trap: Capital, Labor, and Power in the Age of Automation*. Princeton University Press.
Friedman, Milton. 1962. *Capitalism and Freedom*. Chicago: University Of Chicago Press.
Friedman, Gerald. 1988. Strike Success and Union Ideology: The United States and France, 1880–1914. *The Journal of Economic History* 48 (1): 1–25.
Friedman, Milton. 2002. *Capitalism and Freedom*. 40th Anniversary. Chicago: University of Chicago Press.
Friedman, Milton, and Rose D. Friedman. 1988. The Tide in the Affairs of Men. In *Thinking About America: The United States in the 1990s*, edited by Annelise Anderson and Dennis L Bark. Stanford, Calif.: Hoover Institution Press.
Friend, Tad. 2017. Why Ageism Never Gets Old. *The New Yorker*, November 13. https://www.newyorker.com/magazine/2017/11/20/why-ageism-never-gets-old
Fukuyama, Francis. 1989. The End of History? *The National Interest* 16: 3–18.
Fukuyama, Francis. 1992. *The End of History and the Last Man*. Reissue. New York: Free Press.
Gadd, Ian Anders, and Patrick Wallis, eds. 2002. *Guilds, Society and Economy in London 1450–1800*. London: Institute of Historical Research.
Galbraith, John Kenneth. 1952. *American Capitalism*. New York: Boston: Houghton Mifflin/Sentry.
Galbraith, John Kenneth. 1957. *The Affluent Society*. New York: Mentor Books.

Galenson, David W. 1984. The Rise and Fall of Indentured Servitude in the Americas: An Economic Analysis. *The Journal of Economic History* 44 (1): 1–26. https://doi.org/10.1017/S002205070003134X.

Gallagher, Kevin. 2005. International Trade and Air Pollution: Estimating the Economic Costs of Air Emissions from Waterborne Commerce Vessels in the United States. *Journal of Environmental Management* 77 (November): 99–103. https://doi.org/10.1016/j.jenvman.2005.02.012.

Gallagher, Kevin P. 2009. Economic Globalization and the Environment. *Annual Review of Environment and Resources* 34 (1): 279–304. https://doi.org/10.1146/annurev.environ.33.021407.092325.

Gallup. 2019. *10 Gallup Reports to Share With Your Leaders in 2019*. Gallup.Com. January 4. https://www.gallup.com/workplace/245786/gallup-reports-share-leaders-2019.aspx

Gardner, Peter M. 1991. Foragers' Pursuit of Individual Autonomy. *Current Anthropology* 32 (5): 543–572. https://doi.org/10.1086/203999.

Garfield, Zachary H., Christopher von Rueden, and Edward H. Hagen. 2019. The Evolutionary Anthropology of Political Leadership. *The Leadership Quarterly* 30 (1): 59–80. https://doi.org/10.1016/j.leaqua.2018.09.001.

Gat, Azar. 2008. *War in Human Civilization*, 1st ed. Oxford: Oxford University Press.

Gibbon, Edward. 2010. *The Decline and Fall of the Roman Empire, Vol. 1–6*. New York: Everyman's Library.

Gillespie, James. 1965. Towards Freedom in Work. *Anarchy* 4 (1): 1.

Gilligan, James. 2011. *Why Some Politicians Are More Dangerous than Others*. New York: Polity Books.

Gillingham, Peter N. 1979. The Making of Good Work. In *Good Work by E.F. Schumacher*, 147–217. New York: Harper Colophon Books.

Ginsberg, Benjamin. 2013. *The Fall of the Faculty*. Reprint. Oxford: Oxford University Press.

Ginsburg, Helen. 1983. *Full Employment and Public Policy: The United States and Sweden*. Lanham, MD: Lexington Books.

Goldin, Claudia, and Lawrence F. Katz. 2008. *The Race Between Education and Technology*. Cambridge, MA: Harvard University Press.

Goldin, Claudia, and Robert A. Margo. 1992. The Great Compression: The Wage Structure in the United States at Mid-Century. *The Quarterly Journal of Economics* 107 (1): 1–34. https://doi.org/10.2307/2118322.

González-Ricoy, Iñigo. 2014. The Republican Case for Workplace Democracy. *Social Theory and Practice* 40 (2): 232–254. https://doi.org/10.5840/socthe orpract201440215.

Goodman, Paul. 1960. *Growing Up Absurd: Problems of Youth in the Organized Society*. Main. New York: NYRB Classics.

Gordon, Robert J. 2016. *The Rise and Fall of American Growth: The U.S. Standard of Living since the Civil War*. Princeton: Princeton University Press.

Gottschall, Jonathan. 2008. *The Rape of Troy: Evolution, Violence, And The World Of Homer*. Cambridge ; New York: Cambridge University Press.

Gould, Eric D., Bruce Weinberg, and David B. Mustard. 2002. Crime Rates and Local Labor Market Opportunities in the United States: 1979–1997. *Review of Economics and Statistics* 84 (1): 45–61.

Gowen, Peter. 2019. *Right To Own: A Policy Framework to Catalyze Worker Ownership Transitions*. TheNextSystem.Org. https://thenextsystem.org/rto#footnoteref3_ywcp2n7.

Graeber, David. 2012. *Debt: The First 5000 Years*. Reprint. Brooklyn, NY: Melville House.

Graeber, David, and David Wengrow. 2021. *The Dawn of Everything: A New History of Humanity*, 1st ed. New York: Farrar, Straus and Giroux.

Gramlich, John. 2017. Policies Easing Impact of Job Automation Backed by Most in US. *Pew Research Center* (blog). October 9. https://www.pewresearch.org/fact-tank/2017/10/09/most-americans-would-favor-policies-to-limit-job-and-wage-losses-caused-by-automation/

Grandoni, Dino. 2023. Scientists Warn Invasive Pests Are Taking a Staggering Toll on Society. *Washington Post*, September 4. https://www.washingtonpost.com/climate-environment/2023/09/04/invasive-species-un-report/

Gray, Jesse Glenn. 1965. May 1965 Issue Salvation on the Campus Why Existentialism Is Capturing the Students By J. Glenn (Jesse Glenn) Gray. *Harper's Magazine*, May.

Gray, Peter. 2009a. Play as a Foundation for Hunter–Gatherer Social Existence. *American Journal of Play* 1 (4): 476–522.

Gray, Peter. 2009b. *Play Makes Us Human V: Why Hunter–Gatherers' Work Is Play | Psychology Today*. July 2, 2009. https://www.psychologytoday.com/us/blog/freedom-to-learn/200907/play-makes-us-human-v-why-hunter-gatherers-work-is-play

Gray, Peter. 2018. Evolutionary Functions of Play: Practice, Resilience, Innovation, and Cooperation. In *The Cambridge Handbook of Play: Developmental and Disciplinary Perspectives*, edited by Jaipaul L. Roopnarine and Peter K. Smith, 84–102. Cambridge Handbooks in Psychology. Cambridge: Cambridge University Press. https://doi.org/10.1017/9781108131384.006

Gray, Peter. 2021. *How Hunter–Gatherers Maintained Their Egalitarian Ways | Peter Gray, PhD*. October 24, 2021. https://www.madinamerica.com/2021/10/hunter-gatherers-maintained-egalitarian-ways/

Greenhouse Gas Concentrations Surge Again to New Record in 2023. 2024. *World Meteorological Organization. October 25,* https://wmo.int/media/news/greenhouse-gas-concentrations-surge-again-new-record-2023

Grogger, Jeff. 1998. Market Wages and Youth Crime. *Labor Economics* 16 (4): 756–791.

Gulli, Bruno. 2005. *Labor of Fire: The Ontology of Labor between Economy and Culture*. Philadelphia, PA: Temple University Press.

Hacker, Jacob S. 2019. *The Great Risk Shift: The New Economic Insecurity and the Decline of the American Dream,* 2nd ed. New York: Oxford University Press.

Hacker, Jacob S., Gregory A. Huber, Austin Nichols, Philipp Rehm, Mark Schlesinger, Robert Valletta, and Stuart Craig. 2014. The Economic Security Index: A New Measure for Research and Policy Analysis. *Review of Income and Wealth* 60 (S1): S5-32.

Hamlin, Kimberly A. 2014. Sexual Selection and the Economics of Marriage: 'Female Choice' in the Writings of Edward Bellamy and Charlotte Perkins Gilman. In *America's Darwin: Darwinian Theory and U.S. Literary Culture*, 151–80. Atlanta: University of Georgia Press.

Hansen, Hans-Tore. 2005. Unemployment and Marital Dissolution. *European Sociological Review* 21: 133–148.

Harari, Yuval Noah. 2015. *Sapiens: A Brief History of Humankind*, 1st ed. New York: Harper.

Harari, Yuval Noah. 2017. *Homo Deus: A Brief History of Tomorrow*, 1st ed. New York, NY: Harper.

Hardin, Garrett. 1968. The Tragedy of the Commons. *Science* 162 (3859): 1243–1248.

Harris, Marvin. 1991. *Cannibals and Kings: Origins of Cultures*. Reissue. New York: Vintage.

Harris, Kathleen Mullan, Malay K. Majmundar, and Tara Becker, eds. 2021. *High and Rising Mortality Rates Among Working-Age Adults*. Washington, DC: National Academies Press. https://doi.org/10.17226/25976.

Hayek, Friedrich A. 1982. *Law, Legislation and Liberty*. Vol. 1. 3 vols. London: Routledge and Kegan Paul.

Hegel, Georg Wilhelm Friedrich. 1821. *Hegel's Philosophy of Right*. London: Oxford at the Clarendon Press.

Heilbroner, Robert. 1985. *The Act of Work*. Washington, DC: Library of Congress.
Heller, Nathan. 2018. Who Really Stands to Win from Universal Basic Income? *The New Yorker*, July 2. https://www.newyorker.com/magazine/2018/07/09/who-really-stands-to-win-from-universal-basic-income
Herman, Carl. n.d. 'Remaining Awake through a Great Revolution': Dr. King's Last Sermon to You *Washington's Blog*. Accessed January 13, 2016. http://www.washingtonsblog.com/2013/01/remaining-awake-through-a-great-revolution-dr-kings-last-sermon-to-you.html
Herre, Bastian, and Max Roser. 2023. The World Has Recently Become Less Democratic. *Our World in Data*, September. https://ourworldindata.org/less-democratic
Herzberg, Frederick. 1973. *Work and the Nature of Man*. First Printing. New York: Signet.
Hidalgo, Louise. 2011. Dr. Spock's Baby and Child Care at 65. *BBC News*, August 23, 2011, sec. US & Canada. https://www.bbc.com/news/world-us-canada-14534094.
Hobbins, Jennifer. 2016. Young Long-Term Unemployed and the Individualization of Responsibility. *Nordic Journal of Working Life Studies* 6 (2): 43–59. https://doi.org/10.19154/njwls.v6i2.4971.
Holzer, Harry J., Diane Whitmore Schanzenbach, Greg J. Duncan, and Jens Ludwig. 2008. The Economic Costs of Childhood Poverty in the United States. *Journal of Children and Poverty* 14 (1): 41–61. https://doi.org/10.1080/10796120701871280.
Homer. 1944. *The Odyssey*. New York: Walter J. Black.
Horvat, Branko. 1982. *The Political Economy of Socialism: A Marxist Social Theory*. Armonk, NY: M.E. Sharpe.
Houle, Christian. 2009. Inequality and Democracy: Why Inequality Harms Consolidation but Does Not Affect Democratization. *World Politics* 61 (4): 589–622.
Huizinga, Johan. 1938. *Homo Ludens: A Study of the Play-Element in Culture*. Kettering, OH: Angelico Press.
Humphries, Jane. 1990. Enclosures, Common Rights, and Women: The Proletarianization of Families in the Late Eighteenth and Early Nineteenth Centuries. *The Journal of Economic History* 50 (1): 17–42.
Huntington, Samuel P. 1996. *The Clash of Civilizations and the Remaking of World Order*. A. New York: Simon & Schuster.
Inglehart, Ronald. 1989. *Culture Shift in Advanced Industrial Society*. Princeton, NJ: Princeton University Press.

Inglehart, Ronald. 2020a. *Modernization and Postmodernization: Cultural, Economic and Political Change in 43 Societies*. Princeton University Press.
Inglehart, Ronald F. 2020b. Cultural Evolution: People's Motivations Are Changing, and Reshaping the World. *Social Forces* 98 (4): 1–3. https://doi.org/10.1093/sf/soz119.
Inglehart, Ronald, and Wayne E. Baker. 2000. Modernization, Cultural Change, and the Persistence of Traditional Values. *American Sociological Review* 65 (1): 19–51. https://doi.org/10.2307/2657288.
Inglehart, Ronald, and Christian Welzel. 2005. *Modernization, Cultural Change, and Democracy: The Human Development Sequence*. Cambridge, UK ; New York: Cambridge University Press.
Inglis, I. R, Bjorn Forkman, and John Lazarus. 1997. Free Food or Earned Food? A Review and Fuzzy Model of Contrafreeloading. *Animal Behaviour* 53 (6): 1171–91.
Ingraham, Christopher. 2019. *The Share of Americans Not Having Sex Has Reached a Record High*. Washington Post. March 30. https://www.washingtonpost.com/business/2019/03/29/share-americans-not-having-sex-has-reached-record-high/
Ingraham, Jim. 2020. Emancipation: The Caribbean Experience. 2020. https://scholar.library.miami.edu/emancipation/jamaica5.htm
International Labour Organization. 2022. Global Estimates of Modern Slavery. September 12, 2022. https://www.ilo.org/resource/news/50-million-people-worldwide-modern-slavery-0
Irvin, George. 2007. Growing Inequality in the Neo-Liberal Heartland. *Post-Autistic Economics Review* (43): 1–23.
Jacobs, Rose. 2022. *Rising Corporate Concentration Continues a 100-Year Trend*. The University of Chicago Booth School of Business. August 15, https://www.chicagobooth.edu/review/rising-corporate-concentration-continues-100-year-trend
Jaffe, Sarah. 2019. The Road Not Taken. *New Republic* 250 (7/8): 30–36.
Janoff-Bulman, Ronnie. 2023. The Myth of Limited Government. *Yale University Press* (blog). April 28. https://yalebooks.yale.edu/2023/04/28/the-myth-of-limited-government/
Jencks, Christopher. 2015. The War on Poverty: Was It Lost? *The New York Review*, April, 82–85.
Jost, John T., and Brenda Major. 2001. *The Psychology of Legitimacy: Emerging Perspectives on Ideology, Justice, and Intergroup Relations*. Cambridge: Cambridge University Press.

Jost, John T., Brett W. Sheldon, and Bilian Sullivan. 2003. Social Inequality and the Reduction of Ideological Dissonance on Behalf of the System: Evidence of Enhanced System Justification among the Disadvantaged. *European Journal of Social Psychology* 33 (1): 13–36. https://doi.org/10.1002/ejs p.127.
Junger, Sebastian. 2016. *Tribe: On Homecoming and Belonging.* New York: Harper Collins Publishers.
Kaboub, Fadhel. 2012. The Low Cost of Full Employment in the United States. In *The Job Guarantee: Toward True Full Employment*, ed. Mathew Forstater and Michael Murray, 59–72. New York: Palgrave Macmillan.
Kahloon, Idress. 2021. Believe You Me. *The New Yorker*, July, 67–71.
Kahloon, Idrees. 2023. What's the Matter with Men? *The New Yorker*, January 23: 20–27.
Kamerāde, Daiga, Senhu Wang, Brendan Burchell, Sarah Ursula Balderson, and Adam Coutts. 2019. A Shorter Working Week for Everyone: How Much Paid Work Is Needed for Mental Health and Well-Being? *Social Science and Medicine.* https://doi.org/10.1016/j.socscimed.2019.06.006.
Kanazawa, Satoshi. 2009. Evolutionary Psychological Foundations of Civil Wars. *The Journal of Politics* 71 (1): 25–34.
Kane, John, and Haig Patapan. 2012. *The Democratic Leader: How Democracy Defines, Empowers and Limits Its Leaders.* Oxford: Oxford University Press. https://www.oxfordscholarship.com/view/https://doi.org/10.1093/acprof:oso/9780199650477.001.0001/acprof-9780199650477
Karasek, Robert, and Tores Theorell. 1990. *Healthy Work: Stress, Productivity, and the Re-Construction of Working Life.* New York: Basic Books.
Kasmir, Sharryn. 2016. The Mondragon Cooperatives and Global Capitalism: A Critical Analysis. *New Labor Forum* 25 (1): 52–59. https://doi.org/10.1177/1095796015620424.
Kates, Nick, Barrie S. Greiff, and Duane Q. Hagan. 1990. *The Psychosocial Impact of Job Loss*, 1st ed. Washington, DC: American Psychiatric Publisher, Inc.
Katz, Lawrence F., and Claudia Goldin. 2010. *The Race Between Education and Technology.* Cambridge, MA: Belknap Press.
Keeley, Lawrence H. 1997. *War Before Civilization: The Myth of the Peaceful Savage.* Reprint. New York: Oxford University Press.
Keller, Helen. 1911. *Rebel Lives.* Edited by John Davis. Melbourne; New York: Saint Paul, MN: Ocean Press.
Kennedy, David M. 2001. *Freedom from Fear: The American People in Depression and War, 1929–1945.* Reprint. New York: Oxford University Press.

Keynes, John Maynard. 1926. *The End of Laissez-Faire*. London: Hogarth.
Keynes, John Maynard. 1930. Economic Possibilities for Our Grandchildren. In *Essays in Persuasion*, New York: W.W. Norton & Co.: 358–73.
Keynes, John Maynard. 2009. *Essays in Persuasion*. New York: CreateSpace Independent Publishing Platform.
Kieselbach. 2003. Long-Term Unemployment Among Young People: The Risk of Social Exclusion. *American Journal of Community Psychology* 32: 69–76.
Kirp, David L. 2015. It's All About the Money. How America Became Preoccupied with Higher Education's Bottom Line. *The American Prospect*: 119–121.
Kitschelt, Herbert. 1994. *The Transformation of European Social Democracy*. Cambridge: Cambridge University Press.
Klein, Ernest. 1971. *Kleins Comprehensive Etymological Dictionary of the English Language*. Amsterdam, New York: Elsevier Publishing Company.
Koechlin, Tim. 2013. The Rich Get Richer: Neoliberalism and Soaring Inequality in the United State. *Challenge* 56 (2): 5–30.
Kohn, Melvin, and Carmi Schooler. 1983. *Work and Personality: An Enquiry into the Impact of Social Stratification*. Norwood, N.J: Ablex Pub.
Kruse, Douglas. 2016. Does Employee Ownership Improve Performance? *IZA World of Labor*. https://doi.org/10.15185/izawol.311
Kuznets, Simon. 1955. Economic Growth and Income Inequality. *American Economic Review* 45 (1): 1–28.
Laing, R. D. 1965. *The Divided Self: An Existential Study in Sanity and Madness*. Reprint. New York: Penguin Books.
Landes, David S. 1969. *The Unbound Prometheus*. Cambridge: Cambridge University Press.
Lane, Robert E. 1991. *The Market Experience*. Cambridge; New York: Cambridge University Press.
Lasch, Christopher. 1985. *The Minimal Self: Psychic Survival in Troubled Times*. New York, N.Y.: W. W. Norton & Company.
Lawton, Graham. 2020. Human Evolution: The Astounding New Story of the Origin of Our Species. *New Scientist*. April 2020. https://www.newscientist.com/article/mg24532760-800-human-evolution-the-astounding-new-story-of-the-origin-of-our-species/
Layard, Richard. 2006. *Happiness: Lessons from a New Science*. Annotated. New York: Penguin Books.
Leakey, Richard, and Roger Levin. 1978. *People of the Lake: Mankind and Its Beginnings*. New York: Avon Books.

Lebergott, Stanley. 1964. *Manpower in Economic Growth: The American Record since 1800*. New York: McGraw Hill.
Lerman, Robert I. 2016. Reinvigorate Apprenticeships in America to Expand Good Jobs and Reduce Inequality. *Challenge* 50 (5): 372–389.
Lewchuk, W. 1993. Men and Monotony: Fraternalism as a Managerial Strategy at the Ford Motor Company. *Journal of Economic History* 53 (4): 824–856.
Lilley, Sam. 1966. *Men, Machines and History: The Story of Tools and Machines in Relation to Social Progress*. Revised&Enlarged. London: International Publishers.
Lim, Michelle H., Thomas L. Rodebaugh, Michael J. Zyphur, and John F. M. Gleeson. 2016. Loneliness over Time: The Crucial Role of Social Anxiety. *Journal of Abnormal Psychology* 125 (5): 620–630. https://doi.org/10.1037/abn0000162.
Lincoln, Abraham. 1862. *Second Annual Message | The American Presidency Project*. December 1. https://www.presidency.ucsb.edu/documents/second-annual-message-9
Lindbeck, Assar. 1983. The Recent Slowdown of Productivity Growth. *The Economic Journal* 93 (369): 13–34. https://doi.org/10.2307/2232162.
Lindo, Jason M. 2011. Parental Job Loss and Infant Health. *Journal of Health Economics* 30 (5): 869–879. https://doi.org/10.1016/j.jhealeco.2011.06.008.
Long, Heather. 2018. Analysis | The Unhappy States of America: Despite an Improving Economy, Americans Are Glum. *Washington Post*, March 30. https://www.washingtonpost.com/news/wonk/wp/2018/03/30/the-unhappy-states-of-america-despite-an-improving-economy-americans-are-glum/
Loomis, Erik. 2018. *A History of America in Ten Strikes*. New York, NY: The New Press.
Losurdo, Domenico. 2014. *Liberalism: A Counter-History*. Translated by Gregory Elliott. London ; New York: Verso.
Lowrey, Annie. 2018. *Give People Money: How a Universal Basic Income Would End Poverty, Revolutionize Work, and Remake the World*. New York: Crown Publisher.
Lucas, Richard, Andrew E. Clark, Yannis Georgellis, and Edward Diener. 2004. Unemployment Alters the Set Point for Life Satisfaction. *Psychological Science* 15 (1): 8–13.
Lucassen, Jan. 2021. *The Story of Work: A New History of Humankind*. New Haven (Conn.): Yale University Press.
Lumsden, Charles, and Edward O. Wilson. 1983. *Promethean Fire: Reflections on the Origin of Mind*. Cambridge: Harvard University Press.

Lyon, David J. 2021. The Free Market Fallacy. *Challenge* 64 (1): 36–50. https://doi.org/10.1080/05775132.2020.1847528.
Lyon, Larry. 1999. *The Community in Urban Society*. Lone Grove, Ill: Waveland Press, Inc.
Lévi-Strauss, Claude. 2021. *Wild Thought: A New Translation of "La Pensée Sauvage."* Translated by Jeffrey Mehlman and John Leavitt. First edition. Chicago ; London: University of Chicago Press.
Macionis, John J. 1999. *Sociology*, 7th ed. Upper Saddle River, NJ: Prentice Hall.
Macmillan, Gartner, and Rosemary Ross. 1999. When She Brings Home the Bacon: Labor-Force Participation and the Risk of Spousal Violence against Women (in Family Violence). *Journal of Marriage and the Family* 61: 947–958.
Malinowski, Bronislaw. 1922. *Argonauts of the Western Pacific*. New York: Dutton.
Malleson, Tom. 2013. Making the Case for Workplace Democracy: Exit and Voice as Mechanisms of Freedom in Social Life. *Polity* 45 (4): 604–629. https://doi.org/10.1057/pol.2013.20.
Mandeville, Bernard. 1970. *The Fable of the Bees*. Edited by P. Harth. Harmondsworth, Middlesex, England ; New York,: Penguin.
Mandeville, Bernard. 1714. *The Fable of the Bees. Vol. 1*. Edited by F. B Kaye. Oxford University Press.
Mann, Michael. 2012. *The Sources of Social Power: Volume 1, A History of Power from the Beginning to AD 1760*. 2_{nd} edition. New York: Cambridge University Press.
Marcuse, Herbert. 1964. *One-Dimensional Man: Studies in the Ideology of Advanced Industrial Society*, 1st ed. London: Routledge.
Marcuse, Herbert. 1955. *Eros and Civilization*. Boston: Beacon Press.
Marshall, Alfred. 1873. The Future of the Working Classes. In *Memorials of Alfred Marshall*, ed. A. C. Pigou. New York: Augustus M. Kelley: 101–118.
Marshall, Alfred. 1890 (1961). *Principles of Economics. 9th Ed. London, New York: Macmillan*. 9th ed. London, New York: Macmillan.
Marx, Karl. 1859. *A Contribution to the Critique of Political Economy*. Moscow: Progress Publishers.
Marx, Karl. 1867. *Capital: A Critique of Political Economy*, vol. I. New York: Modern Library.
Marx, Karl. 1875. Critique of the Gotha Program. In *The Marx-Engels Reader*, edited by Robert C. Tucker, 2nd ed., 525–41. New York: Norton & Co.

Marx, Karl. 1894. *Capital: A Critique of Political Economy*. Vol. 3. 3 vols. New York: International Publishers Company, Incorporated.

Marx, Karl, and Friedrich Engels. 1848. Manifesto of the Communist Party. In *The Marx-Engels Reader*, edited by Robert C. Tucker, 2nd ed., 469–500. New York: Norton & Co.

Marx, Leo. 2000. *The Machine in the Garden: Technology and the Pastoral Ideal in America*. 35th Anniversary. New York: Oxford University Press.

Maslow, Abraham H. 1954. *Motivation and Personality*. Edited by Robert Frager, James Fadiman, Cynthia McReynolds, and Ruth Cox. 3rd edition. New York: Longman.

Mason, Ronald M. 1982. The Importance of Work. In *Participatory and Workplace Democracy*, 102–227. Carbondale: Southern Illinois University Press.

Mauldin, John. 2016. *Life on the Edge*. MauldinEconomics.Com. May 4, http://www.mauldineconomics.com/frontlinethoughts/life-on-the-edge

May, J. L., and M. Bobele. 1988. Sexual Dysfunction and the Unemployed Male Professional. *Journal of Sex and Marital Therapy* 14 (4): 353–362.

Mazumder, Soumyajit, and Alan N. Yan. 2023. What Do Americans Want from (Private) Government? Experimental Evidence Demonstrates That Americans Want Workplace Democracy. *American Political Science Review*, August, 1–17. https://doi.org/10.1017/S0003055423000667

McCulloch, John Ramsay. 1825. *The Principles of Political Economy: With a Sketch of the Rise and Progress of the Science*. London: W. and C. Tait.

McIntyre, Georgia. 2020. What Is the SBA's Definition of Small Business (And Why)? September 24. https://www.fundera.com/blog/sba-definition-of-small-business

McNally, David. 1993. *Against the Market: Political Economy, Market Socialism and the Marxist Critique*. London: Verso.

McNicholas, Celine, Samantha Sanders, and Heidi Shierholz. 2019. What Workers Need the First Day on the Job. *Challenge* 62 (1): 3–20.

Mellon, Ruby. 2022. As the World Population Hits 8 Billion, Humanity Finds Itself at a Crossroads. *The Washington Post*, November 15.

Merchant, Brian. 2018. *The Presidential Candidate Bent on Beating the Robot Apocalypse Will Give Two Americans a $1000-per-Month Basic Income*. Motherboard. April 19. https://www.vice.com/en/article/pax8a7/andrew-yang-2020-wants-basic-income-because-of-automation

Merrill, Michael. 1995. Putting 'Capitalism' in Its Place: A Review of Recent Literature. *The William and Mary Quarterly* 52 (2): 315–326. https://doi.org/10.2307/2946977.

Mill, John Stuart. 1909. *Principles of Political Economy,* 7th ed. Clifton, NJ: Augustus M. Kelley.
Mill, John Stuart. 1984. The Negro Question. In *Collected Works of John Stuart Mill,* edited by John M. Robson, 11:85–95. Toronto: Toronto University Press.
Moen, Phyllis, Erin L. Kelly, J. Shi-Rong Lee, Michael Oakes, Wen Fan, Jeremy Bray, David Almeida, Leslie Hammer, David Hurtado, and Orfeu Buxton. 2017. Can a Flexibility/Support Initiative Reduce Turnover Intentions and Exits? Results from the Work, Family, and Health Network. *Social Problems* 64 (1): 53–85. https://doi.org/10.1093/socpro/spw033.
Mokyr, Joel. 1990. *The Lever of Riches: Technological Creativity and Economic Progress.* New York: Oxford University Press.
Morin, Rich, and Rakesh Kochhar. 2010. *Lost Income, Lost Friends— And Loss of Self-Respect.* Pew Research Center's Social & Demographic Trends Project (blog). http://www.pewsocialtrends.org/2010/07/22/hard-times-have-hit-nearly-everyone-and-hammered-the-long-term-unemployed/
Muller, Jerry Z. 2003. *The Mind and the Market: Capitalism in Western Thought.* Reprint. New York: Anchor.
Mumford, Lewis. 1961. *The City in History.* New York: Harcourt, Brace, Jovanovich.
Myrdal, Gunnar. 1968. *The Political Element in the Development of Economic Theory.* New York: Simon & Schuster.
NCEO. 2021. *A Visual Guide to Employee Ownership.* 2021. https://www.esopinfo.org/infographics/economic-power-of-employee-ownership.php
National Agricultural Library. 1859. *Lincoln's Milwaukee Speech National Agricultural Library.* https://www.nal.usda.gov/topics/lincolns-milwaukee-speech
National Center for Employee Ownership. 2021. *How an Employee Stock Ownership Plan (ESOP) Works | NCEO.* https://www.nceo.org/articles/esop-employee-stock-ownership-plan
Nikolova, Milena, and Carol Graham. 2020. The Economics of Happiness. 640. *GLO Discussion Paper Series.* GLO Discussion Paper Series. Global Labor Organization (GLO). https://ideas.repec.org/p/zbw/glodps/640.html
Nikolova, Milena, and Femke Cnossen. 2020. What Makes Work Meaningful and Why Economists Should Care about It. *Labour Economics* 65 (August): 101847. https://doi.org/10.1016/j.labeco.2020.101847.
Nordt, Carlos, Ingeborg Warnke, Erich Seifritz, and Wolfram Kawohl. 2015. Modelling Suicide and Unemployment: A Longitudinal Analysis Covering 63 Countries, 2000–11. *The Lancet Psychiatry* 2 (3): 239–245. https://doi.org/10.1016/S2215-0366(14)00118-7.

Nova, Annie. 2019. *Many Americans Who Can't Afford a $400 Emergency Blame Debt*. CNBC. July 20. https://www.cnbc.com/2019/07/20/heres-why-so-many-americans-cant-handle-a-400-unexpected-expense.html

OECD. 2023. *Education Attainment—Population with Tertiary Education—OECD Data*. http://data.oecd.org/eduatt/population-with-tertiary-education.htm

Offer, Avner. 2007. Offer, Avner. 2007. 'The Challenge of Affluence', Interview, Challenge, 50 (2), March/April: 6–19. *Challenge* 50 (2): 6–19.

Olenin, Alice, and Thomas F. Corcoran. 1942. Hours and Earnings in the United States, 1932–40: With Supplement for 1941: Bulletin of the United States Bureau of Labor Statistics, No. 697, January. https://fraser.stlouisfed.org/title/hours-earnings-united-states-1932-40-supplement-1941-408

Orwell, George. 1937. *The Road to Wigan Pier*. New York: Penguin. http://george-orwell.org/The_Road_to_Wigan_Pier/index.html

Osborne, Steve R. 1977. The Free Food (Contrafreeloading) Phenomenon: A Review and Analysis. *Animal Learning & Behavior* 5 (3): 221–35.

Oswald, Andrew J., and N. Powdhavee. 2005. Does Happiness Adapt? A Longitudinal Study of Disability with Implications for Economists and Judges. *Journal of Public Economics*, 92 (5–6), June: 1061-1077.

O'Toole, James. 1974. *Work and the Quality of Life*. Cambridge, MA: MIT Press.

Packer, George. 2021. *Last Best Hope: America in Crisis and Renewal*. New York: Farrar, Straus and Giroux.

Pang, Alex Soojung-Kim. 2018. *Rest: Why You Get More Done When You Work Less*. Huffington Post.

Panksepp, Jaak. 1998. *Affective Neuroscience: The Foundations of Human and Animal Emotions. Affective Neuroscience*. New York: Oxford University Press.

Parenti, Christian. 1999. Atlas Finally Shrugged. *The Baffler* 13: 108–120.

Perelman, Michael. 2007. *The Confiscation of American Prosperity: From Right-Wing Extremism and Economic Ideology to the Next Great Depression*. New York: Palgrave Macmillan.

Peterson, E. Wesley F. 2017. Is Economic Inequality Really a Problem? A Review of the Arguments. *Social Sciences* 6 (4): 1–25.

Pew Research Center. 2017. U.S. Students' Academic Achievement Still Lags That of Their Peers in Many Other Countries. *Pew Research Center* (blog). February 15. https://www.pewresearch.org/short-reads/2017/02/15/u-s-students-internationally-math-science/

Picchio, Matteo, Sigrid Suetens, and Jan C. van Ours. 2018. Labour Supply Effects of Winning a Lottery. *The Economic Journal* 128 (611): 1700–1729. https://doi.org/10.1111/ecoj.12465.
Pieper, Josef, and James V. Schall. 1963. *Leisure: The Basis of Culture*, 1st ed. San Francisco: Ignatius Press.
Piketty, Thomas. 2020. *Capital and Ideology*. Translated by Arthur Goldhammer. Cambridge (Massachusetts); London: Harvard University Press.
Piketty, Thomas. 2022. *A Brief History of Equality*. Translated by Steven Rendall. Cambridge, Massachusetts: Belknap Press: An Imprint of Harvard University Press.
Piketty, Thomas, and Emmanuel Saez. 2006. The Evolution of Top Incomes: A Historical and International Perspective. Working Paper 11955. National Bureau of Economic Research. http://www.nber.org/papers/w11955
Pinker, Steven. 2002. *The Blank State: The Modern Denial of Human Nature*. New York: Penguin Press.
Pinker, Steven. 2011. *The Better Angels of Our Nature: Why Violence Has Declined*. New York: Viking.
Pirsig, Robert M. 1974. *Zen and the Art of Motorcycle Maintenance*. New York: Bantam Books.
Pisani, Bob. 2020. *Wealth Gap Grows as Rising Corporate Profits Boost Stock Holdings Controlled by Richest Households*. CNBC. August 27. https://www.cnbc.com/2020/08/27/wealth-gap-grows-as-rising-corporate-profits-boost-stock-holdings-controlled-by-richest-households.html
Pope Francis. n.d. *Laudato Si' and 'a Correct Understanding of Work.'* Catholic Ecology. Accessed February 27, 2021. https://catholicecology.net/blog/laudato-si-and-correct-understanding-work
Powel, James. 2025. *Majority of Americans Pessimistic About Their Personal Finances, Gallup Poll Finds*. USA TODAY. April 21. https://www.usatoday.com/story/money/2025/04/22/gallup-poll-american-personal-finance/83217865007/
Priestland, David. 2012. *Merchant, Soldier, Sage*. London: Allen Lane.
Prison Inside. 2023. *How Much Does It Cost To Keep a Prisoner?—Prison Inside*. September 30, https://prisoninside.com/how-much-does-it-cost-to-keep-a-prisoner/
Puko, Timothy. 2023a. As Disasters Spike, Superpowers Face Mounting Calls to Forge Climate Deal. *Washington Post*, September 25. https://www.washingtonpost.com/climate-environment/2023/09/25/china-united-states-climate-deal/

Puko, Timothy. 2023b. Canada, a Giant Oil Producer, Urges Others to End Fossil Fuel Subsidies. *Washington Post*, September 22. https://www.washingtonpost.com/climate-environment/2023/09/22/fossil-fuel-subsidies-climate-canada/

Punjwani, Mehdi. 2024. *Small Business Statistics in 2024*. USA TODAY Blueprint. June 5. https://www.usatoday.com/money/blueprint/business/business-formation/small-business-statistics/

Putnam, Robert D. 2000. *Bowling Alone: The Collapse and Revival of American Community*. Revised and Updated. New York: Simon & Schuster.

Raphael, Steven, and Rudolf Winter-Ebmer. 2001. Identifying the Effect of Unemployment on Crime. *Journal of Law and Economics* 44 (1): 259–283.

Rault, Jean-Loup, Susanne Waiblinger, Xavier Boivin, and Paul Hemsworth. 2020. The Power of a Positive Human–Animal Relationship for Animal Welfare. *Frontiers in Veterinary Science* 7 (November): 590867. https://doi.org/10.3389/fvets.2020.590867.

Rawls, John, and Erin Kelly. 2001. *Justice as Fairness: A Restatement*. Cambridge, Massachusetts: Harvard University Press.

Rayo, Luis, and Gary S. Becker. 2007. Evolutionary Efficiency and Happiness. *Journal of Political Economy* 115 (2): 302–337. https://doi.org/10.1086/516737.

Reeves, Richard V, and Kimberly Howard. 2013. The Glass Floor: Education, Downward Mobility, and Opportunity Hoarding. *Brookings* (blog). November 13. https://www.brookings.edu/research/the-glass-floor-education-downward-mobility-and-opportunity-hoarding/

Reich, Robert B. 2010. *The Work of Nations: Preparing Ourselves for 21st Century Capitalism*. 1st edition. New York: Vintage.

Reichert, Arndt, and Harald Tauchmann. 2011. The Causal Impact of Fear of Unemployment on Psychological Health. *SSRN Electronic Journal*. https://doi.org/10.2139/ssrn.1880938.

Richardson, Heather Cox. 2023. *Democracy Awakening: Notes on the State of America*. New York: Viking Press.

Riesman, David. 1950. *The Lonely Crowd: A Study of the Changing American Character*. New Haven, Conn: Yale University Press.

Rodrik, Dani. 1998. Has Globalization Gone Too Far? *Challenge* 41 (2): 81–94. https://doi.org/10.1080/05775132.1998.11472025.

Romeo, Nick. 2022. What Happens When Jobs Are Guaranteed? *The New Yorker*, December 10, https://www.newyorker.com/news/annals-of-inquiry/what-happens-when-jobs-are-guaranteed

Rook, K., David Dooley, and Ray Catalano. 1991. Stress Transmission: The Effects of Husbands' Job Stressors on the Emotional Health of Their Wives. *Journal of Marriage and the Family* 53: 165–167.
Rosanvallon, Pierre. 2013. *The Society of Equals*. Cambridge, MA: Harvard University Press.
Rose, Nancy E. 2013. Bring Back the WPA: Lessons from the Job Creation Programs of the 1930s. In *Employment Guarantee Schemes: Job Creation and Policy in Developing Countries and Emerging Markets*, edited by Mathew Forstater and Michael J. Murray. New York: Palgrave Macmillan.: 155–179.
Roszak, Theodore. 1995. *The Making of a Counter Culture: Reflections on the Technocratic Society and Its Youthful Opposition*. Berkeley: University of California Press.
Rousseau, Jean-Jacques. 1984. *A Discourse on Inequality*. Penguin Classics. Harmondsworth, Middlesex, England ; New York: Penguin Books.
Rousseau, Jean Jacques. 1755. Discourse on the Origin and Foundation of Inequality Among Men. In *The Discourses and Other Early Political Writings*, translated by V. Gourevitch, 111–222. Cambridge: Cambridge University Press.
Russell, Bertrand. 1930. *The Conquest of Happiness*. Edited by Daniel C. Dennett. 1 edition. New York: Liveright.
Sahlins, Marshall. 1974. *Stone Age Economics*. New Brunswick, NJ: Aldine Transaction.
Sahlins, Marshall. 2004. The Original Affluent Society. A Short Essay. In *Investigating Culture: An Experiential Introduction to Anthropology*, edited by Carol Lowery Delaney, 110–33. Oxford: Blackwell.
Salinger, J. D. 1951. *The Catcher in the Rye*. Boston: Little Brown and Company.
Sandel, Michael. 2018. Populism, Trump, and the Future of Democracy. OpenDemocracy. May 9, 2018. https://www.opendemocracy.net/en/populism-trump-and-future-of-democracy/
Sayer, Andrew. 2015. *Why We Can't Afford the Rich*. Cambridge: Policy Press.
Schumacher, E. F. 1979. *Good Work*. New York: Harper Colophon Books.
Schumpeter, Joseph A. 1962. *Capitalism, Socialism, and Democracy*, 3rd ed. New York: Harper Torchbooks.
Scitovsky, Tibor. 1976. *The Joyless Economy: The Psychology of Human Satisfaction*. Oxford: Oxford University Press.
Scott, James C. 2013. Crops, Towns, Government. *London Review of Books*, November 21, 2013.

Scott, James C. 2017. *Against the Grain: A Deep History of the Earliest States*, 1st ed. New Haven: Yale University Press.

Sen, Amartya. 1997. Inequality, Unemployment and Contemporary Europe. *International Labour Review* 136 (2): 155–172.

Serhan, Yasmeen. 2022. How Democracy Fared Around the World in 2022. TIME. December 21. https://time.com/6242188/global-democracy-report-2022/

Shimron, Yonat. 2023. U.S. Faith Groups Do Not View Climate Change as a Crisis, New Poll Finds. *Washington Post*, October 6. https://www.washingtonpost.com/religion/2023/10/06/religion-climate-change-survey/

Sitaraman, Ganesh. 2017. *The Crisis of the Middle-Class Constitution. Why Income Inequality Threatens Our Republic.* New York: Alfred A. Knopf.

Skidelsky, Robert. 2012. Return to Capitalism 'Red in Tooth and Claw' Spells Economic Madness. *The Guardian*, June 21, sec. Business. https://www.theguardian.com/business/economics-blog/2012/jun/21/capitalism-red-tooth-claw-keynes

Slater, Philip. 1970. *The Pursuit of Loneliness: America's Discontent and the Search for a New Democratic Ideal.* 3rd edition. Beacon Press.

Smith, Eric Alden. 2004. Why Do Good Hunters Have Higher Reproductive Success? *Human Nature* 15 (4): 343–364. https://doi.org/10.1007/s12110-004-1013-9.

Smith, Adam. 1763. *Lectures on Jurisprudence.* Edited by Ronald Lindley Meek, D. D. Raphael, and P. G. Stein. Glasgow Edition of the Works and Correspondence of Adam Smith 5. Oxford: Clarendon Press.

Smith, Adam. 1776 (1934). *An Enquiry into the Nature and Causes of the Wealth of Nations.* New York: The Modern Library.

Solnick, Sara, and David Hemenway. 1998. Is More Always Better? A Survey on Positional Concerns. *Journal of Economic Behavior and Organization* 37 (3): 373–383.

Spencer, David A. 2022. *Making Light Work: An End to Toil in the Twenty-First Century,* 1st ed. Medford: Polity.

Spock, Benjamin, and Robert Needlman. 1946. *Dr. Spock's Baby and Child Care:* 9th ed. New York: Pocket Books.

St. Louis Fed. 2024. Average Weeks Unemployed. July 5, 2024. https://fred.stlouisfed.org/series/UEMPMEAN

St. Louis Fed. 2025. *Personal Income per Capita.* January 30, 2025. https://fred.stlouisfed.org/series/A792RC0A052NBEA

Starr, Jared, Craig Nicolson, Michael Ash, Ezra M. Markowitz, and Daniel Moran. 2023. Income-Based U.S. Household Carbon Footprints (1990–2019) Offer New Insights on Emissions Inequality and Climate Finance. *PLOS Climate* 2 (8). https://doi.org/10.1371/journal.pclm.0000190.

Statista. 2022. *Single-Person Households United States 1960–2022*. Statista. https://www.statista.com/statistics/242022/number-of-single-person-households-in-the-us/

Stein, Judith. 2010. Conflict, Change, and Economic Policy in the Long 1970s. In *Rebel Rank and File: Labor Militancy and Revolt from Below in The Long 1970s*, ed. Aaron Brenner, Robert Brenner, and Cal Winslow, London: Verso: 77–102.

Strom, Sara. 2003. Unemployment and Families: A Review of Research. *The Social Science Review* 77: 399–401.

Sullivan, Daniel, and Till von Wachter. 2009. Job Displacement and Mortality: An Analysis Using Administrative Data. *The Quarterly Journal of Economics* 124 (3): 1265–1306.

Suzman, James. 2021. *Work: A Deep History, from the Stone Age to the Age of Robots*. New York: Penguin Press.

Swanson, Ryan. 2019. *The Strenuous Life: Theodore Roosevelt and the Making of the American Athlete*. New York: Diversion Books.

Taleb, Nassim Nicholas. 2010. *The Black Swan: The Impact of the Highly Improbable: With a New Section: "On Robustness and Fragility,"* 2nd ed. New York: Random House Publishing Group.

Tawney, R. H. 1926. *Religion and the Rise of Capitalism*. New York: Harcourt, Brace & World.

Taylor, Frederick Winslow. 1906. *On the Art of Cutting Metals*. New York: Society of Mechanical Engineers.

Taylor, Frederick Winslow. 1911. *The Principles of Scientific Management*. New York: Harper & Row.

Tcherneva, Pavlina R. 2020. *The Case for a Job Guarantee*, 1st ed. Cambridge, England: Polity.

Di Tella, Rafael, Robert J. MacCulloch, and Andrew J. Oswald. 2003. The Macroeconomics of Happiness. *Review of Economics and Statistics* 85 (4): 809–827. https://doi.org/10.1162/003465303772815745.

Temin, Peter. 2008. Real Business Cycle Views of the Great Depression and Recent Events: A Review of Timothy J. Kehoe and Edward C. Prescott's Great Depressions of the Twentieth Century. *Journal of Economic Literature* 46 (3): 669–684. https://doi.org/10.1257/jel.46.3.669.

The Economist. 2015. Digital Taylorism, September 12, 2015. https://www.economist.com/business/2015/09/10/digital-taylorism
The Washington Post. 2025. America's Voice, Silenced, Editorial, Mar.19: A16.
Thomas, Keith. 1964. Work and Leisure in Pre-Industrial Society. *Past and Present* 29: 50–66.
Thompson, E. P. 1963. *The Making of The English Working Class*. New York: Vintage.
Thompson, E. P. 1967. Time, Work-Discipline, and Industrial Capitalism. *Past and Present*, 38: 56–97.
Thompson, Willie. 2015. *Work, Sex, and Power*. London: Pluto Press.
Thompson, Spencer. 2015. Towards a Social Theory of the Firm: Worker Cooperatives Reconsidered. *Journal of Co-Operative Organization and Management*, ICA Global Research Conference 2014, 3 (1): 3–13. https://doi.org/10.1016/j.jcom.2015.02.002
Thoreau, Henry David. 1948. *Walden*. New York: Rinehart.
Thurnwald, Richard. 1932. *Economics in Primitive Communities*. London: Oxford University Press.
Tocqueville, Alexis de. 1835. *Democracy in America*. Edited by Henry Reeve. Vol. 1. 2 vols. New York: Vintage.
Tocqueville, Alexis de. 1840. *Democracy in America*. Translated by Henry Reeve. Vol. 2. 2 vols. New York: Vintage.
Tokumitsu, Miya. 2017. *The United States of Work*. New Republic. April 18, 2017. https://newrepublic.com/article/141663/united-states-work
Twenge, Ph. D., and M. Jean. 2017. *IGen: Why Today's Super-Connected Kids Are Growing Up Less Rebellious, More Tolerant, Less Happy—And Completely Unprepared for Adulthood—And What That Means for the Rest of Us*. 2nd Print. New York: Atria Books.
Tzouliadis, Tim. 2009. *The Forsaken: An American Tragedy in Stalin's Russia*. Reprint edition. Penguin Books.
USDA. 2023. *USDA ERS—Key Statistics & Graphics*. June 20. https://www.ers.usda.gov/topics/food-nutrition-assistance/food-security-in-the-u-s/key-statistics-graphics/
Van Bavel, Bas. 2015. History as a Laboratory to Better Understand the Formation of Institutions. *Journal of Institutional Economics* 11 (1): 69–91. https://doi.org/10.1017/S1744137414000216.
Van Dam, Andrew. 2023. The Mystery of the Disappearing American Vacation. *The Washington Post*, February 19, sec. G 1, 4.
Vatter, Harold G. 1985. *The U.S. Economy in Work War II*. New York: Columbia University Press.

Veblen, Thorstein. 1898. The Instinct of Workmanship and the Irksomeness of Labor. *American Journal of Sociology* 4 (2): 187–201.
Veblen, Thorstein. 1899 (1934). *The Theory of the Leisure Class; an Economic Study of Institutions*. New York: The Modern Library.
Veblen, Thorstein. 1914. *The Instinct of Workmanship and the State of the Industrial Arts*. New York: W. W. Norton & Company.
Veblen, Thorstein. 1919. Some Neglected Points in the Theory of Socialism. In *The Place of Science in Modern Civilization*, 387–408. New York: B. W. Huebsch.
Veenhoven, R. 1993. *Happiness in Nations: Subjective Appreciation of Life in 56 Nations, 1946–1992*. Erasmus University of Rotterdam, Department of Social Sciences, RISBO, Center for Socio-Cultural Transformation.
Vickrey, William. 1992. Chock-Full Employment without Increased Inflation: A Proposal for Marketable Markup Warrants. *American Economic Review* 82 (2): 341–345.
Vonnegut, Kurt. 1970. *God Bless You Mr. Rosewater or Pearls Before Swine*. New York: Dell.
Wade, Nicholas. 2009. *The Faith Instinct: How Religion Evolved and Why It Endures*. New York: Penguin Press.
Waldinger, Robert, and Marc Schultz. 2023. *The Good Life: Lessons from the World's Longest Scientific Study of Happiness*. New York: Simon & Schuster.
Wan, William. 2020. *Workplace Suicides Have Risen to Record High, with More People Killing Themselves at Work than Ever Before*. January 14. https://www.washingtonpost.com/health/2020/01/09/more-americans-are-killing-themselves-work/
Wayback Machine. 2020. September 22 https://web.archive.org/web/20200922084740/https://www.mondragon-corporation.com/2019urtekotxostena/assets/downloads/mondragon-txostena-2019-es.pdf
Wayner, Robert. 2011. The Pursuit of Pleasure in the Animal World. *Saving Earth | Encyclopedia Britannica*, September 19. https://explore.britannica.com/explore/savingearth/the-pursuit-of-pleasure-in-the-animal-world.
West, Darrell M. 2018. Rethinking Work. In *The Future of Work: Robots, AI, and Automation*, ed. Darrell M. West, 63–88. Washington, DC: Brookings Institution Press.
Whyte, William H. 1956. *The Organization Man*. Revised. Philadelphia: University of Pennsylvania Press.
Wilkinson, Richard, and Kate Pickett. 2011. *The Spirit Level: Why Greater Equality Makes Societies Stronger*. Reprint. New York: Bloomsbury Press.

Wilkinson, Richard, and Kate Pickett. 2019. *The Inner Level*. London: Penguin Press.
Willensky, Harold. 1961. The Uneven Distribution of Leisure: The Impact of Economic Growth on 'Free Time'. *Social Problems* 9: 32–56.
Williamson, Jeffrey G. 1991. *Inequality, Poverty, and History: The Kuznets Memorial Lectures*. Cambridge, Mass.: Blackwell.
Wilson, Edward O. 1978. *On Human Nature*. Harvard University Press.
Wilson, Margo, Martin Daly, Stephen Gordon, and Adelle Pratt. 1996. Sex Differences in Valuations of the Environment? *Population and Environment* 18 (2): 143–159. https://doi.org/10.1007/BF02208408.
Wilson, David Sloan, and John M. Gowdy. 2013. Evolution as a General Theoretical Framework for Economics and Public Policy. *Journal of Economic Behavior and Organization*, 90 (June): S3-10. https://doi.org/10.1016/j.jebo.2012.12.008.
Wilson, David Sloan, and John M. Gowdy. 2015. Human Ultrasociality and the Invisible Hand: Foundational Developments in Evolutionary Science Alter A Foundational Concept in Economics. *Journal of Bioeconomics* 17 (1): 37–52.
Wilson, Edward O. 2013. *The Social Conquest of Earth*. New York; London: Liveright.
Winkelmann, Liliana, and Rainer Winkelmann. 1998. Why Are the Unemployed So Unhappy? Evidence from Panel Data. *Economica* 65 (257): 1–15. https://doi.org/10.1111/1468-0335.00111.
Winslow, Cal. 2010. Overview: The Rebellion from Below, 1965–81. In *Rebel Rank and File: Labor Militancy and Revolt from Below in the Long 1970s*, edited by Aaron Brenner, Robert Brenner, and Cal Winslow. London: Verso: 1–36.
Wisman, Jon D. 1991. *Worker Empowerment: The Struggle for Workplace Democracy*. New York: Bootstrap Press.
Wisman, Jon D. 1998. Christianity, John Paul II, and the Future of Work. *International Journal of Social Economics* 25 (11/12): 1658–1671.
Wisman, Jon D. 2003. The Scope and Promising Future of Social Economics. *Review of Social Economy* 61 (4): 1–21.
Wisman, Jon D. 2014. The Financial Crisis of 1929 Reexamined: The Role of Soaring Inequality. *Review of Political Economy* 26 (3): 372–391.
Wisman, Jon D. 2019. The Darwinian Dynamic of Sexual Selection That Thorstein Veblen Missed and Its Relevance to Institutional Economics. *Journal of Institutional Economics* 15 (1): 49–72.

Wisman, Jon D. 2020a. Marx, the Predisposition to Reject Markets and Private Property, and Attractive Alternatives to Capitalism. *Forum for Social Economics* 49 (3): 281–298.

Wisman, Jon D. 2020b. Why Did the Great Recession Fail to Produce a New New Deal in the USA? In *The Palgrave Handbook of Management History*, edited by Bradley Bowden, Jeffrey Muldoon, Anthony M. Gould, and Adela J. McMurray, 951–69. Cham, Switzerland: Springer International Publishing under the imprint Palgrave Macmillan: 951–969.

Wisman, Jon D. 2022. *The Origins and Dynamics of Inequality Sex, Politics, and Ideology*. New York: Oxford Univeristy Press.

Wisman, Jon D. 2025. How the Bourgeoisie's Quest for Status Placed Blame for Poverty on the Poor. *Cambridge Journal of Economics* 49 (1): 41–65. https://doi.org/10.1093/cje/beae040.

Wisman, Jon D., and Kevin W. Capehart. 2010. Creative Destruction, Economic Insecurity, Stress, and Epidemic Obesity. *The American Journal of Economics and Sociology* 69 (3): 963–982.

Wisman, Jon D., and Quentin Duroy. 2020. The Proletarianization of the Professoriate and the Threat to Free Expression, Creativity, and Economic Dynamism. *Journal of Economic Issues* 54 (3): 876–894. https://doi.org/10.1080/00213624.2020.1791651.

Wisman, Jon D., and Michael Cauvel. 2021. Why Has Labor Not Demanded Guaranteed Employment? *Journal of Economic Issues*, 55 (3), September: 677–697.

Wisman, Jon D., and Nicholas E. Reksten. 2024. Nationalism as a Response to Worker Militancy. *American Review of Political Economy* 18 (2): 1–16.

Wolin, Sheldon S. 2010. *Democracy Incorporated: Managed Democracy and the Specter of Inverted Totalitarianism*. Princeton, NJ, Princeton University Press.

Woolf, Steven H., Elizabeth R. Wolf, and Frederick P. Rivara. 2023. The New Crisis of Increasing All-Cause Mortality in US Children and Adolescents. *JAMA* 329 (12): 975–976. https://doi.org/10.1001/jama.2023.3517.

Woolf, Steven H, and Laudan Aron. 2023. *Opinion | American Life Expectancy Is Dropping—And It's Not All Covid's Fault*. Washington Post. June 1. https://www.washingtonpost.com/opinions/2023/06/01/american-life-expectancy-decline-covid/

World Infant Mortality Rate 1950–2023. n.d. Accessed December 22, 2023. https://www.macrotrends.net/countries/WLD/world/infant-mortality-rate

Wrangham, Richard. 2019. *The Goodness Paradox: The Strange Relationship Between Virtue and Violence in Human Evolution*. New York: Pantheon.

Wray, L. Randall, Flavia Dantas, Scott Fullwiler, Pavlina R. Tcherneva, and Stephanie A. Kelton. 2018. *Public Service Employment: A Path to Full Employment | Levy Economics Institute.* April. http://www.levyinstitute.org/publications/public-service-employment-a-path-to-full-employment

Wright, Erik Olin. 2013. Transforming Capitalism through Real Utopias. *American Sociological Review* 78 (1): 1–25. https://doi.org/10.1177/0003122412468882.

Wuthnow, Robert. 1982. The Moral Crisis in American Capitalism. *Harvard Business Review* 60 (2): 76–84.

Yang, Andrew. 2018. *The War on Normal People: The Truth About America's Disappearing Jobs and Why Universal Basic Income Is Our Future*, 1st ed. New York: Hachette Books.

Young, Arthur. 1772. *Political Essays Concerning The Present State Of The British Empire.* London: Kessinger Publishing, LLC.

Index

A

Abundance 2–5, 11, 14, 15, 26, 49, 76, 87, 94, 104, 116, 179, 201, 208–211
Accounting 50
Acemoglu, Daron 79, 80, 133
Adoption of agriculture 32–34, 45–47, 49, 50, 121
Agency problems 188
Agricultural cycle 46
Agriculturalists 24, 46–50
Alcohol and narcotics abuse 149
Alesina, Alberto 43
Allen, Robert 64
Anderson, Elizabeth 57, 140, 176
Anthropologists 8, 14, 25–27, 35, 50, 71
Antitrust 192
Anti-war activism 98
Appendage of the machine 10

Appleby, Joyce 57, 64
Arendt, Hannah 30
Aristotle 23, 36, 57, 73, 191
Artificial intelligence (AI) 19, 157
Austerity 3
Authoritarianism 135
Automatic stabilizers 153, 157
Autor, David H. 91, 106, 112, 156

B

Baby boomers 87, 88, 90, 93, 94
Bailyn, Bernard 61
Barash, David P. 28
Bavel, Bas van 64
Becker, Gary S. 110
Bentham, Jeremy 71
Berger, Peter 209
Berry, John Widdup 50
Betzig, Laura 52

Biden, Joe 85, 101
Biswas-Diener, Robert 41, 92, 125
Blackburn, Robin 57
Blasphemy 51, 203
Bogaard, Amy 49
Boix, Carles 57
Bondage 49, 59, 60
Bosses 8, 19, 24, 27, 66–68, 70, 99, 141, 142, 172, 194, 208
Bourgeoisie 20, 75, 203
Bowles, Samuel 49, 99, 185, 188, 189
Boyce, James K. 130, 131
Brandeis, Louis 134
Bullies 40
Buss, David 37, 148
Byrne, Edmund 68, 74

Cadillac welfare queens 101
Caged 50
Carlyle, Thomas 147
Carter, Jimmy 101
Case, Anne 16, 107, 110–112, 115, 138, 147, 160, 196, 202
Catholic Church 54, 58, 59, 203
Cauvel, Michael 137, 166
Childe, V. Gordon 30
Children 8, 27, 33, 37, 40, 47, 48, 55, 56, 60, 62, 64–66, 80, 87, 88, 91, 92, 94, 97, 99, 103, 104, 110, 112, 113, 138, 152, 164, 166, 178, 185
Chimpanzees 31, 38, 39
Chomsky, Noam 181
Cicero, Marcus Tillius 62
Citizens v. Federal Election Committee 109, 134

Civil rights 58, 90, 98, 131
Civil Works Administration 164
Clocks 63, 64, 66
Communism 18, 79, 86, 87, 168, 206
Community 2–7, 9, 12, 13, 15, 22, 24, 30, 31, 33, 37, 40, 59, 61, 69, 71, 75, 90, 96, 104, 105, 110, 114, 120, 121, 123–127, 129, 141–143, 151, 157, 168, 172, 173, 179, 180, 188, 193, 202, 206, 208, 211
Comparative advantage in violence 51
Competition 13, 53, 63, 67, 68, 70, 100, 121, 123, 124, 140, 144, 154, 172, 187, 193, 203, 210, 211
Concubines 52, 72
Conspicuous consumption 12, 36, 53, 54, 70, 123, 124
Cooperation 33, 36, 130, 187, 188, 191
Corporate income taxes 192, 205
Counter-cultural revolution 88
Crafts guilds 68
Creative destruction 4, 11, 13, 17, 19, 77, 96, 105, 123, 139, 141, 146, 156–158, 163
Creativity 2, 7, 12, 24, 39, 75, 125, 202
Crime 62, 80, 90, 147, 152, 154, 164, 172
Crowd disease 56
Csikszentmihalyi, Mihaly 33, 34, 39, 42, 191
Cultivators 46, 50
Cultural revolution 15, 94
Curle, Adam 25

Daly, Martin 29
Daniels, Ronald J. 104, 113, 133, 138
Darity, William 150, 164, 167
Darwin, Charles 9, 29–31, 35, 37, 148, 187, 210
Death 38, 49, 51, 52, 55, 57, 91, 96, 111, 120, 145, 151, 203
Deaths of despair 16, 111, 202
Deaton, Angus 16, 64, 81, 107, 110–112, 115, 138, 147, 160, 202
Defense 7–9, 37, 90, 172, 191, 208
Degraded neighborhoods 172
Deindustrialization 100
Democracy 4, 5, 17, 18, 21, 78, 88, 96, 103, 113, 120, 131–136, 138, 140, 142, 179, 181, 184–186, 191, 202, 206–208
Democratic Party 17, 85, 86, 101, 146
Deskilling 66
Devaluation of the dollar 100
Dewey, John 181
Diamond, Jared 37, 45, 46, 131
Dignity 73, 74, 82, 153
Disease 16, 46, 49, 57, 62, 80, 110, 111
Divorce 66, 90, 148
Dower, John W. 38
Drug abuse 16
Duroy, Quentin 113
Dutton, Denis 31, 32

Easterlin, Richard A. 125
Eastern European socialism 96
Eastern European state socialism 18, 181
Ecological Armageddon 4, 120, 202, 208
Ecological devastation 97, 103, 119, 127, 128, 140, 141, 147
Ecological disaster 18, 131, 206, 208
Economic dynamism 113, 120, 122, 125, 137, 141, 151, 188, 204, 206, 211
Economic Policy Institute 135
Economics 2, 13, 16, 23, 26, 41, 42, 75, 88, 124, 138, 180, 185, 193, 195, 204
Eden 48, 73
Education 16, 20, 26, 80, 85, 92, 93, 105, 111–114, 138, 155, 159, 163, 166, 178, 195, 198, 206, 207, 212
Efficiency 39, 62, 124, 150, 167, 174, 179, 184, 186–188, 191, 193
Egalitarian 18, 27, 47, 49, 51, 78, 79, 86, 87, 172, 190
Electorate 20, 21, 120, 125, 137, 140, 141, 146, 175, 184, 189, 207
Employee Stock Ownership Plans (ESOPs) 190, 196, 197
Enclosures 61, 62, 65, 69
Enlightenment 74, 79, 204, 212
Entrepreneurship 153, 155, 182, 183, 192
Estate tax 83
Evolution 1, 4, 6, 7, 13, 19, 24, 29–32, 39, 41, 44, 61, 71, 105, 126, 141, 168, 172, 186, 187, 208, 210
Evolutionary biology 21, 29, 126

Evolutionary psychology 29, 30
Exploitation 1, 5, 10, 20, 24, 41, 43, 49, 54, 55, 59, 64, 77, 122, 128, 170, 172, 173, 209, 210, 212
Expropriation 10, 48, 57, 122, 203

Feltman, Rachel 46
Feminism 90
Fire 39, 106
Fisher, Irving 185
Flannery, Kent 8, 55
Flow 42
Fochesato, Mattia 49
Foragers 25, 26, 39, 40, 46, 47, 49, 50, 164
Franchise 62, 79, 132, 133, 136, 166, 205
Franklin, Benjamin 28, 51
Frank, Robert H. 29, 53
Frank, Thomas 137
Freedom 3–6, 15, 17, 18, 20, 21, 47, 58, 63, 64, 73, 88–90, 93, 105, 117, 119, 122, 139–142, 166, 172, 175–178, 182, 186, 192, 202, 206, 207
Free-riding 188
Free trade 156, 157, 193
Free workers 21, 28, 61, 64, 72, 157, 173
Freud, Sigmund 49, 75, 76, 89
Frey, Bruno S. 41, 92, 112, 179
Frey, Carl Benedikt 159
Frictionally unemployed 144
Friedman, Milton 81, 183
Friedman, Rose 81
Fukuyama, Francis 18, 140, 197

Full Employment Bill of 1945 83, 146

Gadd, Ian Anders 68
Galbraith, John Kenneth 88
Galenson, David W. 61
Gallup 107, 110, 138
Gardner, Peter M. 47
Garfield, Zachary H. 8
Gat, Azar 38
Gene-culture co-evolution 29, 36, 39, 173
Gene pool 6
Generosity 31
Generous 98, 121, 210, 211
Genesis 1, 30, 48, 72, 73
Gibbon, Edward 122
Gig economy 107
Gilded Age 53, 205
Gillespie, James 43
Gillingham, Peter N. 46
Gini index 85
Gintis, Hebert 185, 188, 189
Glaeser, Edward 43, 183
Globalization 18, 19, 105, 106, 146, 153, 155, 156, 159, 160, 185
Godwin, William 210
Golden Age of Capitalism 85, 206, 211
Goldin, Claudia 84, 112, 154
Gordon, Robert J. 113
Gordon, Stephen 29
Gottschall, Jonathan 72
Graeber, David 25–28, 55, 60
Graham, Carol 42
Gray, Peter 8, 25–27, 33, 40, 50
Great Compression 84

Great Depression 15, 16, 81, 87, 100, 116, 134, 135, 138, 161, 167, 184, 205, 206
Great Recession 16, 110, 138, 196
Green jobs 154
Growth stunting 152
Growth trap 11, 121, 128, 154
Guaranteed employment 4, 18–21, 83, 140, 141, 145–147, 153–155, 157–159, 162–166, 168, 169, 172, 175, 182, 184, 199, 207, 209, 210
Guidance systems 6, 32
Gulli, Bruno 43

Hagen, Edward H. 8
Hamlin, Kimberly A. 35
Happiness 1, 3, 4, 6, 8, 11–13, 19, 32, 33, 41–43, 49, 65, 75, 92, 95, 96, 103, 112, 119, 125, 126, 147, 173, 179, 182, 195
Happiness research 19, 24, 41, 44, 71, 125, 126, 141, 211
Harari, Yuval 14, 16, 47, 50, 164
Hardin, Garrett 30
Harems 52, 78
Harris, Marvin 27, 110
Hayek, Friedrich A. 201
Heart attacks 44, 148, 178
Hegel, Georg Wilhelm Friedrich 13, 125
Heilbroner, Robert 8, 13
Herzberg, Frederick 177
Hippies 102
Hippy movement 88
Hitler, Adolf 135
Homer 72

Homo sapiens 1, 8, 24, 32, 40, 104, 161
Huizinga, Johan 33
Human capital 18, 147, 150, 151, 154, 156, 204
Humanoid ancestors 31
Humiliation 2, 3
Humphrey-Hawkins Bill 83, 146
Humphries, Jane 62
Hunter gatherers 25
Huntington, Samuel P. 102

Ideology 5, 10, 16, 20, 48, 51, 52, 54, 57, 80, 81, 87, 94, 100, 116, 117, 135, 136, 140, 144, 145, 166, 168, 175, 184, 185, 203, 204, 206, 212
Impotence 120, 149
Incremental Democratization Plan 190
Indebtedness 60
Indebted peasants 10, 48, 52, 104, 144, 173, 203
Indentured servitude 60
Inequality 1, 3–5, 10–12, 14–18, 47, 48, 60, 64, 72, 73, 77, 81, 83–85, 88, 93, 96, 103, 109, 112–117, 119, 122–124, 129, 133, 135–140, 151, 153, 154, 166, 168, 177, 184, 202–206, 208–212
Inglehart, Ronald 15, 89, 90, 92, 93, 102
Inheritance taxes 80, 82, 205
Insecurity 3, 4, 13, 16–19, 49, 88, 93, 94, 96, 99, 100, 103–107, 109, 110, 112, 117, 123, 138,

140, 147, 149, 155, 183, 185, 195, 201, 208
Insurrection 60, 62, 76, 123, 203, 205
International Monetary Fund (IMF) 205

Jencks, Christopher 84, 162
Johnson, Lyndon 84, 97
Jost, John T. 54, 168
Justice 15, 88, 90, 97

Kanazawa, Satoshi xi, 32, 36, 51, 210
Keeley, Lawrence H. 38
Keynesian macroeconomic stabilization policies 101
Keynesian revolution 81
Keynes, John Maynard 88, 91, 124
Kuznets, Simon 84

Labor, attitudes toward 167
Labor, division of 8, 10, 47, 65, 72, 124, 176
Labor-saving technological change 39, 151
Labor, separation of mental and manual 66
Laissez-faire ideology 3–5, 14–16, 18–21, 81–83, 86, 94–96, 100, 103, 104, 116, 117, 119, 120, 130, 131, 135–140, 144, 146, 153, 175, 176, 184, 186, 196, 197, 202–206, 208

Landlords 48, 52, 58, 59, 63, 65
Lane, Robert E. 42, 44, 124, 177
Lasch, Christopher 11
Lawton, Graham 32
Lawton, Philip xi
Layard, Richard 3, 179
Leaders 9, 17, 57, 61, 72, 132, 135, 146, 159, 172, 175, 181, 191
Leaky, Richard 25, 26
Learning by doing 163
Lerman, Robert 163
Levin, Roger 25, 26
Lévi-Strauss, Claude 46
Liberation 3, 14, 17, 22, 103, 117
Life expectancy 17, 46, 64, 78, 80, 88, 110, 148
Lincoln, Abraham 177
Living wage 4, 18–20, 153–155, 157, 161, 162, 169, 172, 207, 208
Loan guarantees 190
Locke, John 57
Loneliness 34, 114, 173, 202
Long, Heather 110, 114
Lordstown 99

Macroeconomic dysfunction 101
Macroeconomic stability 189
Malinowski, Bronislaw 35
Malleson, Tom 178, 184, 190
Mandeville, Bernard 5
Mann, Michael 50
Marcuse, Herbert 89, 98
Marcus, Joyce 8, 55
Margo, Robert A. 84
Markets 3, 4, 16, 18, 20, 21, 58, 59, 63, 64, 69, 72, 97, 106, 120,

122, 139, 140, 144, 159, 165, 181, 186–188, 195, 204, 207, 209, 210
Marshall, Alfred 41
Marx, Karl 10, 13, 30, 79, 136, 180, 209, 212
Maslow, Abraham 42, 88, 89, 113
Mason, Ronald M. 43
Materialist values 90, 94, 97
Material problem 2, 11
Material progress vision 11, 12, 123, 125, 126, 128, 186
McCarthyism 86
Means of production 48, 52, 63, 67, 130, 144, 166, 171
Mental health 108, 147, 152
Mental illness 149
Mercantilism 75, 122
Metallurgy 48
Middle Ages 74, 203
Military organization 10, 48, 203
Mill, John Stuart 180
Mises, Ludwig von 209
Mobility 179
Mokyr, Joel 74
Mondragon 191, 198
Monogamy 78
Monopolies 20, 51, 52, 134, 203, 205
Muller, Jerry Z. 209
Mutual monitoring effect 188
Myrdal, Gunnar 42

Neolithic revolution 34, 45
New Deal 81, 82, 85, 134, 162, 206
Nikolova, Milena 42, 195
No-man's-land 58, 59

Non-accelerating inflation rate of unemployment (NAIRU) 145, 165
Nordhaus, William D. 129

Obesity epidemic 17, 106
Offer, Avner 148
Optimism 79, 86, 95, 99, 103, 109, 130, 211, 212
Organization of Petroleum Exporting Countries (OPEC) 100, 101
Orwell, George 20, 167
O'Toole, James 1

Pain-pleasure guidance system 6
Peak experiences 42
Per capita income 2, 85, 131, 201
Per capita wealth 2, 201
Personal income taxes 205
Pessimism 96, 103, 139, 201, 202, 211
Pickett, Kate 114, 115, 138
Piketty, Thomas 18, 54–56, 80, 83, 84, 191–193, 197
Pinker, Steven 36, 78
Pinnacle of status 53, 70, 123
Pisani, Bob 12, 108
Play 8, 9, 26, 27, 33, 36, 149, 159, 164, 211
Political democracy 19, 131, 174, 181, 184, 189, 193
Pollution 128, 130, 193
Pope Francis 23

Population growth 47, 48, 65, 79, 122
Population-to-land ratio 48
Post-materialist values 96
Poverty 3, 18, 20, 78, 82, 84, 97, 117, 123, 139, 146, 150, 152, 153, 160, 161, 164, 172, 204, 207
Poverty, war on 84
Pratt, Adelle 29
Pregnancy 48
Priesthood 51
Priestland, David 44, 178
Primordial problem of material scarcity 95
Private property 4, 18, 19, 21, 47, 120, 140, 143, 181, 186–188, 195, 207, 209, 210
Privation 11, 14, 17, 78, 87, 88, 91, 98, 99, 103, 104, 116
Problem of scarcity 2, 11, 14, 15, 21, 88, 119, 208, 211
Productive wealth 10–12, 14, 18, 20, 21, 24, 52, 53, 61, 62, 67, 80, 101, 104, 140, 141, 143–145, 166, 169, 172, 173, 181, 187, 207, 209, 210
Productivity 16, 25, 66, 69, 79, 89, 93, 99, 101, 121, 122, 124, 135, 162, 164, 165, 179, 187, 188, 191, 206
Progressive Era 86, 184, 205
Progressive income taxation 83
Proletarianization of labor 61
Prosperity 14, 139, 206
Prostitution 60, 62, 90, 154
Protestantism 75, 79, 203

Provisioning 1, 4, 6–9, 11, 13, 24, 30, 33, 34, 37, 39, 44, 67, 71, 75, 142, 143, 208
Psychological distress 149
Public good 30, 82, 113, 129, 179, 186
Putnam, Robert D. 115

Quit rate 179

Rayo, Luis 6
Reagan, Ronald 86, 100, 101, 136, 196
Recession 16, 86, 91, 100, 103, 158
Red Scare 86, 205
Reich, Robert 159, 188
Reksten, Nicholas 86
Religion 43, 51, 52, 93, 115, 203, 204, 212
Rent seeking 189, 191
Reproductive success 36, 210
Reskilling 4, 19, 20, 145, 146, 154, 156, 157, 162, 163, 165, 207, 208
Revolutionary 210, 212
Ricardo, David 156
Rise of the state 1, 4, 5, 9, 12, 19, 21, 23, 24, 47–50, 52, 55, 60, 67, 70, 72, 73, 77, 104, 116, 123, 132, 144, 169, 173, 203, 207, 211, 212
Robber barons 205
Robinson, James A. 79, 80, 133
Robotization 19, 149, 155, 157, 159
Rodrik, Dani 156

Roosevelt, Franklin Delano 19, 82, 83, 134, 146, 206
Rose, Nancy E. 83
Rousseau, Jean-Jacques 37, 48, 212
Ruling class 52, 136
Runaways 57–59
Russell, Bertrand 42

Sacerdote, Bruce 43
Sahlins, Marshall 25, 26
Sanitation 80, 166
Savannah principle 32
Sayer, Andrew 130
Scarcity 2, 3, 11, 15, 17, 25, 26, 78, 89, 91, 188, 193
Scarring, psychological 147, 150
Scarring, reputational 150
Schultz, Marc 173
Schumpeter, Joseph A. 11, 77, 158
Scientific management 66, 67
Scitovsky, Tibor 13, 124
Scott, James C. 48–50, 56
Sedentary life 47
Self-creation 30, 40, 41
Self-esteem 16, 43, 44, 88, 92, 126, 147, 149, 150, 167, 177
Self-respect 2, 4, 7, 14, 19, 24, 51, 70, 74, 75, 119, 123, 124, 134, 142, 153, 160, 161, 166, 167, 202
Seligman, Martin 43
Sen, Amartya 149–152, 167
Serfdom 23, 58, 59, 72, 75
Serfs 10, 48, 52, 58, 59, 63, 104, 144, 170, 173, 203
Sexual competition 36, 210
Sexual dysfunction 149

Sexual selection 30, 31, 34–36, 44, 148, 187
Sexual services 52
Shirking 66, 188
Sitaraman, Ganesh 85, 86, 132, 176
Slater, Philip 98
Slavery 10, 23, 24, 55–58, 60–62, 72, 75, 77, 78, 124
Slaves 10, 48, 50, 52, 53, 55–59, 61, 63, 72–75, 104, 132, 144, 170, 173, 203
Slums 62, 80, 162, 180
Smith, Adam 10, 36, 48, 53, 65, 70, 79, 123, 136, 139, 162, 176, 212
Smith, Eric Alden 37
Social capital 114, 115, 179
Social coercion 8
Social esteem 24
Socialism 67, 79, 139, 140, 206
Social mobility 16, 139, 152
Social networking 149
Social respect 72
Soviet Union 96, 110, 168, 197, 206
Spencer, David A. 161, 162
Spock, Benjamin 91
Stagflation 16, 101, 206
State control 49
State, rise of 13, 56, 121
State socialism 139, 140
Stone age weapons 40
Stone tools 24
Stone weapons 40
Stress 3, 4, 13, 16, 17, 75, 96, 104, 123, 147, 148, 174, 201, 208
Strikes 59, 98–100, 123, 205
Subsidies 82, 130, 161, 189

Subsistence 5, 25, 50, 52, 53, 55, 59, 61, 63, 64, 70, 71, 98, 116, 121, 123, 141, 170, 203
Suffrage, women's 205
Suicide 16, 110–112, 128, 147, 149, 152
Supply-side economics 16, 100, 117, 135, 206
Supreme Court 109, 134
Surplus 10, 47, 48, 53–55, 57, 59, 70, 72, 104, 116, 122–124, 144, 170, 177, 198, 203
Suzman, James 12, 28, 39, 40, 64, 175, 193

Taleb, Nassim Nicholas 32
Tamir, Maya 41, 92, 125
Tawney, R.H. 59, 122
Tax expenditures 190
Tax preferences 190
Tax revenues 151, 165
Taylor, Frederick Winslow 66, 67
Taylorism 67, 69
Tcherneva, Pavlina R. 146, 152, 164
Teamwork 9, 12
Technological progress 13, 15, 49, 55, 74, 77, 96, 151, 169
Technology 14, 25, 36, 50, 77, 91, 104, 105, 108, 212
Thomas, Keith 62
Thompson, E.P. 28, 64
Thompson, Spencer 188, 191
Thoreau, Henry David 91
Thurnwald, Richard 35
Tocqueville, Alexis de 73
Tokumitsu, Miya 175, 176, 183

Tools 19, 29, 31, 38–40, 121, 171, 176–178, 180
Torture 10, 51, 55, 61, 203
Transactions costs 59
Trinkets and baubles 53
Trump, Donald 101, 113, 128, 131, 135, 137, 155
Trust 99, 115, 138, 177, 190, 195, 197
Tyranny of the majority 151

Unemployed, reserve army of 65, 144, 145, 158
Unemployment insurance 82, 149, 150, 157, 163
Unemployment, natural rate of 145, 158, 165
Unemployment, personal costs of 151
Unemployment, social costs of 151
Unions 82, 85, 86, 98, 106, 107, 115, 181, 185, 197
Universal basic income (UBI) 158–161, 169
US Treasury 205
Usurious interest rates 60
Utopianists 180, 210

Veblen, Thorstein 12, 13, 36, 53, 54, 68, 70, 123, 124
Vertical mobility 137, 139
Vickrey, William 145
Vietnam War 97, 206
Violence 49, 51, 78, 80, 136, 147, 149, 187

Voting Rights Act 134

Wage-price spiral 100
Wage workers 62, 63, 69, 104, 144, 170, 173, 195
Waldinger, Robert 173
Wallis, Patrick 68
War 9, 15, 28, 37, 38, 56, 57, 73, 84, 85, 90, 97, 101, 145, 172, 187
War captives 50, 55
Warring 37, 38, 73, 187
Warrior elites 10, 48, 104, 122, 144, 203
Wealth inequality constraint 189
Welfare cheats 101
Wengrow, David 25–28
Wilkinson. Richard 114, 115, 138
Wilson, David Sloan 29, 191
Wilson, Edward O. 29, 121, 191
Wolin, Sheldon 101, 113, 132

Work, disutility of 2, 13, 24, 67, 75
Worker buyouts 190
Workplace democracy 18–21, 99, 140–142, 174, 175, 179–181, 184–186, 189, 192, 193, 195, 197–199, 207, 209, 210
Works Project Administration (WPA) 161, 162
World Bank 205
World War II 3, 11, 14, 15, 17, 21, 76, 77, 85–87, 89–92, 94–98, 100, 103, 104, 115, 116, 137, 145, 146, 199, 204, 206, 211, 212
Wrangham, Richard 40
Wray, Randall 164
Wright, Erik Olin 139
Writing 23, 28, 50, 167

Yang, Andrew 155, 159
Young, Arthur 48

GPSR Compliance
The European Union's (EU) General Product Safety Regulation (GPSR) is a set of rules that requires consumer products to be safe and our obligations to ensure this.

If you have any concerns about our products, you can contact us on

ProductSafety@springernature.com

In case Publisher is established outside the EU, the EU authorized representative is:

Springer Nature Customer Service Center GmbH
Europaplatz 3
69115 Heidelberg, Germany

www.ingramcontent.com/pod-product-compliance
Lightning Source LLC
LaVergne TN
LVHW012035070526
838202LV00056B/5509